S0-EDJ-629

The First TV Shows

By
Ben
Sonder

A CPI GROUP Book
from
SRA

Photo Credits

Page 4, Kazuhiko Iimura
Pages 6, 7, AT&T Archives
Pages 9, 13, 21, 40, UPI Bettman
Pages 11, 23, Culver Pictures
Pages 12, 16, 26, NBC/Globe Photos
Pages 15, 33, Globe Photos
Pages 19, 28, The Bettmann Archive
Page 31, Laufer/Globe Photos
Page 35, MTM Enterprises, Inc.
Page 37, NBC
Page 42, NASA
Page 44, John Barrett/Globe Photos

Library of Congress Catalog Card Number: 92-75995

Library of Congress Cataloging in Publication Data

Sonder, Ben, 1954–
The first TV shows / by Ben Sonder.

p. cm. — (Famous firsts)
SUMMARY: Discusses the evolution of television programs from the early days of live television with Milton Berle and Ed Sullivan.

ISBN 0-383-03819-7

1. Television programs — United States — History — Juvenile literature. [1. Television programs — History.] I. Title. II. Series.

PN1992.3.U5S59 1994
791.43'75'0973 — dc20 92-75995
CIP
AC

Manufactured in the United States of America

Product Code 87-003819

ISBN 0-383-03819-7

CONTENTS

Home video cameras, or camcorders, allow us to create our own TV shows of happy occasions with family and friends.

How It All Started

Friends and family are enjoying a holiday party. The younger children are playing. The older people are eating picnic foods. You capture this happy occasion by pressing a button on your small video camera. That evening, you're at home, reliving the afternoon fun by watching it all on your own TV set.

As ordinary as this scene now seems, barely 40 years ago it would have been called science fiction. Home video cameras had not been invented. In fact, television in any form did not appear in most American homes until the 1950s. The first TV images had been transmitted long before, but no one could predict how they would change the world.

In 1883, a German scientist named Paul Nipkow rigged a heavy, awkward device in his laboratory. Light, passing through holes in a large spinning disk, was converted into electric signals. These signals created shadows on a mineral-coated tube. Upon close inspection, the shadows seemed to look like whatever was placed in front of the spinning disk. That was the beginning of television.

But most people were not too excited by Nipkow's shadows and hazy images. It was not until the 1920s that a Scottish scientist, John Logie Baird, was able to make a stronger impression. Using a similar spinning disk, Baird asked a young boy to stand in front of his machine. On a tiny TV screen across the room appeared an easily recognizable orange-and-black image of the boy. The boy was so frightened that he ran away! But TV was starting to be taken seriously.

Baird and an American scientist named Charles F. Jenkins tried to market their early televisions. But the pictures were so small, and the machines that produced them so big, that very few people

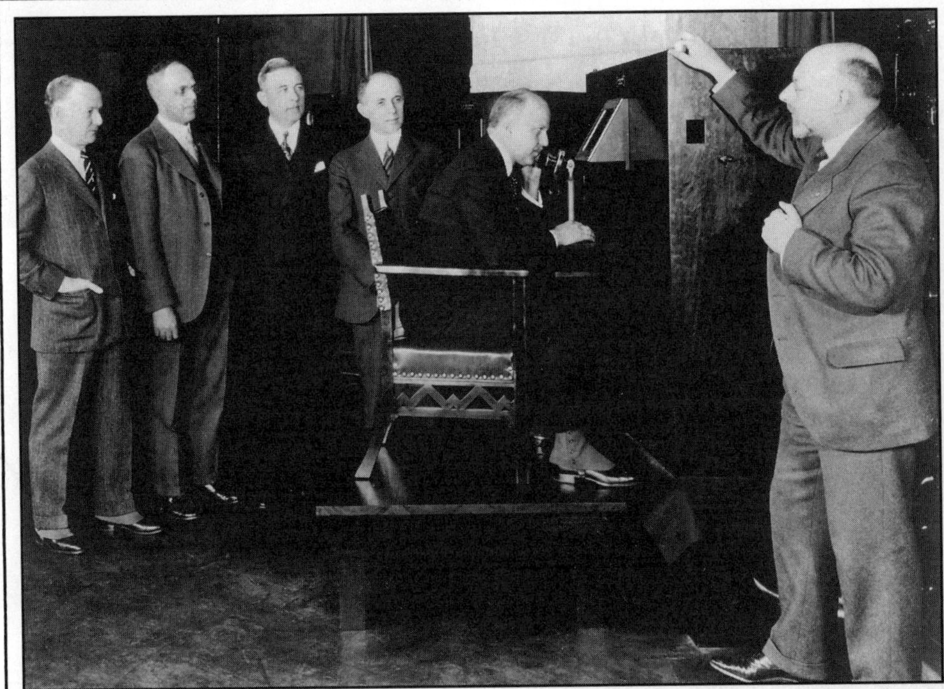

In 1927, Walter Gifford, of the American Telephone and Telegraph Co., saw Secretary of Commerce Herbert Hoover on a small television screen.

were interested. It was not until April 7, 1927, that Americans really sat up and took notice. On that day, Secretary of Commerce Herbert Hoover walked into a kind of TV studio in Washington, D.C. Sitting down in front of a TV camera, he picked up a telephone. Nearly 250 miles away, in New York City, a detailed picture of Hoover appeared on a small screen. The president of the American Telephone and Telegraph Company, Walter J. Gifford, picked up a telephone and talked to Hoover while watching him on television. The two men were using the first "picture telephone"!

But television had a long way to go before it would become a favorite American pastime.

The image of Hoover, seen by Gifford in New York, was televised from Washington, D.C., in that first demonstration of television between cities.

Eventually, the spinning disk method was replaced. By the 1930s, a new system captured the light from an image and converted it into signals. The signals were then encoded for transmission. This method produced sharper pictures and made TV suitable for use in the home.

David Sarnoff, the president of the Radio Corporation of America (later, RCA), had a far-reaching vision for the uses of television. By 1931, he was making tests over an experimental TV station in New York. But few people saw them. Sarnoff had such confidence in the future of television that he invested more than one million dollars.

In 1939, Sarnoff had the chance to show Americans what TV could do. It was the year of the World's Fair in New York City. President Franklin D. Roosevelt would be at the opening. RCA sent a TV camera to film the event, and Roosevelt became the first president ever to appear on television.

Other television images were also being shown at the fair. An RCA exhibit, the "Hall of Television," was seen by hundreds of thousands of people. For many, it was the first time in their lives that they had seen television. Fascinated by its magic, people crowded into the exhibit. There was little doubt that TV would have a tremendous future.

The year 1939 was important for television. Those few hundred people who bought television sets saw the first broadcasts of major league baseball and college football games. In 1941, the first commercial station, WNBT in New York City,

Franklin Delano Roosevelt became the first president to appear on television when he spoke at the 1939 World's Fair in New York.

began offering 15 hours of programs a week. The future of television seemed bright.

Then, on December 7, 1941, the bombing of Pearl Harbor by the Japanese was reported on TV. This was the first television newscast. But the war also signaled a big blow for television. Suddenly, the country had no time for TV. The nation poured its money, its know-how, and its free time into the war effort. TV had all but died even before it was established. It would take several years, new ways of producing TV shows, and TV's first major comedian to bring Americans back to television.

Everyone Gets into the Act

It was not until 1948 that television became popular in American homes. "Uncle Miltie" was TV's first major star. Every Tuesday night, about 750,000 of the one million Americans who then owned TV sets turned them on to watch his comedy-variety show. Others hurried to the home of a friend or relative to catch the program, *The Texaco Star Theater*. The TV screen had become big enough for more than one person to watch — when a special magnifying glass was placed in front of the screen!

More than anything else, it was Milton Berle's wild sense of comedy that sold television to Americans for good. Keep in mind that, until 1958, most TV shows were live. That meant that anything that happened during a broadcast was seen by viewers. Since the shows were live, few special effects could be used. And the pictures were all black and white. Berle realized that television was a medium that required lots of action, a fast pace, and a sense of the absurd.

In the 1940s, those families that had television sets often found themselves with lots of visitors when it came time for a favorite show.

Uncle Miltie's comic routines were wild, nutty, and loud. The guests on his show were chosen to fascinate and amaze. They included singers, dancers, and even acrobats. To keep things moving, Berle relied heavily on slapstick routines. Pies were thrown in faces. People fell off ladders or were tossed into water. Miltie dressed as a clown, a middle-aged woman, a child, or a hobo.

Milton Berle's comedy-variety show ushered in a period of growth for television. By the end of 1948, 127 stations were on the air. In 1950, Americans bought more than 7 million new television sets.

Nearly every TV owner of the time stayed home Tuesday evenings to watch "Mr. Television," Milton Berle, on *The Texaco Star Theater*.

Shortly after Milton Berle's show began, another variety-show host began attracting viewers. Ed Sullivan was stiff and solemn-faced. He began *The Toast of the Town*, later renamed the *Ed Sullivan Show*. Sullivan couldn't have been more different from Uncle Miltie. Sullivan never traded his plain black suit for any comic costumes. He seemed to have difficulty smiling. When he told a joke, it sounded forced. And he couldn't sing, dance, or act. He did, however, have an eye for talent. And he had a feel for the latest entertainment trends. Personalities like Dean Martin, Jerry Lewis, Elvis Presley, and later, the Beatles were invited to

The Beatles (left to right: Ringo Starr, George Harrison, John Lennon, Paul McCartney) rehearse with Sullivan, center, for his television show.

appear on his show — just as they were reaching the height of their popularity.

Sullivan always provided a balance of entertainment for the whole family. Parents who might not have been thrilled by Elvis's performance could still see other entertainers they could enjoy. Children who were too young for either teenage or adult entertainment were delighted by puppet shows or jugglers on Sullivan's show. Highly entertaining programs were becoming available to everyone. And these programs became available through the first TV *networks*.

A TV network was formed as a company to produce or buy TV shows. Then it paid local TV stations across the country to broadcast these shows. At the same time, it charged other companies large sums of money to advertise their products on the shows. This made it possible to present the same, professionally produced programs all over the country. The many commercials you see on TV today are the result of this system. The major networks continue to pay local TV stations to carry their programs. Advertisers pay these networks for the right to air their messages during commercial breaks.

When this system first began, TV shows cost so little that they could be paid for by only one advertiser. Shows had names like *The Goodyear Playhouse*, which was paid for by the Goodyear Tire company, and *Colgate Comedy Hour*, paid for by the makers of Colgate toothpaste.

Howdy Doody, center, with Clarabell the clown and “Buffalo Bob” Smith, who provided Howdy’s voice in full view of the studio audience.

Sitcoms, Drama and the News

Two of the most popular sitcoms that began in the 1950s were *I Love Lucy* and *The Honeymooners*. More than 40 years later, these shows are still popular, and are rerun on many stations. Both shows are about families. Originally, neither show featured children. Later, in the *I Love Lucy* show, a child was added to Lucy's family.

As the fifties advanced, the sitcom family with children became the rule. Comedies about family life, such as *Leave It to Beaver*, *Father Knows Best*, and *The Danny Thomas Show* were very popular. Sometimes, a central character was a child. Usually, a funny or touching adventure would teach the child a lesson about honesty, courage, or other qualities valued by the American family.

Other family shows included westerns and adventure series. *Gunsmoke*, *Davy Crockett*, and *Bonanza* drew viewers of all ages. Adventure series, like *Lassie* and *Superman*, attracted younger viewers. Programs that involved law or police work, such as *Perry Mason* and *Dragnet*, were more

Reruns of *The Honeymooners,* with Jackie Gleason, left, Art Carney, and Audrey Meadows, are still popular today.

suitable for an adult audience. A show about doctors, called *Medic*, started winning viewers. Late at night, old movies that had played in theaters 10 or 20 years before might be broadcast.

In the 1950s there were also programs for the serious or highly educated viewer. Dramas, operas, and ballets scored some of the highest ratings of those years. Programs such as *Playhouse 90*, *The Kraft Television Theater*, and *Hallmark Hall of Fame* aired dramas written especially for television or adapted from Broadway. In 1952, viewers were treated to the first live broadcast of an opera, Gian Carlo Menotti's *Amahl and the Night Visitors*.

For such programs, television had a double advantage. The performance was televised live, so it had the feeling of live theater. However, close-ups, fade-outs, and a variety of camera movements added the excitement usually associated with films.

It was also during this decade that the news became a regular feature of television. What began as local news broadcasts and occasional coverage of special events grew into regular news programs. In the early days of television, the news consisted of a "talking head." Viewers watched a reporter seated at a desk describing what had happened that day or the day before. Charts or still photographs were sometimes shown. At times, film that had been developed the day before could be seen.

Edward R. Murrow changed all this. His *See It Now* series, which began in the 1950s on CBS, took TV cameras to the place where a news event was actually happening. This started a trend in TV news reporting that continues to the present day.

The bringing of news into the living room through TV changed people's response to world events. It allowed viewers to witness an event at the moment it was happening. The 1952 race for president between Dwight D. Eisenhower and Adlai E. Stevenson attracted millions of viewers, making Eisenhower the first "TV president."

In 1956, the program *You Are There* featured CBS news correspondent Walter Cronkite. Through special interviews and footage of the fighting, Cronkite covered rioting on the island of Cyprus. By then, it had become common practice for news reporters to take American audiences into the homes of movie stars, onto the battlefield, or to the site of hurricanes or fires.

Many of the changes in television that occurred throughout the fifties were due to changes in television production. These early years of live TV broadcasting were filled with mistakes, some of them wildly funny. During one live TV drama, two actors were supposed to be sitting at a table by a window, inside a house, while it was snowing outside. To make the "snow," a stagehand sprinkled bits of white paper behind the window. But something went wrong. Suddenly, "snow" was falling in *front* of the window, inside the house!

In those days, the only way to record a broadcast for later showing was to make a *kinescope*. While a live program was being televised, a movie camera, pointed at a television monitor, filmed the TV show. The resulting film, or kinescope, was far from perfect.

One early exception to this method was the *I Love Lucy* show. *I Love Lucy* was filmed by a movie camera in front of a live audience. The film was then edited and broadcast later during the show's regular time slot. The result was a very clear picture. Mistakes were removed and the timing was improved for Lucy's comic routines.

In 1956, *videotape* first began to be used to "prerecord" programs. (The television industry uses the term "prerecord" to mean recording a program for later showing. Of course, the word "record" means the same thing.) However, for the next three years, there were technical problems with playing back videotape. These problems were not solved until 1959.

Videotape provides the advantage of instant replay. Unlike movie camera film, it does not have to be sent away for developing. Parts of a show can be taped, reviewed for mistakes, and then retaped. A videotaped show can be broadcast and rebroadcast seconds, days, weeks, or even years after it was originally recorded.

As the 1950s drew to a close, it seemed that nothing could stop television. The networks were multimillion dollar industries. Nearly every home in America had a television. Still, no one dreamed of the further advances in TV technologies and TV programming that were just around the corner.

Each week, millions of fans watched Lucille Ball, her real-life husband, Desi Arnaz, center, and William Frawley, on the zany *I Love Lucy* show.

Television Comes of Age

With the 1960s and 1970s came a generation of people who had never known life without television! For those born before World War II, television had seemed almost like a miracle. Just seeing in their own living rooms images being sent from some faraway place was enough to amaze and entertain them. But for this new generation of TV viewers, more dazzling thrills were needed.

One of these thrills was color television. Although color TV had been invented in 1928, it did not begin to enter American homes until the late 1950s. The delay was partly due to the fact that several color systems had been developed around the same time.

In 1950, both CBS and RCA each had its own system of color television. The two companies were competing to get their systems licensed. Nowadays, if you do not have a color TV set, you can still view color shows in black and white. In 1950, however, the CBS color system could not be picked up by black-and-white TV sets. RCA's system produced acceptable color images, but poor-quality black-and-white images.

Finally, however, RCA took on the development of a color system that would work for American television. By the late fifties, NBC, the network owned by RCA, was broadcasting 40 hours of color television a week.

Color television opened up a whole new world of TV broadcasting. Suddenly, everything looked more real. New possibilities for television drew big-time movie and recording stars to the industry. These stars — such as Bob Hope, Pearl Bailey, Judy Garland, and Frank Sinatra — took advantage of the effects of color to do *specials*. Specials were one-time programs, featuring a superstar and his or her guests. There were usually sweeping musical numbers. Famous costume designers, makeup artists, and set decorators were called in to dazzle audiences.

Smaller cameras and more advanced lighting methods even made a presidential election an ongoing, prime-time show. In 1960, John F. Kennedy ran for president against Richard M. Nixon. The two agreed to a series of four debates, to be televised to the nation. The debates stirred up enormous interest in the election. A majority of voters decided who they would vote for after watching those debates. When the election results were being broadcast in November, more than 90 percent of people who owned television sets stayed home to watch.

In 1960, John F. Kennedy, left, and Richard Nixon, right, took part in the first Presidential debates ever to be seen on television.

Television's ability to capture news while it was happening really came into its own in the 1960s. In 1965, the launching of a communications satellite allowed live telecasts between Europe and the United States. The satellite was a TV station that orbited Earth, just like a small moon. In it were devices that transmitted television signals beamed up to it from stations on Earth.

Satellite TV turned the planet into what has been called a "global village." Such events as the Olympic Games could be brought into homes as they were happening. Television cameras began going everywhere, capturing images of events as they occurred. The most shocking example of instant TV coverage was the murder of Lee Harvey Oswald, who was suspected of killing President Kennedy. Police guards were taking Oswald from the Dallas city jail to a county jail. A man named Jack Ruby stepped out of the crowd and fired a shot, killing Oswald. People watching television on the morning of November 24, 1963, saw the shooting as it happened! Millions of viewers had seen history being made.

Meanwhile, the rest of TV programming stayed the same in many ways. But programs got more fantastic, more action-packed, and more expensive. The three major networks were competing to win the largest audiences.

In truth, the networks were afraid to make major changes in the kind of programming they created. A pilot, or sample of a new program, cost about $100,000 to make. It might be shown once to determine audience reaction. If it passed this test, it might become a regular program. But a new series that came out of such a pilot could be canceled at any time if audience ratings fell.

Because new programming was so risky and so expensive, networks stuck with the old formulas. They continued to make sitcoms, westerns, variety and adventure shows, police, courtroom, and medical dramas. As time went on, some of these types of shows got better and more advanced. Other types of programs faded away.

The western is one type of TV show that began to die in the late 1960s. In the 1950s, *Gunsmoke* was one of the most acclaimed shows on the air. Similar shows had followed. But by the seventies, westerns were on the way out. Medical shows, not very common in the 1950s, became very popular in the 1960s. Millions of viewers watched dramas about young doctors, like *Ben Casey* and *Dr. Kildare*.

One program that began in 1966 and ended in 1969 left a lasting mark upon television. It was the original *Star Trek*, one of the first television science fiction programs. During its three years, an audience developed that has only grown over time.

Leonard Nimoy appeared as the extremely intelligent Mr. Spock on the popular science fiction series, *Star Trek*.

Throughout the sixties and seventies, interest in police shows soared. The networks responded by making their police and detective dramas more realistic and convincing. Shows with veteran actors, such as *Kojak*, played by Telly Savalas, strove for harsh, action-packed realism. This trend continued into the eighties. Police shows like *Hill Street Blues* won praise for the sensitive way they portrayed police work in big cities.

During the 1960s, educational television began to gain attention. Since the 1950s, these broadcasts had been paid for by private foundations. They carried no advertising. The purpose was to bring educational programs into homes and schools. By 1969, educational television had become part of the Public Broadcasting System (PBS). It became available in more and more cities throughout the country.

The growth of PBS showed that educational television, without advertising, could draw a wide audience. By the 1970s, PBS was airing high-quality dramas imported from England. PBS's news reports and science documentaries were widely praised. *Sesame Street*, a children's show that started on PBS in 1969, combined learning with fun. It became very popular, and many people credit it with improving children's performance in school.

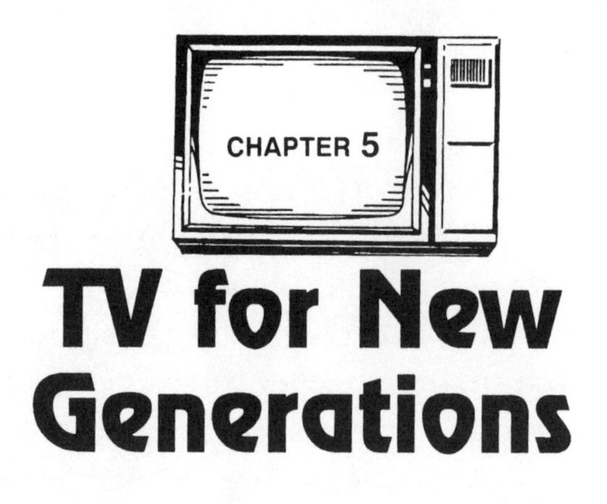

TV for New Generations

By the late 1960s and early 1970s, it was evident that something was changing in commercial television. The old formula shows were still in place. But something about the approach and the material hinted at a new spirit. This was especially true of comedy. One comedy show in particular was getting a lot of attention because of the things it made fun of, the entertainers it used, and the way it was organized.

Rowan and Martin's *Laugh-In* grew out of the variety shows of early television. The routines were quick and easy to understand, and they got broad laughs. Each week, a well-known guest was invited to appear on the show.

Moreover, the humor in *Laugh-In* often had a political edge. Such *Laugh-In* comedians as Goldie Hawn and Lily Tomlin made fun of politicians and other public figures. Their gags rarely lasted more than a few seconds. On TV, the accent had been on comedy since the beginning. But the political messages added a new side to television comedy.

Goldie Hawn, shown here with Arte Johnson, went on to a successful movie career after being featured on *Laugh-In*.

The Flip Wilson Show was like a next-generation Milton Berle show. Like Uncle Miltie, Flip was a gifted comedian. He had a sense of the ridiculous, and a perfect sense of timing. Just as Miltie had put on a dress for laughs, Flip created a female character — "Geraldine" — sending his ratings to the top. What was unusual about *The Flip Wilson Show* was that Flip Wilson was black. Up until this time, television had been led by white performers.

The late 1960s and early 1970s also saw the first African-American newscasters on network TV. And such popular series as *Julia*, *The Mod Squad*, and *I Spy* featured black characters. More and more black entertainers were invited to appear on variety shows. Some, such as Sammy Davis, Jr., had their own specials.

By the mid-seventies, sitcoms had undergone a dramatic change. In the 1950s and early 1960s, they had pictured middle-class, white couples or families. Then, in the early 1970s, Norman Lear developed a series called *All in the Family*. This sitcom shocked many viewers. Its family was very different from the families portrayed in earlier sitcoms. This was a working-class family. The father, Archie Bunker, was white, uneducated, and prejudiced. He was plain-spoken. He complained about blacks, Catholics, Jews — anyone different from him. He argued constantly with his daughter and her husband, who represented the freer life-style of the sixties and seventies generation.

Television viewers around the country often echoed "The devil made me do it," the frequent excuse of Flip Wilson's "Geraldine."

The success of *All in the Family* gave networks the courage to experiment with other types of sitcoms. Norman Lear produced other sitcoms about blacks, Hispanics, middle-aged women, and senior citizens. Many of them were smashing successes.

One of the most popular shows of the 1970s was *The Mary Tyler Moore Show*. It was about a young, unmarried, professional woman, who worked at a TV station. The success of this show gave rise to several other popular sitcoms about single women. Today, sitcoms continue to portray people of both sexes and of all races, ages, and incomes.

As the program content changed, television technology advanced rapidly. Stereo sound and computer technology opened new doors. Special-effects shows began getting larger and larger audiences. *The Six-Million-Dollar Man* starred Lee Majors, playing a "bionic" man — a superhuman figure with many artificial body parts — who could leap to enormous heights or perform feats of amazing strength. It led to *The Bionic Woman*, starring Lindsay Wagner. And there was Lynda Carter as *Wonder Woman*. Special effects helped her do almost as much as Wonder Woman had done in comic books.

With new ideas and technology, it seemed that TV networks and their programs were moving into a new golden age. But no one could have predicted what was about to happen to the all-powerful networks in the 1980s and 1990s.

Mary Tyler Moore, left, played Mary Richards, a single career woman. Here she is seen with Cloris Leachman, as Phyllis, her unlikable neighbor.

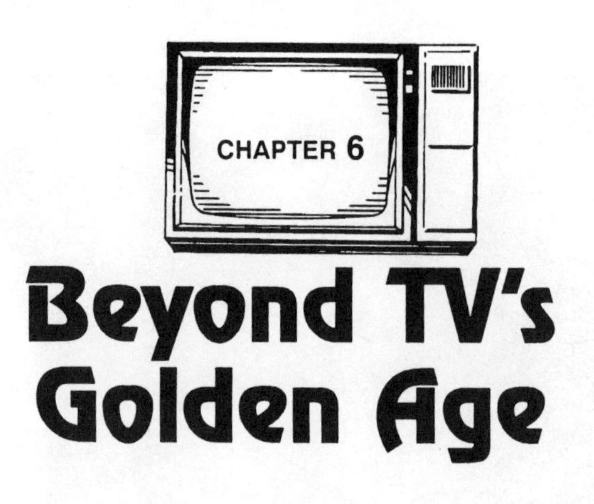

Beyond TV's Golden Age

In the 1980s, fresh, original ideas for TV programming came to full flower. Women lawyers, police officers, and doctors were featured in true-to-life dramas. Sitcoms about well-to-do black families, such as *The Cosby Show*, drew millions of viewers. Talk show hosts, male and female, black and white, became as well-known and as celebrated as their famous guests.

One long-running television show — not reruns — actually began in 1955. The first host of *The Tonight Show* was Steve Allen, who was followed by Jack Parr. In 1962, Johhny Carson began hosting the show. He proved to be so popular that his fans were disappointed when he stepped down nearly 30 years later. He was followed by yet another host, Jay Leno.

During the eighties, soap operas hit prime time. Until then, they had been produced with relatively low budgets for everyday afternooon viewing. Now, shows such as *Dallas*, *Dynasty*, and *Falcon Crest* spent millions on once-a-week productions that

Bill Cosby, seen here with Keshia Knight Pulliam, starred in *The Cosby Show*, about a successful African-American doctor and his family.

were seen in the evening. And these network shows were watched by viewers throughout the world.

News broadcasting also exploded in the 1980s. News spots were lengthened, and some newscasters became stars in their own right. The networks came up with new ideas for documentary shows. Factual programs about real topics, TV documentaries covered everything from interviews with movie stars and sports figures to reports of crime and government corruption. Often, camera crews followed law officers around to record arrests.

In 1972, the video cassette recorder, or VCR, was invented. More and more families were buying VCRs in the early eighties. They could be used at home to record TV programs. A new way of watching TV began to sweep America. Why watch a program when the networks said you had to? And why watch it the way they expected you to?

People began to set the VCR to record favorite programs while they were out, asleep, or busy. This changed the concept of prime time. The prime-time shows ran during the hours between dinner and bedtime. Other shows, which the network did not consider as important, were shown in the middle of the night or during the day, when most people were asleep or at work. Now, with a VCR, viewers could see any programs they wanted, when they wanted. They could just record them and watch them later.

Viewers soon began putting together their own "prime-time" broadcasts on tape. After dinner and before bed, they watched what they wanted to watch — not what happened to be on TV at that time. Another advantage for people using VCRs was that commercials could be left out of a TV recording. Or they could be fast forwarded when a taped program was being watched. VCRs helped limit the absolute power of the networks.

The technology for sending TV signals around the world was becoming less expensive. This led to more and more programs from different countries, minor producers, and small, private broadcasters who created their own mininetworks.

As these networks assembled, they began to face a problem. How could they bring their broadcasts to homes all over the country as the major networks did? The answer lay in the use of cable.

Cable, or underground wires, bring TV signals directly into the home. This differs from the older network-station method of sending these signals through space. Cable TV has existed since 1949. It was intended to bring programs to out-of-the-way areas where it was difficult to receive a television signal. However, legal and technical problems kept it from developing until 1975. At this time, Home Box Office (HBO) came on the scene.

HBO was cable TV that could be ordered and paid for. In exchange, special programs not available on network TV could be seen through cable. One cable event in particular attracted a great deal of attention in 1975. HBO offered Americans a ringside view of the Joe Frazier and

The famous boxing match between Joe Frazier, left, and Muhammad Ali, was seen by millions of viewers on cable television in 1975.

Muhammad Ali boxing match, as it was taking place in the Philippines.

By the 1980s, local stations were reaching millions of homes through cable. WTBS, a station in Atlanta, became national when it joined the cable network. So did WGN-TV from Chicago and WWOR-TV from New York City. Now people from all over the country could order cable and watch programs on these stations.

Rapidly, cable began adding more pay channels. Channels such as Showtime, Cinemax, and The Movie Channel offered viewers recent Hollywood movies, with no advertising interruptions, for a monthly fee. They also produced their own music, comedy, and drama specials.

Cable TV brought something new in television — music TV. The first music TV station, MTV, startled some viewers at first. At the beginning all it offered for 24 hours a day were programs lasting a few minutes each. They featured performances of songs being acted out. These new miniprograms were called *music videos*.

Many people were doubtful about the future of music videos. But the music video industry spread like wildfire. Its audience was enormous. It was composed mostly of young people who wanted to watch their favorite rock singers perform their music. There was a lot of money available to make music videos, as well. Music producers understood that a good rock video might help sell more records, cassettes, or CDs. So they began investing money

Satellites such as this instantly relay television signals across the globe, so viewers around the world can watch the same event at the same time.

in the production of music videos each time a new album was released.

In the 1980s, a rock video of Michael Jackson cost its producers millions of dollars. The video lasted only a few minutes, but it more than paid for itself in additional sales of the recording.

As MTV became established, its horizons widened. Now it offers news, comedy, game shows, interviews, and cartoons — geared mostly to viewers under 30.

In the 1990s, cable stations became more specialized. Now there are stations showing only religious programs, and those for people who want to stay at home while they shop. There are stations showing only old movies, or only programs of interest to retired people. Other stations show sports 24 hours a day. One established cable network offers programs that appeal mainly to blacks. Another station shows only science fiction programs. There is a 24-hour news channel and a channel that allows Americans to watch Congress in session.

In New York and some other cities, there are even public access channels. Public access channels accept programs from just about anyone, and they are broadcast without charge.

In recent years, the marketing of videotapes of movies has cut into both the network and cable market. Video cassette rental stores carry tapes of thousands of programs. These include films, plays, operas, old TV shows, exercise programs, and

Michael Jackson, whose music video productions cost millions of dollars, appeared at the 1993 Super Bowl at the California Rose Bowl.

"how-to" videos. These recorded tapes can be watched at any time. They can be skipped ahead, or rewound so that all of it — or parts of it — can be watched over again.

Often, when a new movie first appears on videotape, it is also offered to television viewers by something called "pay-per-view." Under this system, a cable customer can arrange to watch a special program at home. A charge for this appears on the monthly cable bill.

Television has gone far beyond the limits that could have been imagined just a few years ago. Network and cable stations offer a dizzying choice of programs. New technology will allow viewers to receive as many as 500 channels. Video cassettes and pay-per-view have brought hit movies into homes when they have barely left the theater. Recording TV programs allows us to watch shows when and how we want to.

Now, with the *camcorder*, or TV camera-recorder, people are making their own TV programs. This type of camera was first marketed for home use in 1983. Since that time, it has been growing smaller, lighter, and easier to use.

Because they are now so easy to operate, camcorders are used in classrooms, in courtrooms, and in living rooms across the country. Throughout the world, people are filming birthdays and weddings, school plays, Little League games, and school proms. Later, they relive these events by watching them on television over and over again.

Or they send them to friends and family around the world, to keep in touch in a personal way. Some people even write their own scripts and make their own TV shows.

No one knows where the use of the camcorder will take us. Will home videos decrease the popularity of commercial videos, posing yet another threat to network TV? Perhaps. Or perhaps we shouldn't try to predict the future of television, but simply wait to see and enjoy the changes ahead.

GLOSSARY

surd (uhb-SUHRD) ridiculous

dapt (uh-DAPT) to make something fit or work in a different situation

ssette (kuh-SEHT) a plastic container or case that holds videotape

median (kuh-MEED-ee-uhn) someone whose job is making people laugh

mmercial (kuh-MUHR-shuhl) done for money; a short ad meant to sell a product

mmunications (kuh-myoo-nuh-KAY-shuhnz) sending or receiving messages or signals

vice (dih-VYS) a piece of equipment or a method that serves a special purpose

ama (DRAHM-uh) serious stories acted to show life in a real way

it (EHD-uht) to change or rearrange a piece of work to improve it

code (ihn-KOHD) to change information from one language or system into a code

tertainment (ehnt-uhr-TAYN-muhnt) a performance meant to amuse or give pleasure to people

isode (EHP-uh-SOHD) one part in a continuing story or program

de-out (FAYD-owt) a device in which a TV or movie picture disappears slowly

st forward (fast FAWR-wuhrd) to quickly move a video ahead

foundation (fown-DAY-shuhn) an organization with money to be used for a particular purpose

generation (jehn-uh-RAY-shuhn) the individuals born and living during the same time period

industry (IHN-duhs-tree) a branch of an art, craft, o business having a particular task or activity

makeshift (MAYK-shihft) quickly made, and not likel to last

personality (puhrs-uhn-AL-uht-ee) a person well-know for the qualities of his or her character

political (puh-LIHT-ih-kuhl) of or relating to government

portray (pawr-TRAY) to play the part of, as an actor does; to show

slapstick (SLAP-stihk) comedy that uses broad physical humor and nonsense

studio (STOOD-ee-oh) a place where movies or radio or TV programs are made

technology (tehk-NAHL-uh-jee) the methods and tool made and used by science

telecast (TEHL-ih-kast) to send television signals through the air by radio waves; a progran sent this way

transmit (trans-MIHT) to send radio or television signals from one place to another

trend (trehnd) a pattern of thought or behavior that many people follow for a period of tim

SOURCES OF CIVILIZATION IN THE WEST

Robert Lee Wolff, *General Editor*

LEWIS W. SPITZ, the editor of this volume, received his Ph.D. from Harvard University, and is Professor of History at Stanford University. He is the managing editor of the *Archive for Reformation History,* and is the author of several books, including *The Renaissance and Reformation Movements,* and *Conrad Celtis, The German Arch-Humanist.* He has also edited another volume in the Sources of Civilization in the West series, *The Protestant Reformation.*

OTHER BOOKS IN THE SERIES

The Age of Imperialism, *edited by Robin W. Winks,* S–205

The Ancient World: Justice, Heroism, and Responsibility, *edited by Zeph Stewart,* S–141

Century of Genius: European Thought, 1600–1700, *edited by Richard T. Vann,* S–149

The Conversion of Western Europe, 350–750, *edited by J. N. Hillgarth,* S–203

The Crisis of Church & State, 1050–1300, *by Brian Tierney (with selected documents),* S–102

The English Reform Tradition, 1790–1910, *edited by Sydney W. Jackman,* S–120

The Enlightenment, *edited by Frank E. Manuel,* S–121

The French Revolution, *edited by Philip Dawson,* S–161

Icon and Minaret: Sources of Byzantine and Islamic Civilization, *edited by Charles M. Brand,* S–199

The Image of Rome, *edited by Erich S. Gruen,* S–194

The Italian Renaissance, *edited by Werner L. Gundersheimer,* S–128

Nineteenth-Century Thought: The Discovery of Change, *edited by Richard L. Schoenwald,* S–129

The Protestant Reformation, *edited by Lewis W. Spitz,* S–140

SOURCES OF CIVILIZATION IN THE WEST

Robert Lee Wolff, General Editor

[illegible]

Other Books in this Series

The Age of Imperialism, edited by [illegible]

[illegible]

Century of Genius: European Thought, 1600–1700, edited by [illegible]

[illegible]

The English Reform Tradition, [illegible]

The Enlightenment, edited by [illegible]

The French Revolution, edited by [illegible]

[illegible]

[illegible]

[illegible]

The Italian Renaissance, edited by [illegible]

THE NORTHERN RENAISSANCE

Edited by

Lewis W. Spitz

PRENTICE-HALL, INC.
Englewood Cliffs, New Jersey

 Library of Congress Catalog Card Number 70–178767. Printed in the United States of America.

ISBN: P 0–13–623793–2
C 0–13–623801–7

10 9 8 7 6 5 4 3 2 1

Prentice-Hall International, Inc. (*London*)
Prentice-Hall of Australia, Pty. Ltd. (*Sydney*)
Prentice-Hall of Canada, Ltd. (*Toronto*)
Prentice-Hall of India Private Limited (*New Delhi*)
Prentice-Hall of Japan, Inc. (*Tokyo*)

TO

Robert Heitner

and

Wilbert Rosin

CONTENTS

FOREWORD

This book, a long-desired companion-volume to Professor Gundersheimer's *Italian Renaissance* and Professor Spitz's own *Protestant Reformation* in this series, deals with the Renaissance outside Italy. As Italians spread the new humanism abroad, secular princes and cities and members of the upper classes, as well as learned men, reached out with a passionate enthusiasm for the scholarship, the poetry, the philosophy that now radiated first into the more peaceful Empire, and then into embattled France and England, and into Spain. Professor Spitz not only tells us how this happened, but also enables us to trace the processes in the ebullient words of the leading humanists themselves.

Here is the pioneer German humanist Celtis summoning Apollo to cross the Alps to dissipate the northern darkness with the sunshine of classical learning, and earnestly spurring German youth to make the leap into the new subjects for study. Ulrich von Hutten uses the effective weapons of satire against the perverted piety of those who had attacked the study of Hebrew. A "novel" from Marguerite d'Angoulême's *Heptameron* shows us what happened to the Boccaccio tradition when it came to France, while in a more sober vein, that single-minded humanist Guillaume Budé gives the king of France the new Renaissance credo as effectively as Celtis had given it to his German students. With Rabelais, who tells us how the famous Abbey of Thélème was built, we find ourselves in the presence of a laughing humanist, as towering a figure as one of his own giants; and with Montaigne we meet the first essayist, urbane, learned, and graceful.

Moving across the Pyrenees, Professor Spitz next gives us a sample of *Don Quixote,* which we hope may whet the reader's appetite for more. Cervantes, most Spanish of writers, has been known to trap unwary readers into life-long love affairs with his country and his marvelous book. And across the channel, while John Colet preaches against secular evils at St. Paul's, St. Thomas More introduces us to Utopia, the commonwealth from which the secular evils have virtually disappeared; and Roger Ascham, Queen Elizabeth's own tutor, echoes in England the voices of Celtis in Germany and Budé in France. And at the very end, Erasmus, the incarnation of the new spirit north of the Alps, who felt at home among congenial men in any country, excoriates the stupidities and greed of high men in church and state alike.

The reader of this book will not find all of these selections easy reading. But the effect of each, and still more the cumulative effect of all, is to make us feel the freshness, the sense of energy, discovery, and intellectual excitement that characterized an age in which a fresh wind was blowing. That it blew from the south Professor Spitz makes clear. His choice of materials, his generosity in giving us several entirely new translations into English prepared by his own father, Professor Lewis W. Spitz, sr., and his brisk, compressed, scholarly, and readable general introduction and brief introductory passages preceding each selection have put us greatly in his debt.

Robert Lee Wolff
Coolidge Professor of History
Harvard University

THE NORTHERN RENAISSANCE

Introduction

In the year 1518 the audacious young knight Ulrich von Hutten wrote to his fellow humanist Willibald Pirckheimer, the Nuremberg patrician: "Oh century! Oh letters! It is a joy to be alive! It is not yet time to lapse into repose, Willibald. Studies thrive and minds flourish! Woe to you, barbarism! Accept the noose, look forward to exile!" As proof of the growing strength of the humanists the great propagandist for the new learning cited an international company of men of letters, Oecolampadius, Budé, Erasmus, Lefèvre, Cop, and Ruellius. During the course of the fifteenth century Renaissance culture had indeed spread to the nations beyond Italy.

The changes that the Renaissance underwent as it crossed the Alps and the sea to mix with indigenous elements of the North constitute one of the most interesting studies in intellectual and cultural history. By the term *Northern Renaissance* we really here mean the Renaissance outside of Italy, including Spain as well as countries literally to the north. It took Northern Europe longer than Italy to emerge from what Rabelais called "the Gothic night" just because Gothic culture was northern. Conversely, the Renaissance could scarcely have sprung up spontaneously in lands where learning had not flourished in classical times, in the northern provinces or beyond the *limes* or borders of the Roman Empire.

Two theories have been advanced to explain the origins of the Northern Renaissance. The first of these is the "reception" theory, which holds that Renaissance culture and humanism in the North were derived basically from the Italian Renaissance. Jacob Burckhardt in his great masterpiece *The Civilization of the Renaissance in Italy* (1860) pictured Italy as the cradle of modern individualism and characterized the Renaissance as the rediscovery of the world and of man. The Burckhardtian scholars in this tradition were inclined to portray northern humanism as the result of a process of Italianization: fitting Roman togas on Germanic peoples, building marble forums in place of the rude markets of Gothic cities, and cultivating fluent rhetoricians to replace barbarous scholastic philosophers. They often criticized the northerners for going only half way in changing their life style and in adopting the intellectual formulas of the Italian humanists.

The second theory, the "revisionist" theory, holds that Renaissance culture and humanism in the North were autochthonous, developed continuously out of the medieval past, and fused only gradually and partially with the influences emanating from Italy. The revisionists emphasized the persistence of classical learning from the twelfth-century Renaissance on, the contribution of the Brethren of the Common Life (lay brothers who promoted education and combined religious devotion with respect for the moral teachings of safe classical authors), and the flourishing of culture at the court of Charles IV in Prague.

Today, scholars are more inclined to stress the importance of the Italian influence for what is distinctively "Renaissance" in northern culture, particularly the devotion to the classics not merely as form but as norm for life, while recognizing the continuity in northern traditions and the special patriotic and religious concerns of the northerners.

The diffusion of Italian Renaissance culture to the North resulted from a two-way traffic in men and ideas. During the fourteenth, fifteenth, and sixteenth centuries Italian humanists and artists travelled north as ecclesiastical legates, diplomatic emissaries, lecturers on rhetoric and poetry in the universities, secretaries to northern princes and cities, and business representatives. Many contacts with northerners were made during the course of the church councils of Constance (1414–1418) and Basel (1431–1449). Italian humanists such as Poggio and Vergerio travelled in Germany. Aeneas Silvius served as secretary at the Court of the Habsburgs and wrote a description of Bohemia as well as a treatise praising German culture under the aegis of the Roman church. Not only did Petrarch spend years in Avignon, but Italian humanists throughout the fifteenth century visited France. Artists such as Leonardo da Vinci, Benvenuto Cellini, Andrea del Sarto, Il Rosso, and Francesco Primaticcio accepted the royal invitation to France. Once humanist culture took hold, enthusiasm for the classics exploded. When a second-rate Italian humanist, Aleander, presented lectures on a third-rate Latin poet, Ausonius, one hot summer in Paris, over two thousand people heard him lecture for two and a half hours. On the third day of the lectures the hall was jammed two hours before starting time.

Italians came also to England and brought their Renaissance ideas with them. Poggio arrived in England in 1418 as secretary to the bishop of Winchester and scoured monasteries for classical manuscripts. Polydore Vergil came as a papal subcollector and wrote a remarkable *History of England.* Torrigiano and other Italian artists graced the courts of Henry VII and Henry VIII. Italian bankers and merchants such as the Bardis, Peruzzis, Frescobaldi, and Medici had branches in northern Europe and provided a very real and practical link with the homeland of the Renaissance.

The northerners in turn more and more often journeyed to Italy privately, on business, or for church and state. There had been many close political ties between the Empire and the Italian city states during the Middle Ages. Commercial ties bound Venice and the Italian city-states to the German cities along the Danube and the Rhine. In 1494 the French King Charles VIII invaded Italy and drove all the way to Naples, but for decades before that event the contacts of the French with Italy were many and varied. The ties between Spain and Italy were powerful because of Spain's interest in Sicily, Naples, the papacy, and also, at the end of the century, in northern Italy. A great stream of thousands of students poured into the Italian universities from all parts of Europe for the study of law, medicine, and, increasingly, the liberal arts. At Bologna, Padua, and Pavia the "German nations" were large and restless. The English author William Thomas in his *History of Italy* (1549) observed what a large number of foreigners were in that country, "specially of gentlemen, whose resort thither is under pretence of study." Books were as mobile as the people, and editions of classical and humanist authors flowed north and were reprinted there. There were thus many avenues by which Italian Renaissance ideas made their impact felt in the North.

"These northerners generally have little spirit," observed Vespasiano da Bisticci, author of *The Lives of Famous Men of the Fifteenth Century.* To Italian eyes the progress of Renaissance culture in the North must have seemed painfully slow. Italy had the advantage of an urban society combined with an aristocratic culture. In Northern and Western Europe urbanization was more limited compared with the size of those areas, and social change occurred more slowly there. The feudal nobility in the wooded north was not so easily integrated with the mercantile class as in Italy. Even while financial, political, and military powers were moving gradually from the feudal nobility into the hands of the territorial princedoms and cities in the Empire and into the hands of the rising national monarchs in the West, the feudal classes clung tenaciously to their traditional culture and way of life. During the second half of the fifteenth century the wealthy merchants of the northern cities adapted themselves to the literary standards of the provincial aristocracy, preferring chivalric romances, lives of saints, romantic legends, devotional tracts, and traditional authors to the classics or newer humanist writings. This can be seen by surveying the *incunabula* or books printed up to the year 1500. The humanists poured scorn upon the nobles who preferred the hunt and drunkenness to learned discourse and better books. Nevertheless, a promising beginning in the development of a humanist culture was made in the north already during the fifteenth century.

Humanism was and remained in the north more a matter of the schools and of university learning, less a matter of the councils and forums than in Italy. But by the year 1520 humanism had penetrated the courts of Northern Europe to a much greater extent than historians have until recently realized. Humanism and Renaissance art found a warm welcome in the courts of Emperor Frederick III (1440–1492) and of Emperor Maximilian (1493–1519) in Linz and Vienna. Maximilian was, in fact, a hero of the humanists, who idolized and idealized him as their Maecenas, a brilliant leader who would restore the Empire to greatness. Also the territorial princes and ecclesiastical prince-bishops perceived the usefulness of humanists as Latin secretaries and of rhetoricians as orators. With the revival of Roman law, so congenial to the interests of the princes, legists who combined an interest in ancient letters with their mastery of the *Codex Juris* thrived at courts. The rising imperial cities also began to employ humanist city-secretaries on the Italian model. In France, too, humanism made great headway at the court and at various provincial centers as well. Traditionally King Francis I (1515–1547) has been hailed as the great benefactor of humanism. "Francis I," wrote Jacques Amyot in the preface of his translation of Plutarch's *Lives* (1559), "was the father of good literature, of the study of the ancient languages, and of the neglected arts and sciences in France." [1] There was indeed a flowering of art, architecture, music and letters at the court of Francis I, but there were other centers, notably Lyon, a city with an amazingly free and cosmopolitan atmosphere. Also in Spain the court through the chancellor Cardinal Francisco Ximénez de Cisneros favored a carefully controlled revival of classical languages. In England Henry VIII followed in his father's footsteps in keeping humanists and artists in the service of the court. Humanism was not, then, exclusively a matter of school learning in the North but had begun to penetrate the princely courts, the cities, and the upper ranges of

[1] Werner L. Gundersheimer, ed., *French Humanism 1470–1600* (New York, 1969), p. 9.

society. Consider, to cite but a single instance, the importance of Baldassare Castiglione's *Book of the Courtier* for Elizabethan court society.

Humanism was an international cultural movement, displaying everywhere certain common characteristics, but varying from people to people as it fused with the indigenous cultures of the North. Humanism was an intellectual movement rooted in a desire for the cultural rebirth of classical antiquity. The humanists presupposed that the fountains of antiquity, dried out during the long parched middle ages, could be opened up and would flow forth to nourish a greening of Christendom. They saw antiquity as a closed entity in the distant past separated from their own day by the medieval era. Humanism was more than a mere antiquarian interest in antiquity, for it was a certain way of looking to antiquity for guidance and inspiration. If in the strictest sense antiquity was unique and irrepeatable, classical culture contained the principles for forming and the norms for measuring their own learned culture and style of life. As form, Renaissance humanism was primarily aesthetic; as norm, it involved ethical and spiritual values of critical importance. It differed from medieval humanism in its readier acceptance of classical norms, in the extent of lay participation, and its more secular cast.

The humanists were concerned with the humane studies (*humaniora*), the studies which, as Leonardo Bruni, the Florentine civic humanist, put it in a letter to Niccolò Strozzi, are "best designed to perfect and ornament man." Peter Luder, one of the early "migratory birds" of northern humanism, announced lectures at Heidelberg in 1456 "on the *studia humanitatis,* that is, the books of the poets, orators, and historians." The humanists were opposed to the extended study of scholastic philosophy and theology, based upon Aristotelian dialectic and syllogistic reasoning. They offered an approach to truth and learning which stressed instead the classical languages, poetry and rhetoric, moral philosophy, and history. They believed that truth conveyed by rhetoric that moves the hearer to action is more effective and in some sense therefore more true than a truth that is merely established intellectually by logic and remains inoperative outside the mind. Poetry, too, can move man emotionally as well as intellectually. Moral philosophy provides guidance for life. History was considered useful as a form of philosophy that teaches by examples. There was little formal instruction in history; but the humanists wrote much history, the story of their own times as well as of times past. If these general characteristics were common to humanism in most of Europe, the development of the movement differed from country to country as to time and as to special thrust.

In the year 1507 the young German humanist Nicholas Gerbellius exclaimed "I congratulate myself often on living in this glorious century in which so many remarkable men have arisen in Germany." The two decades just preceding the Reformation marked the high tide of German humanism. The new literary and philological culture came to the Germanies in strength earlier than to the other nations of the North because of their proximity to Italy and because relative peace prevailed in the Empire while England and France were embroiled in the Hundred Years' War.

The course of German humanism developed in three phases. There was a brief flourish of interest in Prague under Emperor Charles IV, whose chancellor, Johann von Neumarkt developed a new book of forms for documents and letters which improved the Latin and German style of public documents. The famous *Plowman of Bohemia,* written by the notary Johann von Tepl, a dialogue of a peasant with death, who had just taken away his wife, reflects the influence of Petrarch and classical authors. This chancellery humanism was later transferred to the court in Vienna by Albert of Austria. The second phase was begun by the Italians that attended the councils of Constance and Basel and carried forward by pioneers of humanism such as Peter Luder, Samuel Karoch, Albrecht von Eyb, Nicholas von Wyle, and Gregor Heimburg. This phase lasted until about 1475. The third phase during the last quarter of the fifteenth century and first two decades of the sixteenth, saw the maturation of German humanism.

During the high tide of German humanism on the eve of the Reformation, a whole generation of outstanding men flourished. Rudolf Agricola (1444–1485) called the "father of German humanism," spent ten years in Italy. As Erasmus put it, "He first brought with him from Italy some gleam of a better literature." He wrote a *Life of Petrarch* and a textbook *On Dialectical Invention* in which he set forth the true function of logic as a basic element of rhetoric: by cultivating accurate thinking and an effective style, logic enables rhetoric to move to the audience conviction and action. At Heidelberg he inspired Conrad Celtis (1459–1508), a lyric poet who was dubbed the "German Arch-humanist." "Oh sacred and mighty work of the poets," Celtis exclaimed, "you alone free all things from fate and lift up mortal ashes to the stars!" He called on Apollo, god of the poets, to leave Italy and to come to the north, and he summoned the German youth to cultural rivalry with the Italians. In the cities men such as Willibald Pirckheimer, a wealthy patrician and councilor in Nuremberg, or Conrad Peutinger, an influential legist in Augsburg, cultivated humanistic disciplines. Aventinus wrote *The Annals of Bavaria.* In Gotha near Erfurt in Saxony a cathedral canon Mutianus Rufus presided over a circle of young humanists, many of whom, like Crotus Rubeanus and Ulrich von Hutten, became embroiled in the Reuchlin controversy.

One of the humanists, Johannes Reuchlin (1455–1522), a lawyer and chancellor to the duke of Württemberg, cultivated the study of Hebrew and wrote two books exploiting the Jewish mystical cabala as an apologetic for Christianity. Ironically he was attacked by a Jew named Pfefferkorn, who had been converted to Christianity and with the zeal of a convert turned against Hebrew letters. He wrote *A Mirror for Jews* in which he urged that all Hebrew books be confiscated. The scholastic doctors, especially the Dominicans at Cologne, in their obscurantist way backed his demand and the emperor even issued a decree that Jews should turn in their books. Pfefferkorn made a vicious attack on Reuchlin in *The Hand Mirror* for defending Hebrew books, and Reuchlin defended himself in a work entitled the *Eye Mirror.* He also published a volume called *Letters of Famous Men* who supported him in the controversy. Taking their cue from this title, two young humanists, Crotus Rubeanus and Ulrich von Hutten published their *Letters of Obscure Men,* a collection of spurious satirical letters mocking the ignorance of Reuchlin's opponents. The Reuchlin controversy was a literary skirmish, like a preliminary fight before the heavyweight title match of the Reformation. Reuchlin's grandnephew Philip Melanchthon, a brilliant young humanist, became Luther's lieutenant and the main author of the evangelical Augsburg Confession. Humanist learning was taken up and promoted zealously by Protestant educators on the secondary school and university levels throughout the sixteenth century. German humanism developed two major drives, the one toward cultural nationalism in rivalry with the Italians, and the other toward religious enlightenment against many medieval practices. When Luther appeared on the scene, most of the humanists at first hailed him as their hero. "Long live liberty!" cried Hutten, and many of the younger humanists joined the Reformation movement. Albrecht Dürer, the great Renaissance artist, hailed Luther as the man who "had brought him certainty."

During the fifteenth century France gained political strength but declined culturally. As political change was followed by social change, a need for a new cultural and artistic expression gradually developed. During the fourteenth century, while Petrarch was in Avignon, the first hints of a French Renaissance culture became discernible. There never ceased to be circles of humanist men of letters and art, not only at the court but in provincial capitals. But usually it was a matter of a small cluster of humanists supported by a single patron such as the chancellor Jean de Montreuil (1354–1418), who had developed an enthusiasm for Petrarch and Italian culture.[2]

During the long reign of King Francis I (1515–1547) Renaissance culture in France truly came alive. The influence of Italian neoclassical design is visually evident in the palace of Fontainebleau, constructed during his reign. His own sister, Marguerite d'Angoulême, was a patroness of humanists, a protector of reformers, and an author and religious poet in her own right. Étienne Dolet (1508–1546), who lived in Lyon, declared in his *Commentaries on the Latin Tongue* that literature was making tremendous progress and urged the king, aristocrats, and men of means to support good letters even more amply. The major figure of French humanism, Guillaume Budé (1468–1540), contributed to the Hellenic revival and persuaded the king to found a Trilingual College as well as a library at Fontainebleau which grew into the National Library of France. The incomparable Erasmus called Budé the "marvel of France."

In addition to the classical revival, French humanism contributed to religious enlightenment. Lefèvre d'Étaples (1455–1536) was the leading figure in that regard. He took his doctorate in Paris, encountered Neoplatonism in Florence, and studied Aristotle in Padua. He read the German mystics, edited Nicholas Cusanus, a fifteenth-century philosopher, and studied the Greek church fathers. In 1509 he published a scholarly edition of the Psalms and in 1512 he published his *Commentary on the Epistles of St. Paul* which combined an edition of the text plus his commentary. He believed with St. Paul that man is saved by God's grace and forgiving mercy alone. He also held that the Scriptures should be understood Christologically and emphasized their spiritual message. In 1522 he also published a *Commentary on the Four Gospels.*

[2] Franco Simone, *The French Renaissance Medieval Tradition and Italian Influence in Shaping the Renaissance in France* (New York, 1969), documents the continuity of humanist learning from Avignon and Petrarch through the fifteenth century in France.

Luther had a high regard for Lefèvre's commentaries and referred to them in his own work on the *Epistle to the Romans* and other Biblical studies. Lefèvre was close to Marguerite d'Angoulême and befriended Gerard Roussel, Guillaume Farel, and John Calvin, young humanists who turned reformers.

The French Renaissance was distinctive for the close alliance of the rebirth of letters with the study of law and particularly of Roman law. Among the leading figures in the area of law and history the most outstanding was Jean Bodin (1530–1596), a political philosopher who lectured on law at Toulouse and practiced in Paris. His *Six Books of the Republic* has been described as the first modern attempt to construct an elaborate system of political science. His *Method for the Easy Comprehension of History* was a study of universal law, human, natural, and divine. He proposed a curious climatic theory of peoples which suggested geographical determinism.

The two leading literary figures of the French Renaissance were the wit and satirist François Rabelais (c. 1495–1553) and the superb essayist Michel de Montaigne (1533–1592). The "prince of the poets" Pierre de Ronsard (1524–1585), was a member of the Pléiades, a brigade or cluster of seven famous poets and dramatists who attempted to "follow the ancients" and were much under Neoplatonic influence. Ronsard called France the "mother of the arts."

In Spain Renaissance culture like so many other things seemed to be handed down from the throne. Cardinal Francisco Ximénez de Cisneros (1436–1517), as archbishop of Toledo, primate of Spain, regent for Ferdinand and Isabella, and from 1508 on grand inquisitor, reformed the church from above and promoted in a safe and limited way a classical literary and educational reform. With the blessing of the monarchs he founded the University of Alcalá, near Madrid, with a trilingual college devoted to the study of Latin, Greek, and Hebrew. He envisioned a Christian humanist reform program which would by returning the clergy to the pure sources of religion bring about spiritual enlightenment and moral reform. He directed the publication of the *Complutensian Polyglot* Bible with Hebrew, Latin and Greek texts in parallel columns. There was a genuine Erasmian tradition, despite the efforts of the Spanish inquisitors to keep out Erasmian and Lutheran influences. Juan Luis Vives and Juan de Valdés were in this tradition. But no literary figure of great importance arose before the giant of Spanish literature Miguel de Cervantes (1547–1616), who lived during the "golden age of Spain." His *Don Quixote* stands as the great Spanish masterpiece of world literature.

The course of humanism in England was far from easy. During the fourteenth and fifteenth centuries England was involved first in the Hundred Years' War and then in the War of the Roses. The English seemed to Italians to be so slow in taking to classical studies that Boccaccio once called them "thick heads." Many students have argued, in fact, that the English Renaissance came only during the age of Elizabeth at the end of the sixteenth and in the early seventeenth centuries with Spenser, Raleigh, and Shakespeare. But we know now that the early centuries were not so barren as was once supposed and that there was much continuity of Renaissance culture during the sixteenth century, which made the flowering of English genius possible during the reign of good Queen Bess.

During the fifteenth century Italians of various callings, including five successive bishops of Worcester, came to England. A brother of King Henry V, Duke Humphrey of Gloucester, used Italian secretaries, gathered a group of *literati* about him, encouraged classical studies at Oxford, and willed a valuable manuscript collection to the university. A number of clergymen had Italian and Greek humanist friends and were classics buffs. William Grey, bishop of Ely, for example, studied with Guarino and was a friend of Poggio and Bessarion. The first printing press set in motion by William Caxton in 1476 stimulated bookish culture. It was only at the end of the century, however, that the study of the classics began in earnest at Oxford, cultivated by Thomas Linacre, William Grocyn, and William Latimer, all three of whom had studied in Florence and had begun there the study of Greek. Grocyn, in turn, became the teacher of the three great humanists John Colet, Thomas More, and Erasmus. John Colet (c. 1467–1519) was an earnest man, influenced by the Florentine neoplatonists, who became the founder of St. Paul's school, a Biblical exegete, and an ecclesiastical reformer. Thomas More (1478–1535) was a prolific author, most famous for his *Utopia,* a defender of the Catholic faith against Protestant reformers, lord chancellor of England, and finally a martyr for conscience' sake when King Henry VIII assumed prerogatives in the church that More thought belonged to the pope alone.

Humanism did not die out with these three giants to be resurrected again by Elizabeth. Rather, Renaissance culture penetrated court circles during the sixteenth century. Young humanists such as Thomas Starkey and Richard Morrison provided the theoretical foundation of Tudor policy, gleaning lessons from Italian political thought and practice. Italian manners were adopted by the court circles. Humanism influenced the schools as Englishmen wrote treatises on education and introduced Renaissance ideas into the schools themselves. Sir Thomas Elyot's *The Governor* (1531) and Roger Ascham's *The Schoolmaster* (1570) became classics of humanist education. Curricular plans of humanists such as the Spaniard Juan Luis Vives were introduced even in some provincial schools. The glories of the age of Elizabeth were made possible by the transmitters of humanist learning from the first bloom early in the sixteenth century to the full flowering late in the century.

In some ways Desiderius Erasmus (1469–1536), the acknowledged "prince of the humanists," was the archetype of northern humanists with his devotion to the classics and his preoccupation with religious enlightenment and reform. But in other respects he differed, for if most of the northern humanists tended toward a cultural nationalism in their rivalry with the Italians, Erasmus remained a perfect cosmopolitan who belonged to all nations or to none. The "Flying Dutchman" grew up in the Netherlands, where he was educated by the Brethren of the Common Life, studied in France, was often in England, lived and worked in Venice, wrote in Louvain, and spent two decades in the upper Rhinelands in Basel and Freiburg in Breisgau. "Where you fare well there is your fatherland," he wrote, citing Cicero. His knowledge of classical and patristic literature was unequalled, and his own writings were unmatched either in volume or in the variety of their literary forms. Among his more popular writings were his *Praise of Folly,* the *Adages,* and the *Colloquies.* His most serious efforts, however, went into his editions of the church fathers, Latin and Greek studies, the 1516 critical edition of the New Testament, his *Paraphrases of the New Testament,* the *Enchiridion,* or *Handbook of a Christian Knight,* and other writings of a religious nature. Twenty-one years after the death of Erasmus a certain Bartholomäus Kalkreuter at the University of Wittenberg delivered an oration (1557) in praise of Erasmus that was actually written by Philip Melanchthon. In it he declaimed that the great Erasmus does not need to be lauded any more than Hercules or Cyrus. The youth should be encouraged to study his useful writings, to consider his virtues, and to reflect on his great talent. "Since, therefore," he concluded, "Erasmus possessed a great power of genius and many outstanding virtues, and since he in the highest degree promoted the language study necessary to the church and the state, we wish to preserve his memory in a thankful heart, to read his literary monuments, and to acknowledge him gratefully."

The Northern Renaissance was more than a pale imitation of the Italian Renaissance. It must be appreciated in its own right as a multifaceted movement varying from people to people, which fused Italian and classical elements with indigenous cultural components into unique amalgams. The Northern Renaissance scored great intellectual, religious, literary and artistic triumphs of its own. By winning the support of the reformers and fusing with the vigorous Reformation movement it continued to be a vital cultural force into modern times.

Conrad Celtis: *Ode to Apollo* and *A Public Oration*

Conrad Celtis, the German arch-humanist, was the best lyric poet among the Empire's humanists. A student of Rudolph Agricola, the "father of German humanism," Celtis lived during the high tide of German humanism. He was born in 1459, the son of a peasant, in a village near Würzburg in the heart of Germany. He ran away to school, studying at Cologne, Heidelberg, Rostock, and Leipzig. He then entered upon a decade of wandering. In 1487 he crossed the Alps for a quick tour of Italy, where he visited Venice, Padua, Bologna, Florence, and Rome. He was offended by the attitude of superiority adopted by the Italian intellectuals toward the barbarians of the north. He hurried back to the University of Cracow, and went from there to Nuremberg and Ingolstadt. After a bumptious career there as a professor of rhetoric he accepted a position at the University of Vienna, on Emperor Maximilian's invitation, in 1497. There he founded the College of Poets and Mathematicians and taught until his death in 1508.

Celtis was the first major German humanist to receive his basic humanist education in the north before his Italian experience. The Holy Roman Emperor Frederick III crowned him the first German poet laureate. He composed three major poetic works, the *Amores,* the *Odes,* and the *Epigrams.* He wrote humanist plays and philosophical poems. He planned a *Germania illustrata,* which was to be like Flavio Biondo's *Italia illustrata;* he composed a book on Nuremberg as his contribution, and gathered topographical and historical sketches from humanists in all parts of the Empire. Gregarious Celtis brought the German humanists together into two loosely organized sodalities, the Rhenish and Danubian, for mutual encouragement in the battle against the scholastic doctors and in the duel with the superior Italian humanists.

Celtis typified the two major tendencies of German humanism, romantic nationalism and an interest in religious enlightenment. His greatest role in cultural history lay in the inspiration he provided for his fellow German humanists. In the *Ode to Apollo* he called for the god of the poets to cross the Alps from Italy to the frozen North. The *Oration Delivered Publicly in the University in Ingolstadt* was his inaugural address delivered on August 31, 1492, when he assumed his professorship of poetry and rhetoric. In it he propounded his ideas on educational reform and called upon the German youth to turn to more cultured study, to rhetoric, philosophy, poetry, drama, and music.

The *Ode to Apollo,* trans. George C. Schoolfield, is from *Conrad Celtis the German Arch-Humanist,* by Lewis W. Spitz (Cambridge, Mass.: Harvard University Press, 1957), 10. Reprinted by permission of Harvard University Press. The *Oration Delivered Publicly in the University in Ingolstadt* presented here is a new translation from the Latin by Dr. Lewis W. Spitz, Sr., based upon the text *Conradus Celtis Protucius Oratio in Gymnasio in Ingelstadio Publice Recitata cum Carminibus ad Orationem Pertinentibus,* ed. Hans Rupprich. (Leipzig: B. G. Teubner, 1932), 1–11.

Ode to Apollo

Phoebus, who the sweet-noted lyre constructed,
Leave fair Helicon and depart your Pindus,
And by pleasant song designated, hasten
    To these our borders.

You perceive how joyous the Muses gather,
Sweetly singing under a frozen heaven;
Come yourself, and with your melodious harp-strings,
    Gaze on these wastelands.

So must he, whom sometime a rude or rustic
Parent fostered, barbarous, all unknowing
Latium's splendors, choose you now as his teacher
    At writing verses.

Just as Orpheus sang to the old Pelasgians,
Orpheus, whom swift stags, beasts of savage custom,
Whom the lofty trees of the forest followed,
    Charmed by his plectrum.

Swift and joyous, once you forswore, and gladly,
Greece for Latium, passing the mighty ocean;

There you wished your delectable arts to broadcast,
Leading the Muses.

Thus it is our prayer you may wish to visit
Our abode, as once those Italian reaches.
May wild tongue take flight, and may all of darkness
Come to destruction.

Oration Delivered Publicly in the University in Ingolstadt

I would not have considered it something special, most excellent fathers and distinguished youths, that I, a German and your fellow countryman, can speak to you in Latin, if those ancient talents of our Germany still flourished, and if that age had returned in which our ambassadors are said to have spoken Greek rather than Latin. But, since through the adverseness of the ages and the change of the times, not only amongst us but even in Italy, the mother and ancient parent of letters, all the past splendor of literature has perished or been extinguished, and all the noble disciplines have been driven away and ruined by barbaric tumults, I am not at all confident that, given the slowness of my mind and the poverty of my powers, I can speak to you adequately in Latin. This is especially true since I have not lacked industry or good teaching, which many of you have up till now experienced and deplored in yourselves. However, lest I be accused of coming in total silence to this place, so richly adorned by your presence, I would rather offend by stammering than lightly pass over by silence your love for me and for the commonwealth of letters. I shall hope for your indulgence if you consider that a little man born in the midst of barbarity and drunkenness, as they say, cannot speak so sensibly as is required by your most sagacious ears and by this auditorium, assigned to me for oratory and poetry by the most illustrious prince, our [Duke] George [the Rich of Bavaria Landshut], and by you most distinguished gentlemen who are privy to all his counsels.

I have decided, moreover, that I can say nothing to you more worthy and pleasant, or more appropriate for me and fitting for you to hear, than to exhort your minds to virtue and the study of the liberal arts. For through them true glory, immortal fame, and happiness can be attained even in this brief life of ours. None of you should be found so sluggish and lazy that you do not regard it as a beautiful, excellent, and magnificent thing to strive toward these lofty goals which can make one truly happy. I have not thought it necessary to discuss with any particular acumen the favors of fortune and the delights of the body, or those sensual pleasures, worthy of slaves, that extinguish the light of the spirit. For these are all perishable, transitory, and destined to die with their body in a brief moment of time or will soon have other masters. Wherefore no wise man is remembered to have striven for these things. Rather, if we examine their lives, we find that these wise men of ancient times so loved learning and wisdom, with which the human spirit is nourished as with nectar and ambrosia, that in order to attain them they left their fatherland, wives, and beloved children, dispersed the richest patrimonies, endured injustices, insults, and infamy at the hands of the common crowd, and suffered exile with the greatest patience and peace of mind. Moreover, it is related that they willingly accepted labors, suffered cold and heat, and undertook arduous journeys because they wished to perceive and to see with their sense what they had learned, tired out by their deepest reflection and constant reading—so great was their incredible zeal to acquire wisdom and their love for searching into celestial things and nature. For these accomplishments they finally attained divine honors and are destined to have an immortal name. Greatly venerated and reverenced by all posterity, they come to be solemnly named "philosophers."

The Scythian race is so brutish, uncultivated, and horrid, like wild beasts, that they wander about in vast and inaccessible solitudes like herds of cattle, protecting themselves from the inclemency of the atmosphere and the harshness of the climate only with the skins of wild animals and their hides, from which they take their name. Nevertheless, glory and the desire for praise have so inspired them that three times they ruled over vanquished Asia. Nor did they carry away any gold or silver, things which we most desire, but considered it more glorious for it to be said of them that by their bravery they added such great splendor and amplitude to their dominion. We thus have great examples of a barbarous people for the pursuit of virtue and glory. While they were not able by genius and learning or by gentle customs, contrary to their nature, to contend with other mortals, they at least seem to have provided for their glory and immortality by their unbridled barbarity and the impetuosity of their spirits, which they regarded as a virtue. But if I were to turn my address to the histories of other tribes and what they did in peace and war, I would have a very broad field for recounting, and this present day would not be long enough to tell them all. So I purposely pass over what you are easily able to apply to this subject from your reading of illustrious authors.

I shall regard it as enough, and more than enough, men of Germany and illustrious youths, if by my presentation today, such as it is, I shall have added, impressed, and as it were, branded upon your spirits some stimulus to glory and virtue, so that you keep ever before your eyes that immortality which you must seek only from the fountain of philosophy and the study of eloquence. I cannot easily declare with what great labors and vigils you must linger and sweat over these two things—that is to say, over the writings of the ancient philosophers, poets, and orators. For they alone have prescribed for us the way to live well and happily and have set before us Nature, which is both the parent of the human race and the cause of all things (as it were), as an example and mirror of life to be imitated. From them you will learn to praise good deeds and to detest evil deeds, and from them you will learn to console yourselves, to exhort, to impel, and to hold back. You will strive to contemplate the Ruler of all things and Nature itself, which is the summit of human happiness. Although all these things can be done by others, nevertheless, and I still do not understand just how, the power to arouse compassion, to reawaken, and to repress the whole spirit lies in the hand of the orator and the poet. Indeed, those ornaments of words and thoughts, which like stars illumine the oration, are the proper instruments of the orator and poet. You must borrow them and use them as the occasion demands for your own use in your daily conversations. For what, by the immortal gods, does it profit us to know many things, to understand the beautiful and the sublime, if we are prevented from speaking of them with dignity, elegance, and gravity, and if we are not able to transmit our thoughts to posterity, which is the unique ornament of human happiness? So it is, by the faith of men: nothing shows a man to be learned and erudite unless it be the pen and the tongue—the two things which eloquence governs.

But to you, excellent gentlemen and noble youths, I now direct my address, to whom, thanks to ancestral virtue and invincible German strength, the empire of Italy has passed and who frequent this university rather than all the other centers of study in our Germany, make it fruitful, and serve as a great adornment and elegance. I exhort you to turn first to those studies that can render your minds gentle and cultured and call you away from the habits of the common crowd, so that you dedicate yourselves to higher studies. Keep before your eyes true nobility of mind, and consider that you are bringing not refinement but dishonor to our empire if you merely feed horses and dogs and pursue ecclesiastical prebends rather than the study of letters. As you seek splendor for your dignities with virtue, knowledge, and erudition, reflect on how to add honor to your holy morals so that men may esteem you worthy of those honors, so that they pursue you, and not you them, like fowlers a flock of birds. Noble men, emulate the ancient Roman nobility who, after they had taken over the empire of the Greeks, combined all their wisdom and eloquence so that it is a question as to whether they equalled or actually surpassed all the Greek faculty of invention and apparatus of learning. So you, too, having taken over the rule of the Italians and having cast off your vile barbarity, must strive after the Roman arts. Take away that infamy of the Germans among the Greek, Latin, and Hebrew writers, who ascribe to us drunkenness, barbarism, cruelty, and whatever is bestial and foolish. Regard it as a great shame for yourselves not to know the histories of the Greeks and the Latins, and beyond all shamelessness not to know the situation, the stars, rivers, mountains, antiquities, peoples of our region and land—briefly, all that foreigners have shrewdly gathered together concerning us. It seems a great miracle to me how the Greeks and Romans with such precise diligence and exquisite learning surveyed our land—"the greatest part of Europe," to use their own words, but rough and crude, I think, compared with the South; and they expressed our morals, affections, and spirits with words like paintings and the lineaments of bodies. Cast out, noble men, cast out and eliminate those villanies which they relate were bestowed among us as proofs of manly excellence. It is a wonder that this native sickness has endured for nearly fifteen hundred years in some parts of Germany. For even now we still do not compel the chiefs of that robber band to surrender, in a happier climate when we have eliminated bogs, cut down vast forests, and peopled our land with famous cities—so difficult is it to correct what has become a custom, spread about for ages, because it is generally approved. Thus it has happened that neighboring peoples make us smart and persecute our name with such awful eternal envy and calumny, proclaiming that with the Empire we have taken on many vices of the foreign nations. They always distrust and fear our talents. We should feel ashamed, noble gentlemen, that certain contemporary historians [Sabellicus], by publishing an edition of new *Decads,* so glory in having equalled the ancient Roman Empire, that they insult and bitterly jeer the German name, and that they call our most glorious princes barbarians, suppressing their natal names. So great has been the old and inexpiable hatred between us and the ancient hatred of our gods, that because of the hostility on both sides we would never have been restrained from mutual slaughter if provident nature had not separated us by the Alps and by cliffs raised up to the stars. Let us feel ashamed, I pray, that although we have successfully waged many memorable wars in Pannonia [Hungary], Gaul, and Italy, and against the most monstrous tyrant of Asia [the Turk], brandishing his sword wet with Christian blood, there is no one found among you today who records for eternity the deeds performed by German courage. But there will be many foreigners who will in their histories, without regard for the law of history, hiss like vipers against our bravery with a great verbal show and enticement of speech, not to say with fictions and mendacious invention, with which that kind of men are most effusive in singing their own praises and belittling the most glorious deeds which we perform. I do not really know whether it is due to our wisdom or to our thoughtlessness that in recent times we returned the insignia of writers and the accompanying imperial laurel beyond to the Tarpeian Hill [Rome]. It is an unhappy omen for our Empire, since having conceded to others the license for bestowing the laurel wreath, that finally no honor of the Empire remains ours.

O men of Germany, assume those ancient passions by which you were so often a dread and terror to the Romans, and turn your eyes to the wants of Germany and consider her lacerated and divided borders. What a shame to have a yoke of servitude imposed on our nation and to pay tributes and taxes to foreign and barbaric kings. O free and strong people, O noble and brave nation, clearly worthy of the Roman Empire, your renowned seaport [Danzig] is held by the Pole and your ocean gateway is occupied by the Dane! In the east the most vigorous tribes are held as slaves; the Marcomanni [Bohemians], Quadi [Moravians], and Bastarnae [Slovaks] live, as it were, separate from the body of our Germany. I do not even speak of the Transylvania Saxons, who also use our national culture and native language. In the west, however, upper Gaul [France] is so friendly and munificent toward us, thanks to the immortal virtue and incredible wisdom of Philipp of the Rhenish

Palatinate, who rules the shore on either side of its renowned river and ever will rule with an auspicious reign, "As long as the pole rotates the stars, as long as the breezes strike the shores." But to the south we are burdened with a kind of distinguished servitude, for new colonies are continually being established, thanks to that ancient and detestable avarice for fostering luxuries by which our land is being emptied of its wonderful natural resources, while we pay from the public treasury to others what we need for ourselves [papal exploitation]. So determined is fortune or fate to pursue and destroy the Germans, the remnants of the Roman Empire. But I fear I have progressed more freely than I desire, so disgusted am I with my Germany when I consider the things in the store of books taken from the Greeks and the Latins and preserved by the power of our Emperors, books which we have till now abandoned like the detested spoils of the enemies, as if locked in a prison, covered with dust, untouched, and not well protected from the rain.

I come back to you, O noble youths, and admonish above all things that you recall to mind before you proceed to the science of law that the knowledge of many things is necessary for you, because that discipline can teach you nothing beyond opinion. For if one is to believe antiquity, the philosophers and poets, the first theologians, called out the people, who were roaming and wandering about, from the haunts and caves of animals to the cities and social abodes, after their crude spirits had been tamed by speech. They taught them religion and the fear of the gods with many and varied arguments and then ruled with laws and ordinances. Who of you will doubt, O most distinguished fathers, that before the study of law it is necessary to pay close attention to true philosophy and especially to those things by which eloquence can be acquired, which you agree are very necessary for the lawyer. Therefore you will also consider those people quite mistaken and responsible for many abuses who, passing by all philosophy (except the low variety), make themselves leaders in law and religion without reflecting on what kind of legislators there were in ancient times—men who spent their day on laws and arms but spent every night on the study of philosophy. Inasmuch as philosophy, like a kind of seminary, teaches fully the knowledge of things human and divine and their jurisdiction, who without drinking of the fountain of philosophy shall judge himself able to manage these two things? I shall not at this point offer as evidence for you the Greeks, Solon, Plato, Alcibiades, Themistocles, or Philip, the father of Alexander

the Great. With what great care he commended his son to Aristotle, the greatest philosopher of that age, and with what great joy he eagerly desired a son born to him at a time when philosophers enjoyed such very great prestige! For that master of arms, so experienced in ruling the state, knew that if his own son were initiated into the precepts and ordinances of philosophy, he would be worthy to be entrusted with the administration of the whole universe. Nor shall I remind you of Anacharsi who, when he introduced his laws to Scythia, first wanted to learn philosophy from the Attic philosophers. I remain silent about the Roman kings, Numa, Cato, the Scipios, the Caesars, and the later ones, the Antonians, the Valerians, the Aurelians, Theodosius, finally also Charlemagne, born of the noble stem of the Franks, by whose learning and by whose concern and zeal for the liberal arts a most glorious empire was procured and preserved, which flourished as long as it maintained philosophy as its partner and assistant. I now pass over Moses the legislator of our ancient religion, most wise in all philosophy, who was a most prudent governor in impelling, curbing, and overcoming the minds of the masses. In writing the sacred laws he began with the creation of the world and with the remembrance of the majesty of Nature and its Maker. He thereby clearly demonstrated that any legislator or student of the legal discipline must first be initiated into the precepts of philosophy as though into sacred rites.

But such great men do not move us, for by the narrow boundary of destiny now among us, by fortune, circumstances, and the dregs of these last times, the Empire grows old; and we, neglecting all philosophy, prostitute our servile spirits to base complaint alone and hire them out for mercenary wages. Hence, when we come from such pursuits to the princes, we suggest to them only those which we have learned. And these are the reasons—I say with great bitterness—why our princes despise learning and always remain unlearned, why they are regarded with derision by others and are ridiculed as "barbarous," because, even in these otherwise prosperous times, they neglect the liberal arts and their proponents. There is nothing more vile and abject at their courts than those who profess with a word or gesture a knowledge of letters—so greatly our barbarity pleases us and the sickness of an intractable mind. Even among our high churchmen and, to use an ancient term, the "sacred flames," to whom the care and protection of letters rightly belongs, they have been so contemptuous of the trifling value of letters and of those devoted to them that they prefer the wild animals of the forests, the long-eared dogs, the snorting and spirited horses, and other pleasures and amusements like Rhea, the wife of Mars [mother of Romulus and Remus], [Emperor] Claudius, and Sardanapalus [effeminate king of Assyria]. We know some bishops, come up from obscure origins, who, when they receive studious men from abroad at their courts, refuse to speak to them to show their knowledge, to such an extent does the silence of Pythagoras please them, lest they seem to be dishonored in their barbarous majesty by the parsimony of the Roman language. Meanwhile they pant with greed like rapacious hawks for money or for the approbations of kings, which they dare exhibit before their doors like common eager whores. So much has Italian luxury and savage cruelty in extorting pernicious silver corrupted us that it would clearly have been more godly and holy had we lived that rude and silvan life of olden times, when we lived within the limits of moderation, rather than bringing in so many instruments of gluttony and luxury, and adopting foreign manners. So it happens that our rulers take those men into their familiar circle who are similarly inclined and exclude those who cherish learning and wisdom. The founders of the Greek and Roman Empire, in contrast, so honored wise men that they bestowed upon them imperial honors and called their secretaries friends. They ordered that those who died should be interred in their own sepulchers, because they believed that power and immortality were preserved for them by those wise men through the benefit and use of letters by which alone immortality is attained. That way they could aid mankind not only while alive but even after they had died. Therefore they live until today and will continue to live as long as Roman and Greek letters exist. I will give no other reason for Italy's flourishing than that they excel us in no other felicity than the love and study of letters. With these they intimidate other nations as though with weapons and lead others to admire them by their talent and industry. But with us there are frequent changes, and among us there is an improper desire for new things, so that a very wise poet says of us:

> Brothers eager to know new things and mad with hate
> Of peace and with genius and quick desire.

So that our horses do not contract the gout and our weapons rust, we raise a tumult among ourselves by dissension like Sulla and Marius of Caesar and Pompey. I cannot be temperate as long as we are involved in our vices and domestic strifes and neglect our very rich territories, whose titles we brandish as though for our own consolation, while we tie bootstraps and stretch out the deliberations in our councils up to the fifth new moon, as a certain historian has written of us, by nature given to worthless goods and eager for small advantages. Meanwhile in the heart of our Germany we tolerate the reign of a pertinacious religion most sumptuous in its use of a foreign tongue [Hussites in Bohemia]. Although their university [Charles University in Prague] weeps and sighs over the ruin of its ancient felicity, they must nevertheless render thanks to the gods because an Italian is their leader [Augustinus Lucianus of Vicenza]. Because the university had no cultivators of true philosophy, it left behind a strong proof by its fall that the foundations of religion can be strengthened and preserved by no one better than by a true philosopher, rather than by those who regard the highest wisdom as ignorance and who merely accommodate themselves by habit to ostentation for the common crowd and set forth only a small shadow of learning and virtue. They are very much like little scarecrows that peasants put up in their orchards and fields to frighten away small birds, but if you come closer you see that they have neither movement nor sense.

I now return to you, then, youths of Germany. Act no longer in a childish manner, but learn to know the secrets of literature, for those writers relate that you flee from them and sing to our shame:

> The Castalian liquids [wines] and the prescient rivers of fate
> No barbarian shall ever drink with his polluted mouth.

It should shame us that such things should be read and applied to you, the possessors of the Roman Empire, and persist down to the present day. Someone might want to argue against me on the basis of the large number of our universities, of which we have fourteen, and might say that because of them barbarity has been eliminated and care has been taken for good morals and honorable arts, and the way has been opened while the crowd flatters and exults us with the titles of masters and doctors! With tears I say it—you will find few who acquire a true knowledge of things and search into the nature and purity of the Roman language or retain it. This is because in our studies of (not to say triflings with) such subjects those who interpret the poets and the writers of the Roman language are repressed and those who uncover the work of nature and the wisdom of its governor with mathematical truthfulness and who think a bit more deeply than the common crowd are regarded as infamous. To such an extent is philosophy trampled underfoot and boiled down by some who have deformed the most beautiful majesty of Nature into incorporeal thoughts and monstrous abstractions and empty chimeras, like poets. For poets with their imagery and apt fables have transposed natural things figuratively so that sacred things should be hidden from the common crowd, for they know that open and naked exposure is inimical to Nature and that Nature must therefore be revealed under respectable coverings and a sacramental veil. For should the common crowd understand certain mysteries as the philosophers do, it might be difficult to restrain their impulses.

Nor shall I now interpret the fables of the Greek and the Latin poets in the manner of the naturalists, who reveal the foundations of all divine inventions under the cloud of poetic fiction to the truly wise. But we accuse such poets of lies and execrate them as imposters and vile men. So much do our baseness and our foul barbarity please us, the gods being hostile, I believe, that we do not, together with the Roman imperium, also assume the splendor of Italian letters and seek to rival them in this most beautiful kind of writing, even though we admire them. We may to be sure find among us those who labor with my vice, usurping for themselves the name "poet" and "orator." But they, ignoring every precept of philosophy and rhetoric, strain every nerve of their genius to produce futile banter and to allure the minds of the adolescents with strange fantasies. They devise smoothness with watery words, spewing forth shamelessly whatever comes into their mouths, making chaste ears drunk with obscene and shameful fables, as if vices should be opened up to us for our understanding, although they always sprout up more densely of their own accord without encouragement, like useless weeds. If someone would give more careful attention to our erudition such as it is, he would come upon an arena without a goal and a voice without blood, although we are quite prepared to fault others for their vocabulary, like schoolboys. But our own stench we do not smell, and I think that the immortal gods have decreed well toward us, for they have conceded to us at least a certain plebeian and vulgar learning. Otherwise by our bleating and vile medley of words we would not permit others who are more learned than we to murmur a sound. Although it pleases us to hear such men, it is not because they nourish our minds with true teaching, while we persecute with hatred those who cry out against and carp at our obsolete manner of teaching, offer new approaches from the true Roman instruction, and compel the aged, trifling grammarians to learn the elements of the Greek language and to cry once again in learning the art of grammar, like infants in the cradle. As if Cato were not at hand as an example, a most serious man and most learned in all erudition and doctrine, who when already an octogenarian began to learn Greek in order to be able to speak Latin correctly. We, boys and old men alike, neglect both languages and, in defense of our slothfulness and inertia, ascribe divine power and miracle to St. James and St. Augustine because they learned so many languages and wrote so many books, which we do not attain in our whole age, rather than crediting their long vigils, the greatest labors, and longest journeys. For by these efforts learning, sanctity, and an eternal name are handed on to all posterity, not by sleep and gluttony, spending on feasting, with dice and Venus, evils with which we are inflamed, thanks to our stupidity; we gormandize our whole life as though we had been born for this alone. But we who wish to appear more cultivated in learning tarry in childish contention about our terms and quiddities on which we grow old and die, as on the rocks of the Sirens. Nor do we want others to know anything except what is stained with our dregs. Therefore we are chosen as leaders and princes of our most beautiful religion. We look longingly with the zeal of avarice and burn with an insatiable thirst for all powers, while we bury away money with ourselves like the corpses of the dead beneath the earth. This is what our vulgar philosophy has taught us with its worthless harvest of empty words, for which we neglect the most restrained and the most fluent writers of our religion. We are able to attain nothing magnificent, high and excellent, while we seek only inferior things, as though certain basic teachings of our religion were not to be found in Plato and Pythagoras, in whom the most beautiful association of the light of nature and of grace may be perceived. But concerning this another time.

For that reason turn, O Germans, turn about to the more gentle studies, which philosophy and eloquence alone can teach you. Consider well that it is not without reason that the Greek and Roman founders of the Empire devoted such great efforts and watchful attentions to those matters and decorated the teachers of those subjects with the highest honors, for they understood that by the power of language and the lessons of wisdom the assemblies of men, cities, religions, the worship of the gods, the most holy morals, and the broadest empires could be preserved and governed. That divine poet [Virgil], the ornament and delight of Roman eloquence, splendidly expressed this truth thus when he sang:

> And, as in times of revolt, which often afflict a great nation,
> When the ignoble throng are roused to a frenzy of passion,
> Firebrands and stones are beginning to fly, for fury finds weapons,—
> Then, if they chance to behold some man, for his faith and his virtue
> Highly revered, they are awed, and attentively listen in silence,
> While he controls their minds by his words, and quiets their passion.
> [Virgil, *Aeneid,* I, 148–53; Harlan Ballard, trans.]

Great indeed was that nearly divine element in administering their state that they aimed to join wisdom with eloquence; and, in order to master these, they instituted public performances in which by sublime persuasion and remarkable inventive faculties, they exhorted the spirits of the viewers to virtue, piety, modesty, fortitude, and endurance of all things. They deterred the idle youth from vices and inflamed them to glory, so that whatever they owed to the fatherland, friends, strangers, and their dear parents, they learned as from living portraits. Therefore that allegory of the poets is not unseemly, according to which Orpheus is said to have tamed wild animals, moved stones, and led them where he wished; for it shows by metaphor the power of eloquence and the duty of the poet, who is able to move ferocious, monstrous, and intractable spirits to gentleness, a right spirit, and love for the fatherland. These things being so, the states of Greece and now of Italy wisely educated their boys from the very beginning with the hymns of poets. In those hymns they learned to perceive musical tunes and the sweetest modulations of harmony, on which that age is very keen; and they provided for those tender spirits, inclined to inertia and laziness, a stimulant to industry so that they were excited to learning with a cheerful zeal, a lively spirit, and eagerness. The gravity of words and meanings imbibed by tender minds will thus endure to a more advanced age and until death, and will continually sprout forth again through an entire lifetime. Aristotle prescribes this plan when he stipulates that adolescents should be educated in musical hymns. Because it—that is, harmony—stirs up the talents of boys and impels them to the acumen of oratory and the production of song. That discipline is very well adapted for relaxing the spirit and for consoling and uplifting minds; it sounds forth in sacred hymns their praises of the gods and carries them off in divine meditations. For this reason Pythagoras and Plato, the loftiest philosophers, named poetry the first philosophy and theology, which uses hymns for its demonstrations and arouses with melodious speech. But the other discipline—that is, oratory—spreads out with humble, loose, and free speech. Poetry is more concise in rhythm and a bit more free with words, but similar and almost equal in many kinds of embellishment. Neither the one nor the other must be neglected; but from the very beginning, O men of Germany, the minds of the boys must be instructed in and, if I may say so, allured with songs. And when the sublime admiration of things resides in these, the beauty and polish of words, the spirits of the youths easily gain strength from them. In an intellectually stronger age, when the youthful spirit has already been hardened by those beginnings, and thought has been invigorated, they are better instructed and better prepared to lead themselves to the reading of more serious philosophers and orators. From these they can finally rise to their own inventions and to the sublimity of the poetic discipline and its figures, attaining to the praises of illustrious authors in writing histories and poems. They will then procure immortality for themselves and glory and praise for the fatherland. I have spoken.

Ulrich von Hutten: *Letters of Obscure Men*

The young poet and polemicist Ulrich von Hutten was born of a noble family in the fortress of Steckelberg on the border of Franconia and Hesse in 1488. When he was eleven his pious family sent him to the ancient monastery at Fulda, but at seventeen he fled from the monastery in order to take up a life of learning. Like Celtis he went first to Cologne University and then wandered from one university to the next, Erfurt, Frankfurt on the Oder, Leipzig, Greifswald, Rostock. "Behold, posterity," he wrote, "the songs of Hutten the poet, whom you are rightly able to call your own!" During his early years he devoted himself to poetry and to opposing the old scholastic learning. During his final years he polemicized for German liberty from the yoke of the Roman church. "Long live liberty!" he called to Luther at the outset of the Reformation. He was too ill to play a role in the Knights' Revolt of 1522 and sought refuge on the island of Ufenau in Lake Zurich where he died in August, 1523.

Hutten's most famous writing, *Letters of Obscure Men,* he did together with Crotus Rubeanus, the son of a Thuringian peasant. Rubeanus received his education largely at the University of Erfurt, where from 1498 to 1509 he studied and served as a tutor. He learned to dislike scholastic philosophy and, like Hutten, joined the circle of poets gathered around mildly skeptical Mutianus Rufus, a canon at near-by Gotha. From 1509 to 1516 he served as principal of the monastery school at Fulda. When a harsh controversy developed over Johannes Reuchlin's promotion of Hebrew letters and opposition to Johannes Pfefferkorn, a converted Jew who wished to burn Jewish books, the humanists aligned themselves with Reuchlin against his obscurantist scholastic critics. Rubeanus and Hutten joined forces to produce *Letters of Obscure Men,* one of the great satires of Renaissance literature. The title was inspired by Reuchlin's *Letters of Famous Men,* a collection of letters supporting him against his enemies which he published in March, 1514.

In *Letters of Obscure Men* (1516) Hutten and Rubeanus

mocked Ortwin Gratius, Arnold von Tungern, the obscurantist scholastic theologians of Cologne, and the Dominican Jakob von Hochstraten, who had cited Reuchlin to appear before his court of inquisition in Mainz and sought his condemnation in Rome. In his letters in the first part of the volume Rubeanus drew a satirical picture of monks and the scholastic doctors for their conceit, stupidity, and loose morals. Hutten added to satire a sharp polemic, and his letters, especially those in the second part of the volume, combined with the assault on obscurantism a sharp attack upon the political problems of the Empire. Soon thereafter Luther appeared upon the scene and became for Hutten another Arminius who would not only free the Germans from cultural inferiority, but would liberate the nation from the bondage of Rome.

The six letters which follow are taken from the *Epistolae Obscurorum Virorum: The Latin Text with an English Rendering, Notes, and an Historical Introduction by Francis Griffin Stokes.* (London: Chatto and Windus, 1909), 301–302, 314–316, 322–324, 434–436, 441–443, 484–486. Reprinted by permission of Chatto and Windus.

Nikolaus Ziegenmelker, Bachelor: to Magister Ortwin Gratius

Abundant greetings, with mighty respect to your worthiness, as is but meet in addressing your magistrality.

Reverend Herr Magister, you must know that there is a notable question that I desire, or entreat, to be by you magistrally determined.

There is a certain Grecian here who readeth in *Urban's* Grammar, and whenever he writeth Greek he always putteth tittles atop.

Thereupon I said, a little while ago, "Magister *Ortwin* of *Deventer* also handleth Greek Grammar, and he is as well qualified therein as that fellow, and yet he never maketh tittles so: and I trow he knoweth his business as well as that Grecian—ay, and can put him to rights." Nevertheless some distrusted me in this matter, wherefore my friends and fellow-students besought me to write to your worthiness so that you might make it known to me whether we ought to put tittles or no. And if we ought not to put them, then, by the Lord, we will roundly harry that Grecian, and bring it to pass that his hearers shall be but few!

Of a truth I took note of you at Cologne, in *Heinrich Quentell's* house, when you were reader, and had to correct Greek, that you would strike out all the tittles that were above the letters and say, "Of what use are these fiddle-faddles?" And it hath just come into my mind that you must have had some ground for this, or you would not have done it.

You are a marvellous man, and God hath given you a large measure of grace, so that you know somewhat of all things knowable. You must praise God, therefore, in your metrification, and the Blessed Virgin, and all the Saints.

Prithee, take it not amiss if I weary your mightiness with such questions as these, seeing that it is for edification that I propound them. Farewell.

LEIPZIG

Magister Conrad of Zwickau: to Magister Ortwin

Greeting.

You have sent me word that you no longer have any mind to wantonness, nor to consort with womankind—save once in a month, or, maybe, twice—yet I marvel that you can write such things. Full well do I know to the contrary. There is a student here who hath just arrived from *Cologne*—you know him right well, he was ever in your company—and he saith that you are intimate with *Johann Pfefferkorn's* wife. He declared this to be true, and made oath, and I believe him. For you are a squire of dames, and know how to wheedle them—besides, you have *Ovid's* "Art of Love" by rote! A certain merchant did tell me, too, that Magister *Arnold von Tungern* was in the lady's good graces as well. But this is false, for I know of a truth that he is a virgin, and hath never bussed a wench. But even if he had done, or were to do, what I cannot believe of him, that would not make him a bad man, for to err is human. You send me whole screeds about that sin—which is not the worst sin in the world—and you quote texts without end. I very well know that it is not a virtue, and yet it is recorded in Holy

Writ that certain men thus erred, and yet were saved. *Samson,* to wit, had dealings with a bona-roba, and nevertheless the spirit of the Lord afterwards came upon him. I can syllogize against you thus: "Whosoever is not unrighteous receiveth the holy spirit; but *Samson* was not unrighteous, ergo, he received the holy spirit." I can prove the major premiss—for it is written, "Into an unrighteous soul the spirit of wisdom shall not enter; but the holy spirit is the spirit of wisdom, ergo, etc." The minor premiss is manifest, for if that sin of incontinence is so grave, then the spirit of the Lord would not have come upon *Samson,* as it is told us in the *Book of Judges.* We read, too, of *Solomon,* how he had three hundred queens, and concubines without number—and he was prince of gallants to his dying day. Nevertheless, the Doctors, with one accord, declare that he found salvation. What then? I am not stronger than *Samson,* nor wiser than *Solomon,* and so I must needs be wanton, once and again. Moreover, the physicians say it is sovran against melancholy. Fie! what booteth it that you cite those dumpish fathers! What saith *The Preacher?* "I know that there is nothing better than that a man should rejoice in his own works." Wherefore, with *Solomon,* I say to my doxy: "Thou hast ravished my heart, my sister, my spouse: thou hast ravished my heart with one of thine eyes, with one chain of thy neck. How beautiful are thy breasts, my sister, my spouse. Thy bosom is fairer than wine . . ." and so forth.

By the Lord, courting the lasses is merry sport! As that Ode of *Samuel* the poet saith:

> "Fail not, jolly cleric, merry maids amare,
> Flattering busses knowing how to you praestare—
> So contriving, many a day, youth's flower conservare!"

"Amor is love, and God is love—therefore Amor is not a bad thing!" Answer me that argument. And *Solomon* saith: "If a man would give all the substance of his house for love, it would utterly be contemned."

But enough of this; let us turn to other matters.

You bid me send you some news—so you must know that there were high jinks here in Lent. There were joustings, and the Prince himself rode in the *Platz,* and he had a fine horse, and a fine saddlecloth too, upon which was painted a woman in brave attire, and near her sitting a youth, with curly locks, who played an organ to her, as saith the *Psalmist:* "Young men and maidens, old men and children, praise the name of the Lord." And when the Prince had entered the town, the University enthroned him with great pomp, and the burghers brewed lashings of beer, and set forth toothsome fare, and royally feasted the Prince and all his train. And afterwards they fell to dancing, and I stood on a scaffold to look on. I can call to remembrance nothing else, save that I wish you all good wishes. So fare ye well, in the name of the Lord.

LEIPZIG

Magister Johann Hipp: to Magister Ortwin Gratius

Greeting.

"Be glad, O ye righteous, and rejoice in the Lord: and be joyful, all ye that are true of heart."—*Psalm xxxi.*

Now, take this not amiss, saying within yourself, "What aileth this fellow with his texts?" But hearken rather, with glee, to a piece of news that will mightily tickle your lordship.

You shall have it in a nut-shell. There was a poet here, calling himself *Joannes Aesticampianus*—a bumptious fellow, ever girding at the Masters of Arts, and decrying them in his lectures. He would dub them dunces, and aver that one Poet was worth ten Masters, and that Poets should always take precedence of Masters and Licentiates in processions. He lectured on *Pliny* and other poets, and declared that the Magisters were not Masters of the Seven Liberal Arts, but of the Seven Deadly Sins, and that they were not grounded in their rudiments, and knew naught save *Peter of Spain* and his Logical Primer. The rantipole was much run after, even by the gentleman-commoners. He used to say that the Scotists and Thomists were piddlers alike, and he uttered blasphemies against the Angelic Doctor himself!

But the Magisters bided their time, to avenge themselves by the help of the Lord. And by the Lord's will, at last he made a speech, and railed at the Magisters, and the Doctors, and the Licentiates and the Bachelors, and extolled his own Faculty, and reviled sacred Theology.

Thereupon mighty indignation arose among the heads of the Faculty. And the Masters and Doctors took counsel together, saying, "What shall we do? For this man hath done many notable things;

and if we send him away, all men will believe that he is more learned than we. And mayhap the Moderns will come and say that their way is better than that of the Ancients, and our University will be defamed, and will become a laughing-stock."

Then Magister *Andrew Delitzsch,* who is a fine poet himself, said that *Aesticampianus* at the University was like a fifth wheel to a coach—for he thwarted the other Faculties, so that the students could not graduate therein. And the other masters were of the same mind, so the long and the short of it was that they determined to either expel or inhibit that poet, at the risk of his everlasting dudgeon. Thereupon they cited him before the Rector, and nailed the citation on the doors of the church.

Then the fellow put in an appearance—an advocate with him—and made as though he would defend himself, nor was he without friends to support him, but the Masters told them to stand aside, if they would not commit perjury in opposing the University. And the Masters waxed valiant in fight, and stuck to their guns, and swore they would spare nobody—for justice' sake.

Nevertheless certain jurists and courtiers pleaded for the fellow. But the Magisters said that this was out of the question, for they had statutes, and by the statutes he ought to be expelled. Then the marvel was that even the Duke put in a word for him; but to no effect, because they replied that he himself ought to observe the statutes of the University, inasmuch as its statutes are to a University as is the binding to a book. If there be no binding, the leaves fall hither and thither; and if there were no statutes order would cease in the University, and the students would be at sixes and sevens, and Chaos would come again—therefore should the Duke work for the good of the University, as did his father before him.

Then the Duke was persuaded, and avouched that he might not oppose the University, and that it was expedient that one man should be expelled, rather than that the whole University should suffer disgrace. The Magisters then were fully content, and cried: "Heaven be thanked, Lord Duke, for this thy righteous judgment!" Then the Rector fastened a decree to the church doors, that *Aesticampianus* should be banished for ten years.

But his disciples murmured much, and declared that the Lords of the Council had done grievous wrong to *Aesticampianus.* But the Doctors swore that they cared not a doit for that.

Some gentlemen-commoners, indeed, have spread it abroad that *Aesticampianus* will avenge the injury, and cite the University before the Roman Curia. But the Magisters laughed, and said: "Pish! what can that vagabond do?"

And now great peace reigneth in the University. Mag. *Delitzsch* lectureth on the humanities, and so doth a Magister from *Rothenburg,* who hath compiled a book full three times as large as all the works of *Virgil;* and in that book he hath put many mighty fine things, both in defence of holy Mother Church and in praise of the saints. And he most of all hath praised our University, and sacred Theology, and the Faculty of Arts—and he hath reproved the secular and heathen poets. The Masters say that his verses are as good as *Virgil's,* and have no faults at all, because he knoweth quite perfectly the Art of Metrification, and hath been a good metrist these twenty years. Therefore the Lords of the Council have allowed him to lecture on that book instead of on *Terence,* because it is more necessary than *Terence,* and is not all about drabs and clowns, as *Terence* is.

You must spread abroad these tidings in your University, and then peradventure *Buschius* will be served in like manner as was *Aesticampianus.* When will you send me your book about *Reuchlin?* You say much, and nothing cometh of it. You promised faithfully that you would send it, but you have sent it not. The Lord forgive you in that you do not love me as I love you, for you are my heart's core. Nevertheless fail not to send it, for with desire have I desired to eat this passover with you—I mean, to read that book. Send me some news—and, just for once, write a little treatise, or some verses, about me, if I am worthy thereof.

And now farewell, *in Chr. D. D. nost.,* world without end. Amen.

Brother Simon Wurst, Doctor of Sacred Theology: to Magister Ortwin Gratius

Greeting.

Ever since *Johann Pfefferkorn's* "Defence," which he composed in Latin, reached us here, daily there have been fresh rumours. One man saith this, another saith that. One man is on *Pfefferkorn's* side, another on *Reuchlin's;* whom one man upholdeth, another blameth. There is sore brangling, and folk would fain be at fisticuffs. If I were to relate all the squabbles that have arisen over that book, a whole Olympiad would fail me.

Briefly, however, I will glance at one or two matters. Many folk—especially the lay Magisters, and the priests and friars of the Franciscan Order—roundly declare it to be a thing impossible that *Pfefferkorn* composed that book, seeing that he never learned a word of Latin. I reply that this objection is futile, though it hath been for the undoing of great men even to this day, but with injustice—for *Johann Pfefferkorn,* who beareth with him a pen and an ink-horn, can jot down that which he heareth at public preachments, or at assemblies, or when students and Dominicans come to his house, or when he goeth to the baths. Sonty! how many sermons hath he not heard in twelve years! How many exhortations! How many opinions of the holy fathers! And these he could either lay up in his own mind, or dictate to his wife, or scratch upon the walls, or enter in his notebook. I added, moreover, that *Johann Pfefferkorn* avoweth of himself—without boasting—that he can apply, without help, everything contained in the Bible or in the Holy Gospel, to any purpose, good or evil, and that in German or in Hebrew. He knoweth too, by rote, all the gospels that are read throughout the year, and he can recite them to the letter—and this is more than the Jurists and Poets can do. He hath, moreover, a son named *Lorenz*—a right towardly youth—who studieth until he hath grown pale; I marvel however, that he is allowed to study those diabolical poets. He gathereth for his father saws from the Orators and poets—both personally and from the lips of his teachers—to be applied to any subject and any argument; moreover he can quote *Hugo. Johann Pfefferkorn,* forsooth, hath profited much from this sagacious youth, inasmuch as what he for lack of learning cannot attain to, his son despatcheth.

Let them therefore be put to shame who have falsely spread it abroad that *Johann Pfefferkorn* hath not composed his own books, but that they have been written by the Doctors and Magisters at *Cologne:* let *Johann Reuchlin,* too, blush, and groan to all eternity, in that he declared that Pfefferkorn composed not the *Handspiegel* himself—concerning which there hath been before now much discussion amongst the learned—since three men furnished him with the authorities he citeth therein. One asked me, saying, "What three men be they?" And I replied that I knew not, but that I deemed them to be the same three men who appeared unto *Abram,* of whom we read in the Book of Genesis. But when I said this they all made mouths at me, and mocked me as if I was a greenhorn. Would that the devil would smite them with heavy blows, as it is written in the book of *Job,* which just now in our monastery we are reading in the refectory. Exhort *Johann Pfefferkorn* to have patience, for I trust that the Lord will sooner or later work a miracle. Greet him, too, in my name. Prithee salute also his wife for me—you well know how: but privily. And now, farewell.

ANTWERP: written in hot haste, and without deliberation.

Magister Berthold Häckerling: to Magister Ortwin Gratius

Brotherly love, by way of salutation.

Honoured Sir, having in remembrance the promise I made you on parting, that I would tell you all the news, and how I fared, I would have you know that I have now been two months at *Rome,* but as yet have found no patron. An assessor of the Rota would fain have bespoken me, and I was well pleased, and said, "I am nothing loth, Sir; but I pray your magnificence to apprize me what my charge will be." He replied, that my lodgment would be in the stable, to minister unto a mule, serve it with victuals and drink, curry-comb it, and keep it clean; and that I must have a care that he was ready to carry his master, with bridle and saddle and so forth. And then it would be my office to run by his side to the court, and home again.

Thereupon I made answer that it was not meet for me, who am a Master of Arts of *Cologne,* to drudge thus. Quoth he, "If not, the loss is yours." I am resolved, therefore, to return to the fatherland. I, to curry-comb a mule and mundify a stable! The Devil run away with the stable and the mule! I verily believe it would be flying in the face of the Statutes of the University! For a Magister must needs comport himself as a Magister. It would be a scandalous thing for a Master of Arts of *Cologne* to do such drudgery. Nay, for the honour of the University I will return to the fatherland.

Rome moreover pleaseth me not in other ways. You would not believe how arrogant are the Clerks and Curialists. One of them said but yesterday that he would besquatter a *Cologne* Magister. "Besquatter the gallows!" quoth I. Then he made answer that he, too, was a Magister, to wit of the Curia, and that a Magister of the Curia took precedence of a Master of Arts of *Germany*. "That," said I, "is impossible. Would you fain make yourself out my equal, seeing that you have never offered yourself for examination, as did

I when five Magisters sifted me with rigour? You are naught but a Magister by diploma."

Then began he to dispute with me, saying, "And what is a Magister?"

"A Magister," I answered, "is a person duly qualified, promoted, and graduated in the Seven Liberal Arts, having first undergone a magistral examination; he is privileged to wear a gold ring, and a silken lining to his cope, and he comporteth himself towards his pupils as doth a king towards his subjects. The name 'Magister' hath a fourfold derivation. First, from *magis* and *ter,* for a Magister knoweth three times as much as a lewd person. Secondly, from *magis* and *terreo,* for a Magister is terrible in the sight of his disciples. Thirdly, from *magis* and *theron* (that is, rank), for a Magister is of higher rank than his disciples. Fourthly, from *Magis* and *sedere,* for a magister ever sitteth in a higher room than any of his disciples."

Then quoth he, "What is your authority?" I answered that I had read all this in the *Vademecum.* Forthwith he began to carp at that book, and declared that it was in no way authentic. Then said I, "You find fault with the Ancients, because you know no better. But I never heard of any man at *Cologne* making light of that book. Have you no sense of shame?" And in high dudgeon I departed from him.

So, be well assured, I shall hie me back to *Germany;* for there Magisters are paramount; and rightly. I can prove it by the Gospel: Christ called himself Magister, and not Doctor, saying, "Ye call me Master and Lord, and ye say well, for so I am."

But I can now write no more, for paper faileth me, and it is a great way to the *Campo dei Fiori.* Farewell.

From the Court of Rome.

Magister Konrad Unckebunck sendeth to Magister Ortwin Gratius

Abundant Greetings.

"Mouths have they and they speak not; eyes have they and they see not; ears have they and they hear not," saith the Psalmist: and these words will serve as preamble and text of my discourse:

Magister *Ortwin* hath a mouth and speaketh not—else would he have said to some Curialist setting out for Rome, "Salute Herr *Konrad Unckebunck* for me:" Eyes hath he and he seeth not—for I have written him many letters and he replieth not, as though he could neither read nor see them: and, in the third place, ears hath he and he heareth not—for I have commissioned many a comrade departing hence for the provinces to greet him, but he cannot have heard my salutations, inasmuch as he reciprocateth them not.

In this you sorely err, for I love you, and you therefore ought to love me in return. Howbeit you do not—for you write naught to me. It would gladden me exceedingly were you to write to me very oft, for when I read your letters they inwardly rejoice the cockles of my heart.

Nevertheless I have learnt that you have of pupils but a few, and complain that *Buschius* and *Caesarius* lure the students from you—notwithstanding that they lack your skill to expound the poets allegorically and to cite thereanent the Scriptures. The Devil, I trow, is in those Poets. They are the bane of the universities.

An old Magister of *Leipzig,* who hath been Master for these thirty years, told me that when he was a lad, then did the University greatly prosper: those were the days when there was not a Poet within twenty miles. He told me, too, how that the students then diligently attended lectures—whether public or bursarial; it was deemed a great scandal that a student should walk in the street without having *Peter of Spain* or the *Parva Logicalia* under his arm; or, if they were grammarians, then they would carry with them Alexander's *Doctrinale,* or his *Opus Minus,* or the *Vade Mecum,* or the *Exercitium Puerorum,* or Johann Sinthen's *Dicta.* Then were there zealous students in the Schools, who held the Masters of Arts in honour, and if they spied a Magister they fell to trembling as if they had seen a devil. He told me that in those days there were four promotions of bachelors each year, and many a time fifty or sixty graduated at once. In those days the University was in full bloom; and when a student had resided for a year and a half he was made Bachelor, and after three years, or two and a half years, in all, a Magister. Thus it came to pass that his parents were well pleased, and freely sent him money when they saw that their son had attained a place of honour. But nowadays all the students must needs attend lectures on *Virgil* and *Pliny* and the rest of the newfangled authors—what is more, they may listen to them for five years and yet get no degree: and so, when they return home, their parents ask them, saying, "What art thou?" And they reply that they are naught, but that they have been reading Poetry! And then the parents are perplexed—but they see that their sons are not grammarians, and therefore they are disgruntled at the University, and begrudge sorely the money they have spent. Then they say to others, "Send not your sons to the University—they'll learn naught, but go trapesing in the streets anights; money given for such a bringing-up is but thrown away."

The old Magister furthermore told me that in his time there were full two thousand students at *Leipzig,* and a like number at *Erfurt;* four thousand at *Vienna* and as many at *Cologne*—and so with the rest. Nowadays there are not as many students at all the Universities put together as there were then in one or two. The Magisters at *Leipzig* bitterly lament the scarcity of scholars. It is the Poets that do them this hurt. Even when students are sent by their parents to hostels and colleges they will not stay there, but are off to the Poets to learn stuff and nonsense. He told me that at *Leipzig* he used to have two score pupils, and when he went to the Church, or to the market, or to stroll in the Rosengarten, they would all follow after him. In those days it was a grave offence to study poetry. If a penitent admitted in the confessional that he had privily listened to a Bachelor lecturing upon *Virgil,* the priest would impose upon him a thumping penance—to wit, to fast every Friday, or to rehearse daily the seven penitential Psalms. He swore to me, on his conscience, that he saw a candidate rejected because he had once been detected by one of the Examiners reading *Terence* on a feast day. Would that it were thus in the Universities now; then I should not have to drudge here at the Curia. For what work is there for us at the Universities? We cannot make a living. Students no longer will dwell in Hostels under Magisters. Among twenty students you will scarce find one with a mind to graduate. Yet all of them are eager to study the Humanities. When a Magister lectureth he findeth no audience; but, as for the Poets, when they discourse it is a marvel to behold the crowd of listeners. And thus the Universities throughout all *Germany* are minished and brought low. Let us pray God, then, that all the Poets may perish, for "it is expedient that one man should die" that is that the Poets, of whom there are but a handful in any one University, should perish, rather than so many Universities should come to naught.

And now you will surely send me a letter—or long will be my lamentations over your neglect. Farewell.

FROM ROME.

Marguerite d'Angoulême: *Novel XII*

Marguerite was a most remarkable lady of letters, a choice pearl of the French Renaissance. "She had," observed Clément Marot, "a woman's body, a man's heart, and an angel's head." Not only was she a patroness of humanists and a protector of reformers; she was also an author in her own right and a woman of exquisite spirituality. Marguerite was born at Angoulême in 1492 and was two years older than her brother King Francis I. In 1509 she was married to Charles, duke d'Alencon, who left her a widow in 1525. In 1527 she married young Henri d'Albret, who was titular king of Navarre. King Francis I did not reconquer Navarre for them, as he had promised, but at Nérac and Pau Marguerite and Henry maintained miniature courts where many French men of letters gathered. She died in 1549.

Marguerite's mother, Louise of Savoy, had looked after her education well, for she learned Latin, some Greek, and sufficient Italian to read Dante and Petrarch's sonnets. She was the belle of the court, beautiful and vibrant, intellectually gifted and inclined toward a deep mystical piety. Her literary output was truly remarkable, for she wrote reams of poetry, many short stories, and intense, searching religious mystical treatises. Her religious spirit found expression in poetry and in her treatise, *Mirror of a Sinful Soul.*

Her most famous work was the *Heptameron,* a collection of seventy-two short stories, some risqué and nearly as crude as Rabelais, reflecting the nature of the court society in which she lived. The *Heptameron,* obviously written under the influence of Boccaccio's *Decameron,* consisted of a collection of tales related to each other by a company of ladies and gentlemen who were delayed by a swollen river on their way home from Canterets, a fashionable watering-place. This delightful book, strongly characteristic of the courtly French Renaissance, was marked with sensuality, but after the story is told the participants in the dialogue discuss its merits and frequently also the morality of the action recounted. Most of the stories seem to relate the experiences of real people although a few are conventional and appear in earlier collections of tales. The *Heptameron* is peopled by blithe spirits, beautiful light-minded ladies, exquisite creatures, who read *La Belle Dame sans Merci,* and devised clandestine rendezvous with their lovers. But it is also peopled by cruel and domineering men, dukes who had the power of life and death, who could hire an assassin for ten crowns. The tale presented here, the second told on the second day, is based upon one of the most celebrated incidents in the annals of Florence. Duke Alessandro was lured to the house of his cousin, Lorenzo de' Medici, by the prospect of an "interview" with a Florentine lady, and there he was murdered.

This story is from *The Heptameron of the Tales of Margaret, Queen of Navarre,* ed. M. Le Roux de Lincy. (London: D. Trenor for the Bibliophilist Library, 1902), 106, 113–22.

At Florence there lived, about ten years ago, a duke of the house of Medicis, who had married Madame Margaret, natural daughter of the Emperor Charles the Fifth. As the princess was still very young, and the duke would not sleep with her until she was of more mature age, he treated her very tenderly; and to spare her he amused himself with some other ladies of the city, whom he used to visit by night whilst his wife slept. Among others, he took a fancy to a lady as beautiful as she was good and virtuous, the sister of a gentleman whom the duke loved as himself, and to whom he conceded such authority that he was obeyed like the duke himself. The latter had no secrets which he did not communicate to him, so that, in a manner, he might be called his second self. The duke, knowing that the gentleman's sister was a lady of the highest virtue, durst not at first speak to her of his passion; but after having tried every other expedient, he at last addressed his favourite on the subject.

"If there was anything in the world, my friend," he said, "which I would not do for you, I should be afraid to tell you what is in my thoughts, and still more to ask your aid. But I have so much friendship for you, that if I had a wife, a mother, or a daughter who could save your life, you may be assured you should not die. I am persuaded that you love me as much as I love you. If I, who am your master, have such an affection for you, that which you should have for me should be no less. I have a secret, then, to tell you. Through trying to conceal it, I have fallen into the state in which you now see me, from which I have no hope of escaping but by death, or by the service you may render me, if you will."

Touched by these representations on the part of his master, and seeing his face bathed in tears, the gentleman felt so much pity that he said, "I am your creature, my lord; it is from you I hold all my wealth and honours, and you may speak to me as to your own soul, being sure that whatever I can do is at your command."

The duke then declared the passion with which he was possessed for his favourite's sister, and told him it was impossible he should live long unless the brother enabled him to enjoy her; for he was quite sure that prayers or presents would be of no avail with her. "If, then," said the duke, in conclusion, "you love my life as much as I love yours, find means to secure me a bliss I can never obtain but through your aid." The gentleman, who loved his sister and the honour of his house more than his master's pleasure, remonstrated with him, and implored him not to reduce him to the horrible necessity of soliciting the dishonour of his family, protesting there was nothing he would not do for his master, but that his honour would not suffer him to perform such a service as that. The duke, inflamed with intolerable anger, bit his nails, and replied, furiously, "Since I find no friendship in you, I know what I have to do." The gentleman, who knew his master's cruelty, was alarmed, and said, "Since you absolutely insist on it, my lord, I will speak to her." "If you set store by my life, I will set store by yours," were the duke's last words as he went away.

The gentleman knew well what this meant, and remained a day or two without seeing the duke, pondering over the means of extricating himself from so bad a dilemma. On the one hand, he considered the obligations he was under to his master, the wealth and honours he had received from him; on the other hand, he thought of the honour of his house, and the virtue and chastity of his sister. He knew very well that she never would consent to such infamy, unless she were overcome by fraud or violence, which he could not think of employing, considering the shame it would bring upon him and her. In fine, he made up his mind that he would rather die than behave so vilely to his sister, who was one of the best women in Italy; and he resolved to deliver his country from a tyrant who was bent on disgracing his house; for he saw clearly that the only means of securing the lives of himself and his kindred was to get rid of the duke. Resolved, then, without speaking to his sister, to save his life and prevent his shame by one and the same deed, he went after two days to the duke, and told him that he had laboured so hard with his sister that at last, with infinite difficulty, he had brought her to consent to the duke's wishes, but on condition that the affair should be kept secret, and that no one should know of it but they three. As people readily believe what they desire, the duke put implicit faith in the brother's words. He embraced him, promised him everything he could ask, urged him to hasten the fulfilment of his good tidings, and appointed a time with him for that purpose.

When the exulting duke saw the approach of the night he so longed for, in which he expected to conquer her whom he had thought invincible, he retired early with his favourite, and did not forget to dress and perfume himself with his best care. When all was still, the gentleman conducted him to his sister's abode, and showed him into a magnificent chamber, where he undressed him, put him to bed, and left him, saying, "I am going, my lord, to bring you one who will not enter this room without blushing; but I hope that before day dawns she will be assured of you."

He then went away to his own room, where he found one trusty servant awaiting him by his orders. "Is thy heart bold enough," he said to him, "to follow me to a place where I have to revenge myself on the greatest of my enemies?" "Yes, my lord," replied the man, who knew nothing of the matter in hand, "though it were upon the duke himself." Thereupon, without giving the man time for reflection, the gentleman hurried him away so abruptly that he had not time to take any other weapon than a poniard with which he was already armed.

The duke, hearing his favourite's footsteps at the door, believed that he was bringing him the object of his passion, and threw open the curtains to behold and welcome her; but instead of her he saw her brother advance upon him with a drawn sword. Unarmed, but undaunted, the duke started up, seized the gentleman round the middle, saying, "Is this the way you keep your word?" and for want of other weapons used his nails and his teeth, bit his antagonist in the thumb, and defended himself so well that they fell together beside the bed. The gentleman, not feeling confident in his own strength, called his man, who, seeing his master and the duke grappling each other so desperately that he could not well distinguish which was which in that dark spot, dragged them both out by the heels into the middle of the room, and then set about cutting the duke's throat with his poniard. The duke defended himself to the last, until he was exhausted by loss of blood. Then the gentleman and his man laid him on the bed, finished him with their poniards, drew the curtains upon the body, and left the room, locking the door behind them.

Having slain his enemy and liberated the republic, the gentleman thought that his exploit would not be complete unless he did the same by five or six near relations of the duke. To this end he ordered his man to go and fetch them one by one; but the servant, who had neither vigour nor boldness enough, replied, "It strikes me, my lord, that you have done enough for the present, and that you had much better think of saving your own life than of taking that of others. If every one of them should take as long to despatch as the duke, it would be daylight before we had finished, even should they be unarmed." As the guilty are easily susceptible of the contagion of fear, the gentleman took his servant's advice, and went with him alone to a bishop, whose place it was to have the gates opened and to give orders to the postmasters. The gentleman told the prelate he had just received intelligence that one of his brothers was at the point of death; that the duke had given him leave to go to him, and therefore he begged his lordship would give him an order to the postmasters for two good horses, and to the gatekeepers to let him pass. The bishop, to whom his request seemed almost equivalent to a command from the duke his master, gave him a note, by means of which he at once obtained what he required: but instead of going to see his brother, he made straight for Venice, where he had himself cured of the bites inflicted by the duke, and then passed over into Turkey.

Next morning the duke's servants, not seeing or hearing anything of him, concluded that he had gone to see some lady; but at last becoming uneasy at his long absence, they began to look for him in all directions. The poor duchess, who was beginning to love him greatly, was extremely distressed at hearing that he could not be found. The favourite also not making his appearance, some of the servants went for him to his house. They saw blood at his chamber door, but no one could give any account of him. The trace of blood led the duke's servants to the chamber where he lay, and finding the door locked, they broke it open at once, saw the floor covered with blood, drew the curtains, and beheld the duke stark dead on the bed. Picture to yourselves the affliction of these servants, as they carried the body to the palace. The bishop arrived there at the same time, and told them how the gentleman had fled in the night under pretence of going to see his brother. This was enough to lead every one to the conclusion that it was he who had done the deed. It clearly appeared that his sister had known nothing about it. Though she was surprised at so unexpected an event, she loved her brother for it, since, without regard to his own life, he had delivered her from a tyrant who was bent on the ruin of her honour. She continued always to lead the same virtuous life; and though she was reduced to poverty by the confiscation of all the family property, her sister and she found husbands as honourable and wealthy as any in Italy. Both of them have always lived subsequently in the best repute.

Here is a fact, ladies, which should make you beware of that little god, who delights in tormenting princes and private persons, the strong and the weak, and who so infatuates them that they forget God and their conscience, and even the care of their own lives. Princes and those who are in authority ought to fear to outrage their inferiors. There is no man so insignificant but he can do mischief when it is God's will to inflict vengeance on the sinner, nor any so great that he can do hurt to one whom God chooses to protect.

This story was listened to by the whole company, but with very different sentiments. Some maintained that the gentleman had done well in securing his own life and his sister's honour, and delivering his country from such a tyrant. Others, on the contrary, said that it was enormously ungrateful to take the life of a man who had loaded him with wealth and honours. The ladies said he was a good brother and a virtuous citizen; the gentlemen, on the contrary, maintained that he was a traitor and a bad servant. It was amusing to hear the opinions and arguments delivered on the one side and on the other: but the ladies, as usual, spoke more from passion than from judgment, saying that the duke deserved death, and that blessed was the brother who had slain him. "Ladies," said Dagoucin, who saw what a lively controversy he had excited, "pray do not put yourselves in a passion about a thing that is past and gone; only take care that your beauties do not occasion murders more cruel than that which I have related."

" 'The Fair Lady without Compassion,' "[1] said Parlamente, "has taught us to say that people hardly ever die of so agreeable a malady."

"Would to God, madam," rejoined Dagoucin, "that every lady here knew how false is this notion. They would not then, I im-

[1] *La Belle Dame sans Merci* is the title of a poem by Alain Chartier, in the form of a long metaphysical dialogue between a lady and her lover.

agine, desire the reputation of being pitiless, or like to resemble that incredulous fair one who let a good servant die for want of responding favourably to his passion."

"So, then," said Parlamente, "to save the life of a man who says he loves us, you would have us violate our honour and our conscience?"

"I do not say that," replied Dagoucin, "for he who loves thoroughly would be more afraid of hurting the honour of his mistress than she herself. Hence it seems to me that a gracious response, such as is called for by a seemly and genuine love, would only give more lustre to the honour and conscience of a lady. I say a seemly love, for I maintain that those who love otherwise do not love perfectly."

"That is always the upshot of your orisons," said Ennasuite. "You begin with honour, and end with its opposite. If all the gentlemen present will tell us the truth of the matter, I will believe them on their oaths."

Hircan swore that he had never loved anyone but his wife, and that it was far from his wish to make her offend God. Simontault spoke to the same effect, and added that he had often wished that all women were ill-natured except his own wife. "You deserve that yours should be so," retorted Geburon; "but for my part, I can safely swear that I loved a woman so much that I would rather have died than have made her do anything capable of diminishing the esteem in which I held her. My love was so founded upon her virtues, that I would not have seen a stain upon them for the most precious favours I could have obtained from her."

"I thought, Geburon," said Saffredent, laughing, "that the love you have for your wife, and the good sense with which nature has endowed you, would have saved you from playing the lover elsewhere; but I see I was mistaken, for you use the very phrases which we are accustomed to employ to dupe the most subtle of dames, and under favour of which we obtain a hearing from the most discreet. Where is the lady, indeed, who will not lend us an ear when we begin our discourse with honour and virtue? But if we were all to lay open our hearts before them just as they are, there is many a man well received by the ladies whom then they would not condescend so much as to look upon. We hide our devil under the form of the handsomest angel we can find, and so receive many a favour before we are found out. Perhaps, even, we lead the ladies so far, that thinking to go straight to virtue, they have neither time nor opportunity to retreat when they find themselves face to face with vice."

"I thought you quite a different sort of man," said Geburon, "and imagined virtue was more agreeable to you than pleasure."

"Why," said Saffredent, "is there any greater virtue than to love in the way God has ordained? To me it seems much better to love a woman as a woman, than to make her one's idol, as many do. For my part, I am convinced that it is better to use than to abuse."

All the ladies coincided in opinion with Geburon, and bade Saffredent hold his tongue. "Very well," said he, "I am content to say no more on the subject, for I have fared so badly with regard to it that I don't want to have any more to do with it."

"You may thank your own bad thoughts for having fared badly," said Longarine, "for where is the woman with a proper sense of decorum who would have you for a lover after what you have just said?"

"There are those," he retorted, "who did not think me intolerable, and who would not have exchanged their own sense of decorum for yours. But let us say no more about it, in order that my anger may shock no one, and may not shock myself. Let us think to whom Dagoucin will give his voice."

"I give it to Parlamente," he replied at once, "persuaded as I am that she must know better than anyone what is honourable and perfect friendship."

"Since you elect me to tell a story," said Parlamente, "I will relate to you one which occurred to a lady who had always been one of my good friends, and who has never concealed anything from me."

Guillaume Budé: *On Establishing the Study of Letters*

1468–1540

Étienne Dolet called his friend Guillaume Budé the "chief captain" of the French humanists. Budé was a formidable scholar and a multifaceted intellectual, who embodied the major trends of French humanism in his dedication to the classics, devotion to religious enlightenment, and desire for a reformation of society. Budé was born in 1468 into a family of civil servants and was himself headed for a career in government. He began the study of law, but developed such a passion for the classics that he devoted himself to the study of Latin and Greek. Even on his wedding day he spent three hours working on an ancient manuscript. He often stayed up all night reading Greek and writing letters in Greek to correspondents such as Erasmus. The story was told that once when his house caught on fire a servant rushed into his study to tell him, but he merely replied, "Tell my wife that she is in charge of the housekeeping!" He wrote *Annotations* on the Pandects or digest of Justinian's law. He published *De Asse,* a treatise on numismatics in which he analyzed the ancient monetary system. His most important work, however, was his *Commentaries on the Greek Language*. King Francis I esteemed him as a cultural ornament at his court. Perhaps Budé's greatest contribution to learning was in persuading the king to found in 1530 a school in which Latin, Greek, and Hebrew were to be taught with a few other subjects. This school, called at the time the *Corporation of the royal readers,* survives today as the *Collège de France*. Budé died in 1540.

The selection presented here reveals Budé's evaluation of the importance of the liberal arts, the new way of making man's earthly existence meaningful. In this selection, which is itself turgid and artificially rhetorical, Budé praises the power of speech, the contribution of sophists and rhetoricians, relates the tale of Hercules addressed by Inertia and Virtue, rejoices over the revival of learning after a thousand years of medieval mud, and describes the importance of rhetoric for all the disciplines, including philosophy and theology.

This translation by Dr. Lewis W. Spitz, Sr., is based upon the text *De Studio Literarum Recte et Commode Instituendo*, dedicated to Francis I and published by Ascensius in Paris, 1523, reproduced in facsimile by Friedrich Frommann Verlag, Stuttgart-Bad Cannstatt, 1964.

On Establishing the Study of Letters Rightly and Properly, to the Most Invincible and Powerful Prince Francis, King of France

"Honor nourishes the arts" is a proverb worn out by long use. It does not so much pertain to sedentary occupations and to earning money and gifts as to the arts which the ancients believed should be called "noble" or "liberal." They doubtless wanted this term to be understood in this way, that these worthy arts are for people who do not serve in slavery and have not been born with a degenerate and servile mind. Roman antiquity granted to these very arts the honor of declaring them to be "humane sciences," that is, that moral men could hardly preserve and firmly embrace true humanity without them. Indeed, since Providence has given the human race by far the most noble among all creatures, two natural excellences, namely mind and speech, the ancients saw that those who passed their years of childhood and adolescence far from literary schools were either nearly half-wild or rustic, like children who cannot speak.

We see many of the kind turn up who use only common sense for their preceptor and master. But the manner of speaking tends to deteriorate with time and to pass over gradually from the patricians (if I may say so) to the plebeians, the number of the unskilled certainly surpassing the skilled many times. Then the human mind, imbued with erratic and blemished morals immediately from childhood and the apprenticeship of life, does not sense that by continual contact with powerful ignorance it is finally in a measure brought back step by step to the order of the other animals, even though it has in rank, as is said, indeed been freed by the privilege of a distinguished and noble origin. Truly the notion of things human and divine is gradually added to a person's nature as he grows up, as if by a teacher. Thus in the assembly of many men, the common understanding arises as in a game, and in time clearly grows in the man proportionally to his age. Moreover, it is itself merely begun and is not a full, true knowledge, and not sufficient for the understanding of those things that must be provided for instructing and governing life.

Therefore both in forensic debates that are to be judged and in legal disputes that are to be resolved, however great the prudence of common sense may be, it nevertheless lacks the knowledge of civil law and the equity produced by those men who render legal opinion. And the notion of the things mentioned above, anticipated by the benefit of nature and then increased and strengthened by public conversation, is nevertheless too dull to equal the mental darkness of perception that weighs upon our life. Within that mental darkness and dense fog, so to speak, of fallacious images and empty forms, the retinue of philosophy has begun to explore hidden truth and the nature of the supreme good, and to follow the tracks of nature with truly keen and ardent zeal. Not a few men, who had entered the family of philosophy with its various branches of schools, managed by the keenest contention of their minds (neglecting both their body and their fortunes) to prepare for themselves first of all the resources of the most honorable disciplines. Then they handed down a way to retain them for posterity, secured and made easy by method and precepts as fully as possible. Indeed the most noble of them considered it shameful that human nature through ignorance of itself and through moral corruption, which had long ago begun to grow among mortals, had been cast down from the rank of sublime nature, which itself from the beginning of things was of the same stock as and related to the divine. For this reason and the feeling of shame, men were stirred up and began to inquire eagerly why the human race itself, having lost the right way, should lie through inertia, as it were, at the public places and crossroads of life in those small gatherings of the multitudes that are called city-states.

Therefore among the Greeks some men appeared, more cultured in morals and language than others, who were sometimes called sophists and sometimes philosophers. When these men observed that barbarous solecisms had increased in reason and morals in the duties of public life and in speech, they began to profess the discipline of an honest and improved life, and persuaded many to nurture and retain it. This teaching, furthermore, like a sculptor and teacher who polishes, and cultivates humanity, is now designated with the name "good letters." In the opinion of a large number of men the goals of this teaching are, however, much less limited and much more ample than the name itself indicates, for it includes all communication and the whole world that can be shared with the Muses—indeed, the varied and multiplex itself, toward whatever end it widely pertains.

Particularly philosophy, the teacher of a more distinguished life, the master of right conduct, and the interpreter of its oracles, is truly believed to have produced and to have left behind aids for life by which men, who had given too much attention to the body (and for that reason crept on earth like brute animals), could finally bestir themselves, rise to self-knowledge, and from that level of intelligence, turn their faces toward and aspire to heaven. Moreover, that this was once the unique goal of philosophy, which was cultivated and approved by good, honest men, that noble precept is the proof: "Know thyself!" This precept is heeded and weighed with sufficient gravity by few, I think, and perhaps even by very few, although at one time it was consecrated in the most noble temple of the entire world as the most important of the oracles of prudence. For the summit of human wisdom extends up to this. Philosophy has chiefly deliberated about this in discussing nature and morals. Finally heaven admonished mortals, once represented among the gods and gifted by decrees with divine honors in all the world, to look up to heaven and to despise the temporal things below. At least this was the feeling, it seems likely, in those most ancient days which are said to have produced heroes.

There is that noble fable of Hercules, whom the learned Prodicus [a fifth-century sophist] described in Xenophon's second book of *Remembrances*. When Hercules first reached manhood—the time given by nature for choosing one's way of life—he had gone into solitude and, sitting there, had been in great doubt for a long time. He observed two ways—one of pleasure, the other of virtue—and wondered which of the two it would be better to enter upon. In the meantime two women, great of stature, appeared to him. One was of decent aspect and noble mind, of refined dress, manifesting chastity in look and modesty in posture, and clothed in a white garment. The other was of a more fleshy appearance and simple education, ornamented with exquisite make-up so artfully colored that the appearance feigned greater whiteness and redness of the skin than was true. The movement of her body and deportment were so affected that she appeared to be taller than her natural size. With her eyes wide open and with a garment that effected the greatest charm of the body, she meanwhile examined herself, cast her eyes here and there, looking constantly to see whether anyone was turning his eyes upon her, and observing her own shadow.

When she had already approached Hercules more closely (the first woman mentioned had also hastened to advance), she ran up to him, eager to arrive before the other woman, and began to speak with these words: "I see that you, Hercules, are in doubt as to which way of life you should ultimately enter upon. If you have been persuaded to use me as a friend and author, I shall lead you in the most happy way, at the same time also the easiest way, and I shall truly give you a taste of all delightful things. But I shall make you free of grievous things forever. In the first place, you shall indeed be free from the care of wars and negotiations. Finally, you will live securely in this thought, that first of all you must consider what food and what drink you shall find to be most pleasant for you, what pleases your eyes, what your touch, what smell will be most agreeable to you, with which amours to indulge your spirit, how to sleep most sweetly, in which way you will be able to indulge all your desires effortlessly. But beware lest the thought of danger enter your mind and that you need fear losing at some time the things from which the delights I have mentioned are customarily supplied. I forbid you to fear such things, for in no wise shall I entice you to a life of labor and enduring worry either in mind or body, so that thereby pleasant delights of this kind may be in store for you. And when indeed you enjoy the labors of other men, then you will abstain from nothing from which some gain could possibly be derived. Yes, I give to my followers this kind of unrestrained liberty to procure and increase their advantages from anywhere." When Hercules had heard this, he said: "But what, then, is your name, woman?" She said: "My friend, my name is Happiness, but those who have hated me, wanting to belittle the force of this word, call me Inertia."

Meanwhile the first woman arrived. "I also," she said, "come to you, Hercules, as one who knew your parents and knows your talent to perceive my instruction, and I hope if you enter upon the way leading safely to me, you will strenuously perform difficult and honorable things, and thereupon I myself shall appear more honorable and for the most part more distinguished. You shall, furthermore, in no way expect me to deceive you with a voluptuous and more carefully arranged dress, for as the gods have established, so I shall simply recount the truth of things. But the gods themselves are indeed wont to give men none of those things that are good and honorable without labor and care. If you desire the gods to be propitious to you, you must worship them. If you wish to be loved by friends, the friends must also be gained by favors. If in any state honor is bestowed upon you, you must prove yourself useful to that state. For if the spirit is to stir up admiration for you throughout all of Greece, you must some time bestow a benefaction upon Greece itself. Moreover, if you want the earth to pour out her fruits for you in abundance, you must cultivate the earth itself. And if you have determined to make more money in the cattle business, you must diligently care for the cattle themselves. But if you have caught the urge for affairs of war, to exalt your dignity by freeing your freinds and delivering up the enemies to servitude, when this seems right to you, you must by all means see to it that you learn the arts of war from those who are capable and apt to teach them. And when you have learned their use, you must confirm them with practice. Finally, if you intend to acquire the physical fitness of an athlete, you must accustom the body to serve the mind, to exercise it by labor and sweat."

Listening to her speech, Inertia, according to Prodicus, said: "Do you note, O Hercules, how difficult and long a way to gladness that woman has set before you? But I shall lead you on a short declining road to happiness."

Then Virtue replied: "O you miserable one! What good do you possess in the end? Have you yourself come to know any delights at all? Do you therefore support doing any of these things that must be prepared for—you who do not even have a need for the desire and longing characteristic of those who are truly happy? Should you accustom yourself to be sated with all these things and prefer them to true desire? Before you are hungry, taking food; before you are thirsty, drinking! In order to feast sumptuously, you carefully search out the masters of food; in order to drink sweetly, you purchase precious wines; and in the summer, if it please the gods, you desire to have snow all around. Moreover, to be lulled joyfully to sleep with luxury you not only spread out beds but even soft sedans, taking care that their seats are made soft for you, which you doubtless have arranged not so that you can alternate between sleep and work, but for sleep only, because you have nothing else better to do. Then, listless, you will incite love with carefully contrived devices, unmoved by the power of love itself. Consider what your friends desire to learn from you that they may spend the nights with wantonness and the best part of the day in a stupor. Therefore, though you are immortal, you are ejected from the assembly of the gods. Finally, you are deprived of the most joyful gratification to the ear, for you never hear that you have been praised. At the same time you are deprived of a spectacle that truly should be seen, for you will never have viewed any beautiful or honorable work of your own."

Most illustrious and excellent Prince, such for the most part are the tales of Hercules and certainly the students of his Heraclean philosophy today, a philosophy which the ancient Greeks called "circular erudition" and which not only embraced an immense circumference and, as it were, a circular play and choral dance of disciplines, but also arduous and difficult digressions of the way. But in our age they are more passable with considerable labor than in time past, because our age has with effort begun to produce the choruses of the Muses, wearing the toga [Roman] and at the same time dressed in the pallium [Greek], reproduced and brought back from the once most celebrated heights that already seemed inaccessible and deserted.

Yes indeed, it is worth the effort to value the greatness of the ancient geniuses from their own images, which one or another age has restored and which stand out clearly to this day. Having found them in withered and squalid documents, they have almost wiped them clean and polished them to their original brightness. Although a large part of these documents is believed not to have survived unharmed to this day, we must often remember and give thanks to Providence that we already have the best part of them, I think, and they have been rescued from a deluge of more than a thousand years. For a calamitous flood had so swallowed up and absorbed literature and the kindred arts worthy of the name and kept them buried in barbarian mud that it is a miracle that they have survived till now. Obviously, this must be due to Providence, which wanted to return to us the remnants and images of the ancient minds in order to cultivate and adorn life.

One discipline [rhetoric] of those we have mentioned comprehends the wonderful power of speaking, flowing and gushing forth continuously from the fountain of wisdom and, in addition, the immense and varied masses of eloquence, as well as the limits of that law and empire, an orb long and wide-open, if indeed they can be circumscribed by any circumference. At one time men, or rather certain demigods of the literary ilk, were wont to traverse this orbit of great spirits not by one or another spirit but by a single effort and an unhindered course. We see this appropriately demonstrated in the fictions of the most ancient fables: of what nature are the golden rods of Mercury, the shield of Pallas, finally, the songs of the Muses, so also the torchbearers of their Calliope [Muse of epic poetry], as Hesiod says, "This one is the eldest of all." Indeed the poets hid their choruses away in lonely mountains and, as if united ropelike by their joined hands the Muses signify and manifestly demonstrate the consensus of the sciences and the relationships of all the studies in that they regard the one or the other to be imperfect without the rest and lacking the necessary supports. But the misfortune of many centuries, which brought on a calamitous desolation in literature never produced anything of lasting value.

Truly, what is more unworthy and more shameful for this splendor of letters than what is happening now through our indolence and idleness, or because customs hardened by age into crookedness refuse to apply a correcting hand, so that the circle of disciplines that once had coalesced has now been dissolved into parts or cut to pieces? And that the functions of each profession and of individual men have been divided into very many? It has already reached the point where those who profess themselves to be either medics or students of law or followers of any other science whatever, if at any time it happens that they must speak on one of the other subjects whose academic title they themselves had not taken up—indeed if they have to deliver an oration somewhat more cultivated—unless they prefaced it with a plea for indulgence, they seem to do so impudently and improperly, like those who go to collect a bundle from a strange harvest. . . .

But most notable is the error and the guilt of those who want to appear to be most experienced in the divine law, when without the divine will of Mercury, the defender and master of interpretations, they assert that the explanation of the most wonderful oracles can be correctly given—which, if I may say so, contain the horn of plenty of all knowledge and wisdom. They indeed, if it please the gods, maintain that this is being done more appropriately and even in a holier way, as if this one part of teaching [theology] truly either had no genius of speech except with a few or had a preposterous and contentious one. But to uphold and to declare this obstinately is an aspect of men's inertia and the rusticity of its defenders, not of the sanctimony and truth of the students, if Mercury is indeed today sacred through the knowledge of ancient letters, whom those masters of our theology and the Platos of orthodox philosophy thought should be very much cultivated and venerated. And yet many Latins have fallen upon times calamitous to letters. . . .

Nor in truth is the faculty of speaking faultlessly with a certain proper eloquence of speech oratory, as it is generally believed to be. It is fused throughout all the disciplines, since it is formed and compressed from the knowledge of all of them. Therefore it can take from each one what it believes to be applicable. On the other hand, oratory must serve each science as occasion and opportunity presents itself, and apply its labor generously to the appropriate extent. For what branch of knowledge, what faculty, as long as it is liberal, can gather even one small bundle of glory in its harvest without the ability of this kind of speech? Even omitting glory, how could any discipline share the fruit of its labor and dissertations with posterity? The study of this profession [rhetoric], which is capable of so many great functions, being circumscribed by no bounds, is restrained by no annual laws [university regulations], although the studies of the other arts have their curricula measured by certain years, by spaces, as it were, and by the customs and rules of the scholars. Truly this faculty of speaking . . . can in this manner properly and honestly deserve the attention of all the sciences and the arts, as well as of theology.

François Rabelais: from *Gargantua and Pantagruel*

Few intellectuals have puzzled historians so much as has François Rabelais, for they have described him as a skeptical free-thinker, a forerunner of Voltaire, as a crypto-Protestant, a truly pious Catholic, or as an Erasmian humanist. Born around 1495, as a child he was placed with the Franciscans and spent his youth as a Franciscan. He studied the Greek and Latin classics in his spare time. Not happy with the unintellectual mendicants, he joined the Benedictine order, which had a longer tradition of learning. Still dissatisfied he became a secular priest in order to travel about. In 1530 he enrolled in the school of medicine at Montpellier and the following year he lectured on Hippocrates and Galen. In 1532 he moved to Lyon, where a lively circle of writers and publishers were at work. There he began to write *Gargantua and Pantagruel* to which he was to return in his leisure time for many years thereafter. He journeyed to Rome in 1533 and 1535 with Jean du Bellay, who was made a cardinal. He rejoined the Benedictines and became a canon of St. Maur. He took his doctorate in medicine at Montpellier in 1537 and served as a physician in Metz, a city in the Empire, during the last repressive years at the end of the reign of Francis I. His major work was, in fact, censured by the Sorbonne and the Parlement forbade its sale. He died in the year 1553.

The plot of his yarn can be simply told. Rabelais borrowed the names Gargantua and Pantagruel from some stories already in circulation at the time. Gargantua's giant parents celebrate the birth of their gigantic infant with a fantastic feast at which the guests gorge themselves with food and drink. As a young man Gargantua founded the Abbey of Thélème, which is the ideal monastery, welcoming both sexes. Its inhabitants are pure spirits who shun evil and cultivate the good, and learn freely, without restraint. The motto of Thélème is "Do what thou wouldst!" Gargantua's son, Pantagruel, while a student at Paris learns to know Panurge, a lecherous fellow, a hard drinker, and a coward. Panurge declares his intention of marrying, but seeks oracular advice.

He and Pantagruel set sail for the Land of the Lanterns to consult the Oracle of the Bottle. When they at last arrive the Oracle instructs Panurge to "Drink a Toast!" This he takes as a sanction for marriage, but the book ends at this point. The entire yarn is full of digressions, satires, seemingly irrelevant incidents, puzzles, and mysterious poems. It reflects the intellectual currents of French humanist society during Rabelais' life. "To laugh is proper to man!" wrote Rabelais. He is the best-known of the French vernacular writers of the early sixteenth century.

The following selections on "The Abbey of Thélème," Book I, chaps. LII to LVII, and on "The Joys of Learning," a letter from Gargantua to Pantagruel, Book II, chap. VIII, are taken from *All the Extant Works of François Rabelais,* trans. Samuel Putnam, © 1929 by Corici Fríede, Inc. Used by permission of Crown Publishers, Inc.

How Gargantua Had the Abbey of Thélème Built for the Monk

There remained the monk to provide for. Gargantua wanted to make him Abbot of Seuilly, but the friar refused. He wanted to give him the Abbey of Bourguêil or that of Saint-Florent, whichever might suit him best, or both, if he had fancy for them. But the monk gave a peremptory reply to the effect that he would not take upon himself any office involving the government of others.

"For how," he demanded, "could I govern others, who cannot even govern myself? If you are of the opinion that I have done you, or may be able to do you in the future, any worthy service, give me leave to found an abbey according to my own plan."

This request pleased Gargantua, and the latter offered his whole province of Thélème, lying along the River Loire, at a distance of two leagues from the great Forest of Port-Huault. The monk then asked that he be permitted to found a convent that should be exactly the opposite of all other institutions of the sort.

"In the first place, then," said Gargantua, "you don't want to build any walls around it; for all the other abbeys have plenty of those."

"Right you are," said the monk, "for where there is a wall (*mur*) in front and behind there is bound to be a lot of *murmur*—ing, jealousy and plotting on the inside."

Moreover, in view of the fact that in certain convents in this world there is a custom, if any woman (by which, I mean any modest or respectable one) enters the place, to clean up thoroughly after her wherever she has been—in view of this fact, a regulation was drawn up to the effect that if any monk or nun should happen to enter this new convent, all the places they had set foot in were to be thoroughly scoured and scrubbed. And since, in other convents, everything is run, ruled, and fixed by hours, it was decreed that in this one there should not be any clock or dial of any sort, but that whatever work there was should be done whenever occasion offered. For, as Gargantua remarked, the greatest loss of time he knew was to watch the hands of the clock. What good came of it? It was the greatest foolishness in the world to regulate one's conduct by the tinkling of a time-piece, instead of by intelligence and good common sense.

Another feature: Since in those days women were not put into convents unless they were blind in one eye, lame, hunchbacked, ugly, misshapen, crazy, silly, deformed, and generally of no account, and since men did not enter a monastery unless they were snotty-nosed, underbred, dunces, and troublemakers at home—

"Speaking of that," said the monk, "of what use is a woman who is neither good nor good to look at?"

"Put her in a convent," said Gargantua.

"Yes," said the monk, "and set her to making shirts."

And so, it was decided that in this convent they would receive only the pretty ones, the ones with good figures and sunny dispositions, and only the handsome, well set-up, good-natured men.

Item: Since in the convents of women, men never entered, except underhandedly and by stealth, it was provided that, in this one, there should be no women unless there were men also, and no men unless there were also women.

Item: Inasmuch as many men, as well as women, once received into a convent were forced and compelled, after a year of probation, to remain there all the rest of their natural lives—in view of this, it was provided that, here, both men and women should be absolutely free to pick up and leave whenever they happened to feel like it.

Item: Whereas, ordinarily, the religious take three vows, namely, those of chastity, poverty and obedience, it was provided that, in this abbey, one might honorably marry, that each one should be rich, and that all should live in utter freedom.

With regard to the lawful age for entering, the women should be received from the age of ten to fifteen years, the men from the age of twelve to eighteen.

How the Abbey of the Thelemites Was Built and Endowed

For the building and furnishing of the abbey, Gargantua made a ready-money levy of two-million-seven-hundred-thousand-eight-hundred-thirty-one of the coins known as "big woolly sheep"; and for each year, until everything should be in perfect shape, he turned over, out of the toll-receipts of the Dive River, one-million-six-hundred-sixty-nine-thousand "sunny crowns" and the same number of "seven-chick pieces." For the foundation and support of the abbey, he made a perpetual grant of two-million-three-hundred-sixty-nine-thousand-five-hundred-fourteen "rose nobles," in the form of ground-rent, free and exempt of all encumbrances, and payable every year at the abbey gate, all of this being duly witnessed in the form of letters of conveyance.

As for the building itself, it was in the form of a hexagon, so constructed that at every corner there was a great round tower sixty paces in diameter, all these being of the same size and appearance. The River Loire flowed along the north elevation. Upon the bank of this river stood one of the towers, named Arctic, while, proceeding toward the east, there was another, named Calaer, following it another, named Anatole, then another, named Mesembrine, another after it, named Hesperia, and finally, one named Cryere. Between every two towers, there was a distance of three-hundred-twelve paces. To the building proper, there were six stories in all, counting the underground cellars as one. The second story was vaulted, in the form of a basket handle. The rest were stuccoed with plaster of Paris, in the manner of lamp bottoms, the roof being covered over with a fine slate, while the ridge-coping was lead, adorned with little mannikins and animal figures, well grouped and gilded. The eaves-troughs, which jutted out from the walls, between the mullioned windows, were painted with diagonal gold and blue figures, all the way down to the ground, where they ended in huge rainspouts, all of which led under the house to the river.

This building was a hundred times more magnificent than the one at Bonivet, at Chambord, or at Chantilly; for in it there were nine-thousand-three-hundred-thirty-two rooms, each equipped with a dressing-room, a study, a wardrobe, and a chapel, and each opening into a large hall. Between the towers, in the center of the main building, was a winding stair, the steps of which were partly of porphyry, partly of Numidian stone, and partly of serpentine marble, each step being twenty-two feet long and three fingers thick, with an even dozen between each pair of landings. On each landing were two fine antique arches, admitting the daylight, while through these arches, one entered a loggia of the width of the stair, the chair itself running all the way to the roof and ending in a pavilion. From this stair one could enter, from either side, a large hall, and from this hall the rooms.

From the tower known as Arctic to the one called Cryere, there were fine large libraries, in Greek, Latin, Hebrew, French, Tuscan, and Spanish, separated from each other according to the different languages. In the middle of the building was another and marvelous stairway, the entrance to which was from outside the house, by way of an arch thirty-six feet wide. This stair was so symmetrical and capacious that six men-at-arms, their lances at rest, could ride up abreast, all the way to the roof. From the tower Anatole to Mesembrine, there were large and splendid galleries, all containing paintings representative of deeds of ancient prowess, along with historical and geographical scenes. In the center of this elevation was still another gateway and stair, like the one on the river-side. Over this gate, there was inscribed, in large old-fashioned letters, the following poem:

Inscription Over the Great Portal of Thélème

You hypocrites and two-faced, please stay out:
Grinning old apes, potbellied snivelbeaks,
Stiffnecks and blockheads, worse than Goths, no doubt,
Magogs and Ostrogoths we read about;
You hairshirt whiners and you slippered sneaks;
You fur-lined beggars and you nervy freaks;
You bloated dunces, trouble-makers all;
Go somewhere else to open up your stall.

Your cursed ways
Would fill my peaceful days
With nasty strife;
With your lying life,
You'd spoil my roundelays—
With your cursed ways.

Stay out, you lawyers, with your endless guts,
You clerks and barristers, you public pests,
You Scribes and Pharisees, with your "if's" and "but's,"
You hoary judges (Lord, how each one struts!):
You feed, like dogs, on squabbles and bequests;
You'll find your salary in the hangman's nests;
Go there and bray, for here there is no guile
That you can take to court, to start a trial.

No trials or jangles
Or legal wrangles:
We're here to be amused.
If your jaws must be used,
You've bags full of tangles,
Trials and jangles.

Stay out, you usurers and misers all,
Gluttons for gold, and how you hoard the stuff!
Greedy windjammers, with a world of gall,
Hunchbacked, snubnosed, your money-jars full, you bawl
For more and more; you never have enough;
Your stomachs never turn, for they are tough,
As you heap your piles, each miser-faced poltroon:
I hope Old Death effaces you, right soon!

That inhuman mug
Makes us shrug:
Take it to another shop,
And please don't stop,
But elsewhere lug
That inhuman mug!

Stay out of here, at morning, noon and night,
Jealous old curs, dotards that whine and moan,
All trouble-makers, full of stubborn spite,
Phantom avengers of a Husband's plight,
Whether Greek or Latin, worst wolves ever known;
You syphilitics, mangy to the bone,
Go take your wolfish sores, and let them feed at ease—
Those cakey crusts, signs of a foul disease.

Honor, praise, delight
Rule here, day and night;
We're gay, and we agree;
We're healthy, bodily;
And so, we have a right
To honor, praise, delight.

But welcome here, and very welcome be,
And doubly welcome, all noble gentlemen.
This is the place where taxes all are free,
And incomes plenty, to live merrily,
However fast you come—I shan't "say when":
Then, be my cronies in this charming den;
Be spruce and jolly, gay and always mellow,
Each one of us a very pleasant fellow.

Companions clean,
Refined, serene,
Free from avarice;
For civilized bliss,
See, the tools are keen,
Companions clean.

And enter here, all you who preach and teach
The living Gospel, though the heathen raves:
You'll find a refuge here beyond their reach,
Against the hostile error you impeach,
Which through the world spreads poison, and depraves:
Come in, for here we found a faith that saves;
By voice and letter, let's confound the herd
Of enemies of God's own Holy Word.

The word of grace
We'll not efface
From this holy place;
Let each embrace,
And himself enlace
With the word of grace.

Enter, also, ladies of high degree!
Feel free to enter and be happy here,
Each face with beauty flowering heavenly,
With upright carriage, pleasing modesty:
This is the house where honor's held most dear,
Gift of a noble lord whom we revere,
Our patron, who's established it for you,
And given us his gold, to see it through.

Gold given by gift
Gives golden shrift—
To the giver a gift,
And very fine thrift,
A wise man's shift,
Is gold given by gift.

What Kind of Dwelling the Thelemites Had

In the middle of the lower court was a magnificent fountain of beautiful alabaster, above which were the three Graces with cornucopias, casting out water through their breasts, mouths, ears, eyes, and the other openings of their bodies.

The interior of the portion of the dwelling that opened upon this court rested upon great pillars of chalcedony and of porphyry, fashioned with the finest of antique workmanship. Above were splendid galleries, long and wide, adorned with paintings, with the horns of deer, unicorns, rhinoceroses, and hippopotamuses, as well as with elephants' teeth and other objects interesting to look upon.

The ladies' quarters extended from the tower Arctic to the Mesembrine gate. The men occupied the rest of the house. In front of the ladies' quarters, in order that the occupants might have something to amuse them, there had been set up, between the first two outside towers, the lists, the hippodrome, the theatre, and the swimming-pools, with wonderful triple-stage baths, well provided with all necessary equipment and plentifully supplied with water of myrrh.

Next the river was a fine pleasure-garden, in the center of which was a handsome labyrinth. Between the towers were the tennis courts and the ball-grounds. On the side by the tower Cryere was the orchard, full of all sorts of fruit trees, all of them set out in the form of quincunxes. Beyond was the large park, filled with every sort of savage beast. Between the third pair of towers were the targets for arquebus, archery, and crossbow practice. The servants' quarters were outside the tower Hesperia and consisted of one floor only, and beyond these quarters were the stables. In front of the latter stood the falcon-house, looked after by falconers most expert in their art. It was furnished annually by the Canadians, the Venetians, and the Sarmatians, with all kinds of out-of-the-ordinary birds: eagles, gerfalcons, goshawks, sakers, lanners, falcons, sparrowhawks, merlins, and others, all so well trained and domesticated that, when these birds set out from the castle for a little sport in the fields, they would take everything that came in their way. The hunting kennels were a little farther off, down toward the park.

All the halls, rooms and closets were tapestried in various manners, according to the season of the year. The whole floor was covered with green cloth. The bedding was of embroidered work. In each dressingroom was a crystal mirror, with chasings of fine gold, the edges being trimmed with pearls; and this mirror was of such a size that—it is the truth I am telling you—it was possible to see the whole figure in it at once. As one came out of the halls into the ladies' quarters, he at once encountered the perfumers and the hair-dressers, through whose hands the gentlemen passed when they came to visit the ladies. These functionaries each morning supplied the women's chambers with rose, orange, and "angel" water; and in each room a precious incense-dish was vaporous with all sorts of aromatic drugs.

How the Monks and Nuns of Thélème Were Clad

The ladies, when the abbey was first founded, dressed themselves according to their own fancy and good judgment. Later they of their own free will introduced a reform. In accordance with this revised rule, they went clad as follows:

They wore scarlet or kermes-colored stockings, and these extended above their knees for a distance of three inches, to be precise, the borders being of certain fine embroideries and pinkings. Their garters were of the same color as their bracelets, and clasped the leg above and below the knee. Their shoes, pumps, and slippers were of brilliant-colored velvet, red or violet, shaped in the form of a lobster's barbel.

Above the chemise, they wore a fine bodice, of a certain silk-camlet material, and a taffeta petticoat, white, red, tan, gray, etc. Over this went a skirt of silver taffeta, made with embroideries of fine gold or elaborate needlework, or, as the wearer's fancy might dictate, and depending upon the weather, of satin, of damask, or of velvet, being orange, tan, green, ash-gray, blue, bright yellow, brilliant red, or white in color, and being made of cloth-of-gold, silver tissue, thread-work, or embroidery, according to the feast-days. Their gowns, which were in keeping with the season, were of gold tissue or silver crisping, and were made of red satin, covered with gold needle-work, or of white, blue, black, or tan taffeta, silk serge, silk-camlet, velvet, silver-cloth, silver-tissue, or of velvet or satin with gold facings of varying design.

In summer, on certain days, in place of gowns they wore cloaks of the above-mentioned materials, or sleeveless jackets, cut in the Moorish fashion and made of violet-colored velvet, with crispings of gold over silver needlework, or with gold knots, set off at the seams with little Indian pearls. And they always had a fine plume, matching the color of their sleeves and well trimmed with golden spangles.

In winter, they wore taffeta gowns of the colors mentioned, trimmed with the fur of lynxes, black-spotted weasels, Calabrian or Siberian sables, and other precious skins. Their chaplets, rings, gold-chains, and goldwork necklaces contained fine stones: carbuncles, rubies, balas rubies, diamonds, sapphires, emeralds, turquoises, garnets, agates, beryls, and pearls great and small.

Their head-dress, likewise, depended upon the weather. In winter, it was after the French fashion; in spring, after the Spanish style; in summer, after the Tuscan. That is, excepting feast-days and Sundays, when they wore the French coiffure, for the reason that it is more respectable and better in keeping with matronly modesty.

The men dressed after a fashion of their own. Their stockings were of broadcloth or of serge, and were scarlet, kermes-hued, white, or black in color. Their hose were of velvet and of the same colors, or very nearly the same, being embroidered and cut to suit the fancy. Their doublets were of cloth-of-gold, silver-cloth, velvet, satin, damask, or taffeta, of the same shades, all being cut, embroidered, and fitted in a most excellent fashion. Their girdles were of the same-colored silk, the buckles being of well enameled gold. Their jackets and vests were of cloth-of-gold, gold-tissue, silver-cloth, or velvet. Their robes were as precious as the ladies' gowns, the girdles being of silk, of the same color as the doublet. Each one carried a fine sword at his side, with a gilded handle, the scabbard being of velvet, of the same shade as the stockings, while the tip was of gold or goldsmith-work, with a dagger to match. Their bonnets were of black velvet, trimmed with a great many berry-like ornaments and gold buttons, and the white plume was most prettily divided by golden spangles, from the ends of which dangled handsome rubies, emeralds, etc.

Such a sympathy existed between the men and women that each

day they were similarly dressed; and in order that they might not fail on this point, there were certain gentlemen whose duty it was to inform the men each morning what livery the ladies proposed to wear that day, for everything depended upon the will of the fair ones. In connection with all these handsome garments and rich adornments, you are not to think that either sex lost any time whatsoever, for the masters of the wardrobe had the clothing all laid out each morning, and the ladies of the chamber were so well trained that in no time at all their mistresses were dressed and their toilets completed from head to foot.

In order to provide the more conveniently for these habiliments, there was, near the wood of Thélème, a large group of houses extending for half a league, houses that were well lighted and well equipped, in which dwelt the goldsmiths, lapidaries, embroiderers, tailors, gold-thread-workers, velvet-makers, tapestry-makers, and upholsterers; and there each one labored at his trade and the whole product went for the monks and nuns of the abbey. These workmen were supplied with material by my Lord Nausicletus, who every year sent them seven ships from the Pearl and Cannibal Islands, laden with gold-nuggets, raw silk, pearls, and precious stones. And if certain pearls showed signs of aging and of losing their native luster, the workmen by their art would renew these, by feeding them to handsome cocks, in the same manner in which one gives a purge to falcons.

How the Thelemites Were Governed in Their Mode of Living

Their whole life was spent, not in accordance with laws, statutes, or rules, but according to their own will and free judgment. They rose from bed when they felt like it and drank, ate, worked, and slept when the desire came to them. No one woke them, no one forced them to drink or to eat or do any other thing. For this was the system that Gargantua had established. In the rule of their order there was but this one clause:

DO WHAT THOU WOULDST

for the reason that those who are free born and well born, well brought up, and used to decent society possess, by nature, a certain instinct and spur, which always impels them to virtuous deeds and restrains them from vice, an instinct which is the thing called honor. These same ones, when, through vile subjection and constraint, they are repressed and held down, proceed to employ that same noble inclination to virtue in throwing off and breaking the yoke of servitude, for we always want to come to forbidden things; and we always desire that which is denied us.

In the enjoyment of their liberty, the Thelemites entered into a laudable emulation in doing, all of them, anything which they thought would be pleasing to one of their number. If anyone, male or female, remarked: "Let us drink," they all drank. If anyone said: "Let us play," they all played. If anyone suggested: "Let us go find some sport in the fields," they all went there. If it was hawking or hunting, the ladies went mounted upon pretty and easy-paced nags or proud-stepping palfreys, each of them bearing upon her daintily gloved wrist a sparrowhawk, a lanneret, or a merlin. The men carried the other birds.

They were all so nobly educated that there was not, in their whole number, a single one, man or woman, who was not able to read, write, sing, play musical instruments, and speak five or six languages, composing in these languages both poetry and prose.

In short, there never were seen knights so bold, so gallant, so clever on horse and on foot, more vigorous, or more adept at handling all kinds of weapons than were they. There never were seen ladies so well groomed, so pretty, less boring, or more skilled at hand and needlework and in every respectable feminine activity. For this reason, when the time came that any member of this abbey, either at the request of his relatives or from some other cause, wished to leave, he always took with him one of the ladies, the one who had taken him for her devoted follower, and the two of them were then married. And if they had lived at Thélème in devotion and friendship, they found even more of both after their marriage, and remained as ardent lovers at the end of their days, as they had been on the first day of their honeymoon.

The Letter Which Pantagruel at Paris Received from His Father Gargantua

Pantagruel studied very hard, you may be sure of that, and profited greatly from it; for he had a two-fold understanding, while his memory was as capacious as a dozen casks and flagons of olive oil. And while he was residing there, he received one day a letter from his father, which read as follows:

My very dear Son:

Among all the gifts, graces, and prerogatives with which that sovereign plastician, Almighty God, has endowed and adorned human nature in its beginnings, it seems to me the peculiarly excellent one is that by means of which, in the mortal state, one may acquire a species of immortality, and in the course of a transitory life be able to perpetuate his name and his seed. This is done through that line that issues from us in legitimate marriage. By this means, there is restored to us in a manner that which was taken away through the sin of our first parents, of whom it was said that, inasmuch as they had not been obedient to the commandment of God the Creator, they should die, and that, through their death, the magnificent plastic creation which man had been should be reduced to nothingness. By this means of seminal propagation, there remains for the children that which was lost to the parents, and for the grandchildren that which, otherwise, would have perished with the children; and so, successively, down to the hour of the last judgment when Jesus Christ shall have rendered to God the Father His specific realm, beyond all danger and contamination of sin; for then shall cease all begettings and corruptions, and the elements shall forego their incessant transmutations, in view of the fact that the peace that is so desired shall then have been consummated and perfected, and all things shall have been brought to their period and their close.

It is not, therefore, without just and equitable cause that I render thanks to God, my Saviour, for having given me the power to behold my hoary old age flowering again in your youth: for when, by the pleasure of Him who rules and moderates all things, my soul shall leave this human habitation, I shall not feel that I am wholly dying in thus passing from one place to another, so long as, in you and through you, my visible image remains in this world, living, seeing, and moving among men of honor and my own good friends, as I was wont to do. My own conduct has been, thanks to the aid of divine grace—not, I confess, without sin, for we are all sinners, and must be continually beseeching God to efface our sins—but at least, without reproach.

For this reason, since my bodily image remains in you, if the manners of my soul should not likewise shine there, then you would not be held to have been the guardian and the treasury of that immortality which should adhere to our name; and the pleasure I should take in beholding you would accordingly be small, when I perceive that the lesser part of me, which is the body, remained, while the better part, which is the soul, through which our name is still blessed among men, had become degenerate and bastardized. I say this, not out of any doubt of your virtue, of which you have already given me proof, but to encourage you, rather, to profit still further, and to go on from good to better. And I am now writing you, not so much to exhort you to live in this virtuous manner, as to urge you to rejoice at the fact that you are so living and have so lived, that you may take fresh courage for the future. In order to perfect and consummate that future, it would be well for you to recall frequently the fact that I have spared no expense on you, but have aided you as though I had no other treasure in this world than the joy, once in my life, of seeing you absolutely perfect in virtue, decency, and wisdom, as well as in all generous and worthy accomplishments, with the assurance of leaving you after my death as a mirror depicting the person of me, your father—if not altogether as excellent and as well formed an image as I might wish you to be, still all that I might wish, certainly, in your desires.

But while my late father of blessed memory, Grandgousier, devoted all his attention to seeing that I should profit from and be perfected in political wisdom, and while my studious labors were equal to his desires and perhaps even surpassed them, nevertheless, as you can readily understand, the times were not so propitious to letters as they are at present and I never had an abundance of such tutors as you have. The times then were dark, reflecting the unfortunate calamities brought about by the Goths who had destroyed all fine literature; but through divine goodness, in my own lifetime light and dignity have been restored to the art of letters, and I now see such an improvement that at the present time I should find great difficulty in being received into the first class of little rowdies—I who, in the prime of my manhood, and not wrongly so, was looked upon as the most learned man of the century. I do not say this in any spirit of vain boasting, even though I might permissibly do so—you have authority for it in Marcus Tullius, in his book on *Old Age,* as well as in that maxim of Plutarch's that is to be found in his book entitled *How One May Praise One's Self Without Reproach*—but I make the statement, rather, to give you the desire of climbing higher still.

Now all the branches of science have been reestablished and languages have been restored: Greek, without which it is a crime for anyone to call himself a scholar, Hebrew, Chaldaic, and Latin; while printed books in current use are very elegant and correct. The latter were invented during my lifetime, through divine inspiration, just as, on the other hand, artillery was invented through the suggestion of the devil. The world is now full of scholarly men, learned teachers, and most ample libraries; indeed, I do not think that in the time of Plato, of Cicero, or of Papinian, there ever were so many advantages for study as one may find today. No one, longer, has any business going out in public or being seen in company, unless he has been well polished in the workshop of Minerva. I see brigands, hangmen, freebooters, and grooms nowadays who are more learned than were the doctors and preachers of my time. What's this I'm saying? Why, even the women and the girls have aspired to the credit of sharing this heavenly manna of fine learning. Things have come to such a pass that, old as I am, I have felt it necessary to take up the study of Greek, which I had not contemned, like Cato, but which I never had had the time to learn in my youth. And I take a great deal of pleasure now in reading the *Morals* of Plutarch, the beautiful *Dialogues* of Plato, the *Monuments* of Pausanias, and the *Antiquities* of Athenaeus, as I wait for the hour when it shall please God, my Creator, to send for me and to command me to depart this earth.

For this reason, my son, I would admonish you to employ your youth in getting all the profit you can from your studies and from virtue. You are at Paris and you have your tutor, Epistemon; the latter by word-of-mouth instruction, the former by praiseworthy examples, should be able to provide you with an education.

It is my intention and desire that you should learn all languages perfectly: first, the Greek as Quintilian advises; secondly, the Latin; and finally, the Hebrew, for the sake of the Holy Scriptures, along with the Chaldaic and the Arabic, for the same purpose. And I would have you form your style after the Greek, in imitation of Plato, as well as on the Latin, after Cicero. Let there be no bit of history with which you are not perfectly familiar. In this you will find the various works which have been written on cosmography to be of great help.

As for the liberal arts, geometry, arithmetic, and music, I gave you some taste for these while you were still a little shaver of five or six; keep them up; and as for astronomy, endeavor to master all its laws; do not bother about divinatory astrology and the art of Lully, for they are mere abuses and vanities.

As for civil law, I would have you know by heart the best texts and compare them with philosophy.

As for a knowledge of the facts of nature, I would have you apply yourself to this study with such curiosity that there should be no sea, river, or stream of which you do not know the fish; you should likewise be familiar with all the birds of the air, all the trees, shrubs, and thickets of the forest, all the grasses of the earth, all the metals hidden in the bellies of the abysses, and the precious stones of all the East and South: let nothing be unknown to you.

Then, very carefully, go back to the books of the Greek, Arabic, and Latin physicians, not disdaining the Talmudists and the Cabalists, and by means of frequent dissections, see to it that you acquire a perfect knowledge of that other world which is man. And at certain hours of the day, form the habit of spending some time with the Holy Scriptures. First in Greek, the New Testament and the Epistles of the Apostles; and then, in Hebrew, the Old Testament.

In short, let me see you an abysm of science, for when you shall have become a full-grown man, you will have to forsake your quiet life and leisurely studies, to master the art of knighthood and of arms, in order to be able to defend my household and to succor my friends in all their undertakings against the assaults of evildoers.

In conclusion, I would have you make a test, to see how much profit you have drawn from your studies; and I do not believe you can do this in any better fashion than by sustaining theses in all branches of science, in public and against each and every comer, and by keeping the company of the learned, of whom there are as many at Paris as there are anywhere else.

But since, according to the wise Solomon, wisdom does not enter the malevolent soul, and since science without conscience is but the ruin of the soul, it behooves you to serve, love, and fear God and to let all your thoughts and hopes rest in Him, being joined to Him through a faith formed of charity, in such a manner that you can never be sundered from Him by means of sin. Look upon the scandals of the world with suspicion. Do not set your heart upon vain things, for this life is transient but the word of God endures eternally. Be of service to all your neighbors and love them as yourself. Respect your teachers, shun the company of those whom you would not want to be like, and do not receive in vain the graces which God has bestowed upon you. And when you feel that you have acquired all the knowledge that is to be had where you now are, come back to me, so that I may see you and give you my blessing before I die.

My son, may the peace and grace of Our Lord be with you! Amen.

From Utopia, this seventeenth day of the month of March.

Your Father,

GARGANTUA

When he had received and read this letter, Pantagruel took fresh courage, and was inflamed to profit more than ever from his studies; to such a degree that, seeing him so study and profit, you would have said that his mind among his books was like a fire among brushwood, so violent was he and so indefatigable.

Michel de Montaigne: *Of Friendship*

Montaigne, the most exquisite intellectual of the French Renaissance, was a wise, erudite, tolerant aristocrat. He is believed by many to have been the greatest writer in French literature. Michel Eyquem, Lord of Montaigne, was born in 1533 at the family estate in southern France. His father, a merchant who held several municipal offices in Bordeaux, was fascinated by education, hired tutors for his son in Latin and Greek, and had him awakened each morning by soft music. At six Montaigne was sent to study at the College of Guinne at Bordeaux. At thirteen he left the college to study law, probably at Toulouse. In 1555 he became a councilor in the Bordeaux parlement. In 1565 he married Françoise de la Chassaigne, daughter of another member of the parlement. When his father died in 1568 Montaigne inherited the family estate and in 1571 he retired to his chateau to devote himself to a life of study and reflection. He built a tower of refuge which contained a bedroom, a small chapel, and a library of over a thousand volumes, including his favorite Plutarch and other classics. There he meditated, read, wrote, inscribed moral sentences which are still to be seen on the walls and beams, and lived a life of learned leisure. In 1581 he was elected mayor of Bordeaux, an office which he accepted reluctantly on the insistence of King Henry III, and served two terms. His last years were plagued with illness and, always of frail health, he succumbed in 1592.

Montaigne has been called the creator of the personal essay. His whole life he strove to understand man's nature and behavior, beginning with a determined and honest effort to understand himself. He offers his thoughts as *Essays,* undogmatic and tentative reflections, on life. The longest and most famous of the 107 essays is the "Apology for Raymond Sebond" which is a treatise on human presumption and the vanity of human reason. It was a skeptical step on the way to the psychological and moral convictions of the essays in the third and final book.

Montaigne had a capacity for true friendship. During his last years he was very close to Marie de Gournay, a young intellectual and his ardent admirer. In his earlier years, he developed a close friendship with Étienne de la Boétie, a fellow councilor in Bordeaux, who was a keen intellectual and an attractive personality. When he died in 1563 Montaigne was deeply grieved. This friendship inspired Montaigne's famous essay *Of Friendship*, which is presented here.

Of Friendship is taken from *The Complete Works of Montaigne. Essays. Travel Journal. Letters*, trans. Donald M. Frame (Stanford, Calif.: Stanford University Press, 1957), 135–44. Reprinted by permission of the Stanford University Press.

As I was considering the way a painter I employ went about his work, I had a mind to imitate him. He chooses the best spot, the middle of each wall, to put a picture labored over with all his skill, and the empty space all around it he fills with grotesques, which are fantastic paintings whose only charm lies in their variety and strangeness. And what are these things of mine, in truth, but grotesques and monstrous bodies, pieced together of divers members, without definite shape, having no order, sequence, or proportion other than accidental?

> A lovely woman tapers off into a fish.
>
> HORACE

I do indeed go along with my painter in this second point, but I fall short in the first and better part; for my ability does not go far enough for me to dare to undertake a rich, polished picture, formed according to art. It has occurred to me to borrow one from Étienne de la Boétie, which will do honor to all the rest of this work. It is a discourse to which he gave the name *La Servitude Volontaire*; but those who did not know this have since very fitly rebaptized it *Le Contre Un*. He wrote it by way of essay in his early youth, in honor of liberty against tyrants. It has long been circulating in the hands of men of understanding, not without great and well-merited commendation; for it is a fine thing, and as full as can be. Still, it is far from being the best he could do; and if at the more mature age when I knew him, he had adopted a plan such as mine, of putting his ideas in writing, we should see many rare things which would bring us very close to the glory of antiquity; for particularly in the matter of natural gifts, I know no one who can be compared with him. But nothing of his has remained except this treatise—

and that by chance, and I think he never saw it after it left his hands—and some observations on that Edict of January, made famous by our civil wars, which will perhaps yet find their place elsewhere. That was all I could recover of what he left—I, to whom in his will, with such loving recommendation, with death in his throat, he bequeathed his library and his papers—except for the little volume of his works which I have had published.

And yet I am particularly obliged to this work, since it served as the medium of our first acquaintance. For it was shown to me long before I had seen him, and gave me my first knowledge of his name, thus starting on its way this friendship which together we fostered, as long as God willed, so entire and so perfect that certainly you will hardly read of the like, and among men of today you see no trace of it in practice. So many coincidences are needed to build up such a friendship that it is a lot if fortune can do it once in three centuries.

There is nothing to which nature seems to have inclined us more than to society. And Aristotle says that good legislators have had more care for friendship than for justice. Now the ultimate point in the perfection of society is this. For in general, all associations that are forged and nourished by pleasure or profit, by public or private needs, are the less beautiful and noble, and the less friendships, in so far as they mix into friendship another cause and object and reward than friendship itself. Nor do the four ancient types—natural, social, hospitable, erotic—come up to real friendship, either separately or together.

From children toward fathers, it is rather respect. Friendship feeds on communication, which cannot exist between them because of their too great inequality, and might perhaps interfere with the duties of nature. For neither can all the secret thoughts of fathers be communicated to children, lest this beget an unbecoming intimacy, nor could the admonitions and corrections, which are one of the chief duties of friendship, be administered by children to fathers. There have been nations where by custom the children killed their fathers, and others where the fathers killed their children, to avoid the interference that they can sometimes cause each other; and by nature the one depends on the destruction of the other. There have been philosophers who disdained this natural tie, witness Aristippus: when pressed about the affection he owed his children for having come out of him, he began to spit, saying that that had come out of him just as well, and that we also bred lice and worms. And that other, whom Plutarch wanted to reconcile with his brother, said: "I don't think any more of him for having come out of the same hole."

brothers

Truly the name of brother is a beautiful name and full of affection, and for that reason he and I made our alliance a brotherhood. But that confusion of ownership, the dividing, and the fact that the richness of one is the poverty of the other, wonderfully softens and loosens the solder of brotherhood. Since brothers have to guide their careers along the same path and at the same rate, it is inevitable that they often jostle and clash with each other. Furthermore, why should the harmony and kinship which begets these true and perfect friendships be found in them? Father and son may be of entirely different dispositions, and brothers also. He is my son, he is my kinsman, but he is an unsociable man, a knave, or a fool. And then, the more they are friendships which law and natural obligation impose on us, the less of our choice and free will there is in them. And our free will has no product more properly its own than affection and friendship. Not that I have not experienced all the friendship that can exist in that situation, having had the best father that ever was, and the most indulgent, even in his extreme old age, and being of a family famous and exemplary, from father to son, in this matter of brotherly concord:

> Known to others
> For fatherly affection toward my brothers.
>
> HORACE

women

To compare this brotherly affection with affection for women, even though it is the result of our choice—it cannot be done; nor can we put the love of women in the same category. Its ardor, I confess—

> Of us that goddess is not unaware
> Who blends a bitter sweetness with her care
>
> CATULLUS

—is more active, more scorching, and more intense. But it is an impetuous and fickle flame, undulating and variable, a fever flame, subject to fits and lulls, that holds us only by one corner. In friendship it is a general and universal warmth, moderate and even, besides, a constant and settled warmth, all gentleness and smoothness, with nothing bitter and stinging about it. What is more, in love there is nothing but a frantic desire for what flees from us:

> Just as a huntsman will pursue a hare
> O'er hill and dale, in weather cold or fair;

> The captured hare is worthless in his sight;
> He only hastens after things in flight.
>
> ARIOSTO

As soon as it enters the boundaries of friendship, that is to say harmony of wills, it grows faint and languid. Enjoyment destroys it, as having a fleshly end, subject to satiety. Friendship, on the contrary, is enjoyed according as it is desired; it is bred, nourished, and increased only in enjoyment, since it is spiritual, and the soul grows refined by practice. During the reign of this perfect friendship those fleeting affections once found a place in me, not to speak of my friend, who confesses only too many of them in these verses. Thus these two passions within me came to be known to each other, but to be compared, never; the first keeping its course in proud and lofty flight, and disdainfully watching the other making its way far, far beneath it.

As for marriage, for one thing it is a bargain to which only the entrance is free—its continuance being constrained and forced, depending otherwise than on our will—and a bargain ordinarily made for other ends. For another, there supervene a thousand foreign tangles to unravel, enough to break the thread and trouble the course of a lively affection; whereas in friendship there are no dealings or business except with itself. Besides, to tell the truth, the ordinary capacity of women is inadequate for that communion and fellowship which is the nurse of this sacred bond; nor does their soul seem firm enough to endure the strain of so tight and durable a knot. And indeed, but for that, if such a relationship, free and voluntary, could be built up, in which not only would the souls have this complete enjoyment, but the bodies would also share in the alliance, so that the entire man would be engaged, it is certain that the resulting friendship would be fuller and more complete. But this sex in no instance has yet succeeded in attaining it, and by the common agreement of the ancient schools is excluded from it.

And that other, licentious Greek love is justly abhorred by our morality. Since it involved, moreover, according to their practice, such a necessary disparity in age and such a difference in the lovers' functions, it did not correspond closely enough with the perfect union and harmony that we require here: *For what is this love of friendship? Why does no one love either an ugly youth, or a handsome old man?* [Cicero.] For even the picture the Academy paints of it will not contradict me, I think, if I say this on the subject: that this first frenzy which the son of Venus inspired in the lover's heart at the sight of the flower of tender youth, in which they allow all the insolent and passionate acts that immoderate ardor can produce, was simply founded on external beauty, the false image of corporeal generation. For it could not be founded on the spirit, the signs of which were still hidden, which was only at its birth and before the age of budding. If this frenzy seized a base heart, the means of his courtship were riches, presents, favor in advancement to dignities, and other such base merchandise, which were generally condemned. If it fell on a nobler heart, the means were also noble: philosophical instruction, precepts to revere religion, obey the laws, die for the good of the country; examples of valor, prudence, justice; the lover studying to make himself acceptable by the grace and beauty of his soul, that of his body being long since faded, and hoping by this mental fellowship to establish a firmer and more lasting pact.

When this courtship attained its effect in due season (for whereas they do not require of the lover that he use leisure and discretion in his enterprise, they strictly require it of the loved one, because he had to judge an inner beauty, difficult to know and hidden from discovery), then there was born in the loved one the desire of spiritual conception through the medium of spiritual beauty. This was the main thing here, and corporeal beauty accidental and secondary; quite the opposite of the lover. For this reason they prefer the loved one, and prove that the gods also prefer him, and strongly rebuke the poet Aeschylus for having, in the love of Achilles and Patroclus, given the lover's part to Achilles, who was in the first beardless bloom of his youth, and the handsomest of all the Greeks.

After this general communion was established, the stronger and worthier part of it exercising its functions and predominating, they say that there resulted from it fruits very useful personally and to the public; that it constituted the strength of the countries which accepted the practice, and the principal defense of equity and liberty: witness the salutary loves of Harmodius and Aristogeiton. Therefore they call it sacred and divine. And, by their reckoning, only the violence of tyrants and the cowardice of the common people are hostile to it. In short, all that can be said in favor of the Academy is that this was a love ending in friendship; which corresponds pretty well to the Stoic definition of love: *Love is the attempt to form a friendship inspired by beauty* [Cicero].

I return to my description of a more equitable and more equable kind of friendship. *Only those are to be judged friendships in which the characters have been strengthened and matured by age* [Cicero].

For the rest, what we ordinarily call friends and friendships are nothing but acquaintanceships and familiarities formed by some chance or convenience, by means of which our souls are bound to each other. In the friendship I speak of, our souls mingle and blend with each other so completely that they efface the seam that joined them, and cannot find it again. If you press me to tell why I loved him, I feel that this cannot be expressed, except by answering: Because it was he, because it was I.

Beyond all my understanding, beyond what I can say about this in particular, there was I know not what inexplicable and fateful force that was the mediator of this union. We sought each other before we met because of the reports we heard of each other, which had more effect on our affection than such reports would reasonably have; I think it was by some ordinance from heaven. We embraced each other by our names. And at our first meeting, which by chance came at a great feast and gathering in the city, we found ourselves so taken with each other, so well acquainted, so bound together, that from that time on nothing was so close to us as each other. He wrote an excellent Latin satire, which is published, in which he excuses and explains the precipitancy of our mutual understanding, so promptly grown to its perfection. Having so little time to last, and having begun so late, for we were both grown men, and he a few years older than I, it could not lose time and conform to the pattern of mild and regular friendships, which need so many precautions in the form of long preliminary association. Our friendship has no other model than itself, and can be compared only with itself. It is not one special consideration, nor two, nor three, nor four, nor a thousand: it is I know not what quintessence of all this mixture, which, having seized my whole will, led it to plunge and lose itself in his; which, having seized his whole will, led it to plunge and lose itself in mine, with equal hunger, equal rivalry. I say lose, in truth, for neither of us reserved anything for himself, nor was anything either his or mine.

When Laelius, in the presence of the Roman consuls—who, after condemning Tiberius Gracchus, prosecuted all those who had been in his confidence—came to ask Caius Blossius, who was Gracchus' best friend, how much he would have been willing to do for him, he answered: "Everything." "What, everything?" pursued Laelius. "And what if he had commanded you to set fire to our temples?" "He would never have commanded me to do that," replied Blossius. "But what if he had?" Laelius insisted. "I would have obeyed," he replied. If he was such a perfect friend to Gracchus as the histories say, he did not need to offend the consuls by this last bold confession, and he should not have abandoned the assurance he had of Gracchus' will. But nevertheless, those who charge that this answer is seditious do not fully understand this mystery, and fail to assume first what is true, that he had Gracchus' will up his sleeve, both by power over him and by knowledge of him. They were friends more than citizens, friends more than friends or enemies of their country or friends of ambition and disturbance. Having committed themselves absolutely to each other, they held absolutely the reins of each other's inclination; and if you assume that this team was guided by the strength and leadership of reason, as indeed it is quite impossible to harness it without that, Blossius' answer is as it should have been. If their actions went astray, they were by my measure neither friends to each other, nor friends to themselves.

For that matter, this answer has no better ring than would mine if someone questioned me in this fashion: "If your will commanded you to kill your daughter, would you kill her?" and I said yes. For that does not bear witness to any consent to do so, because I have no doubt at all about my will, and just as little about that of such a friend. It is not in the power of all the arguments in the world to dislodge me from the certainty I have of the intentions and judgments of my friend. Not one of his actions could be presented to me, whatever appearance it might have, that I could not immediately find the motive for it. Our souls pulled together in such unison, they regarded each other with such ardent affection, and with a like affection revealed themselves to each other to the very depths of our hearts, that not only did I know his soul as well as mine, but I should certainly have trusted myself to him more readily than to myself.

Let not these other, common friendships be placed in this rank. I have as much knowledge of them as another, and of the most perfect of their type, but I advise you not to confuse the rules of the two; you would make a mistake. You must walk in those other friendships bridle in hand, with prudence and precaution; the knot is not so well tied that there is no cause to mistrust it. "Love him," Chilo used to say, "as if you are to hate him some day; hate him as if you are to love him." This precept, which is so abominable in this sovereign and masterful friendship, is healthy in the practice of ordinary and customary friendships, in regard to which we must use the remark that Aristotle often repeated: "O my friends, there is no friend."

In this noble relationship, services and benefits, on which other friendships feed, do not even deserve to be taken into account; the reason for this is the complete fusion of our wills. For just as the friendship I feel for myself receives no increase from the help I give myself in time of need, whatever the Stoics say, and as I feel no gratitude to myself for the service I do myself; so the union of such friends, being truly perfect, makes them lose the sense of such duties, and hate and banish from between them these words of separation and distinction: benefit, obligation, gratitude, request, thanks, and the like. Everything actually being in common between them—wills, thoughts, judgments, goods, wives, children, honor, and life—and their relationship being that of one soul in two bodies, according to Aristotle's very apt definition, they can neither lend nor give anything to each other. That is why the lawmakers, to honor marriage with some imaginary resemblance to this divine union, forbid gifts between husband and wife, wishing thus to imply that everything should belong to each of them and that they have nothing to divide and split up between them.

If, in the friendship I speak of, one could give to the other, it would be the one who received the benefit who would oblige his friend. For, each of them seeking above all things to benefit the other, the one who provides the matter and the occasion is the liberal one, giving his friend the satisfaction of doing for him what he most wants to do. When the philosopher Diogenes was short of money, he used to say that he asked it back of his friends, not that he asked for it. And to show how this works in practice, I will tell you an ancient example that is singular.

Eudamidas of Corinth had two friends, Charixenus, a Sicyonian, and Aretheus, a Corinthian. When he came to die, he being poor and his two friends rich, he made his will thus: "I leave this to Aretheus, to feed my mother and support her in her old age; this to Charixenus, to see my daughter married and give her the biggest dowry he can; and in case one of them should chance to die, I substitute the survivor in his place." Those who first saw this will laugh at it; but his heirs, having been informed of it, accepted it with singular satisfaction. And when one of them, Charixenus, died five days later, and the place of substitute was opened to Aretheus, he supported the mother with great care, and of five talents he had in his estate, he gave two and a half to his only daughter for her marriage, and two and a half for the marriage of the daughter of Eudamidas, holding their weddings on the same day.

This example is quite complete except for one circumstance, which is the plurality of friends. For this perfect friendship I speak of is indivisible: each one gives himself so wholly to his friend that he has nothing left to distribute elsewhere; on the contrary, he is sorry that he is not double, triple, or quadruple, and that he has not several souls and several wills, to confer them all on this one object. Common friendships can be divided up: one may love in one man his beauty, in another his easygoing ways, in another liberality, in one paternal love, in another brotherly love, and so forth; but this friendship that possesses the soul and rules it with absolute sovereignty cannot possibly be double. If two called for help at the same time, which one would you run to? If they demanded conflicting services of you, how would you arrange it? If one confided to your silence a thing that would be useful for the other to know, how would you extricate yourself? A single dominant friendship dissolves all other obligations. The secret I have sworn to reveal to no other man, I can impart without perjury to the one who is not another man: he is myself. It is a great enough miracle to be doubled, and those who talk of tripling themselves do not realize the loftiness of the thing: nothing is extreme that can be matched. And he who supposes that of two men I love one just as much as the other, and that they love each other and me just as much as I love them, multiplies into a fraternity the most singular and unified of all things, of which even a single one is the rarest thing in the world to find.

The rest of this story fits in very well with what I was saying, for Eudamidas bestows upon his friends the kindness and favor of using them for his need. He leaves them heirs to this liberality of his, which consists of putting into their hands a chance to do him good. And without doubt the strength of friendship is shown much more richly in his action than in that of Aretheus.

In short, these are actions inconceivable to anyone who has not tasted friendship, and which make me honor wonderfully the answer of that young soldier to Cyrus, who asked him for how much he would sell a horse with which he had just won the prize in a race, and whether he would exchange him for a kingdom: "No indeed, Sire, but I would most willingly let him go to gain a friend, if I found a man worthy of such an alliance." That was not badly spoken, "if I found one"; for it is easy to find men fit for a superficial acquaintance. But for this kind, in which we act from the very bottom of our hearts, which holds nothing back, truly it is necessary that all the springs of action be perfectly clean and true.

In the relationships which bind us only by one small part, we need look out only for the imperfections that particularly concern that part. The religion of my doctor or my lawyer cannot matter. That consideration has nothing in common with the functions of the friendship they owe me. And in the domestic relationship between me and those who serve me, I have the same attitude. I scarcely inquire of a lackey whether he is chaste; I try to find out whether he is diligent. And I am not as much afraid of a gambling mule driver as of a weak one, or of a profane cook as of an ignorant one. I do not make it my business to tell the world what it should do—enough others do that—but what I do in it.

> That is my practice: do as you see fit.
>
> TERENCE

For the familiarity of the table I look for wit, not prudence; for the bed, beauty before goodness; in conversation, competence, even without uprightness. Likewise in other matters.

Just as the man who was found astride a stick, playing with his children, asked the man who surprised him thus to say nothing about it until he was a father himself, in the belief that the passion which would then be born in his soul would make him an equitable judge of such an act, so I should like to talk to people who have experienced what I tell. But knowing how far from common usage and how rare such a friendship is, I do not expect to find any good judge of it. For the very discourses that antiquity has left us on this subject seem to me weak compared with the feeling I have. And in this particular the facts surpass even the precepts of philosophy:

> Nothing shall I, while sane, compare with a dear friend.
>
> HORACE

The ancient Menander declared that man happy who had been able to meet even the shadow of a friend. He was certainly right to say so, especially if he spoke from experience. For in truth, if I compare all the rest of my life—though by the grace of God I have spent it pleasantly, comfortably, and, except for the loss of such a friend, free from any grievous affliction, and full of tranquillity of mind, having accepted my natural and original advantages without seeking other ones—if I compare it all, I say, with the four years which were granted me to enjoy the sweet company and society of that man, it is nothing but smoke, nothing but dark and dreary night. Since the day I lost him,

Which I shall ever recall with pain,
Ever with reverence—thus, Gods, did you ordain—

VIRGIL

I only drag on a weary life. And the very pleasures that come my way, instead of consoling me, redouble my grief for his loss. We went halves in everything; it seems to me that I am robbing him of his share,

Nor may I rightly taste of pleasures here alone,
—So I resolved—when he who shared my life is gone.

TERENCE

I was already so formed and accustomed to being a second self everywhere that only half of me seems to be alive now.

Since an untimely blow has snatched away
Part of my soul, why then do I delay,
I the remaining part, less dear than he,
And not entire surviving? The same day
Brought ruin equally to him and me.

HORACE

There is no action or thought in which I do not miss him, as indeed he would have missed me. For just as he surpassed me infinitely in every other ability and virtue, so he did in the duty of friendship.

Why should I be ashamed or exercise control
Mourning so dear a soul?

HORACE

Brother, your death has left me sad and lone;
Since you departed all our joys have gone,
Which while you lived your sweet affection fed;
My pleasures all lie shattered, with you dead.
Our soul is buried, mine with yours entwined;
And since then I have banished from my mind
My studies, and my spirit's dearest joys.
Shall I ne'er speak to you, or hear your voice?
Or see your face, more dear than life to me?
At least I'll love you to eternity.

CATULLUS

Miguel de Cervantes Saavedra: from *Don Quixote*

Cervantes, the greatest Spanish author of all times, was born at Alcalá de Henares in 1547. He went to school in Madrid and made his literary debut with a few undistinguished poems dedicated to the "most serene queen of Spain Isabella." He seems to have wounded a man in a duel and fled Spain to avoid the sentence of having his hand cut off. In Rome he entered the service of Cardinal Giulio Acquaviva. In 1570 he enlisted in the army, and in September, 1571, he sailed on a ship which was part of the armada under Don John of Austria. He fought fiercely in the battle of Lepanto with the Turks, October 7, 1471, and suffered several wounds. He fought in several other naval encounters and assisted in the capture of Tunis. Sailing back to Spain where he hoped for preferments, his ship, *El Sol,* was captured by Barbary pirates who sold Cervantes and his brother into slavery. After several futile escape attempts, he was finally ransomed in 1580. Back in Spain he resumed his writing with *Pictures of Algiers,* in which he described his life as a slave, with a pastoral romance entitled *La Galatea,* and poems. He married and took a post in the civil service to support himself. He was jailed when discrepancies were discovered in his accounts and he was dismissed from the civil service, sinking into abject poverty. From 1600 to its publication in 1605 Cervantes wrote his masterpiece *Don Quixote,* which proved to be an immediate and lasting success. To offset the damage done by a pseudonymous author who had faked a continuation of the story, Cervantes in 1615 published a genuine second part which he deliberately concluded with his hero's death. Literary success, however, did not bring with it financial prosperity and Cervantes continued his life of refined poverty. His later works, *Exemplary Novels* and *Persiles and Sigismunda* did not rise to the level of his masterpiece. He died in Madrid on April 23, 1616, the same day on which Shakespeare died in England.

Cervantes stated quite plainly that his main purpose in writing *Don Quixote* was to ridicule chivalric romances, but the story unfolds into a brilliant panorama of Spanish society, of its knights and poets, gentlemen and scoundrels, priests and merchants, peasants and barbers, courtly ladies and country girls, passionate dames and Moorish beauties. The Romantic knight Don Quixote and his man Sancho Panza have become two of the best known figures in all literature. As the story unfolds the reader sees them grow as human beings. The wealth of comic incidents, the satire, the thrusts at folly and evil, the reticent pathos, penetrating criticism and large humanity make *Don Quixote* the literary gem it is.

The station in life and the pursuits of the famous gentleman, Don Quixote de la Mancha

In a village of La Mancha the name of which I have no desire to recall, there lived not so long ago one of those gentlemen who always have a lance in the rack, an ancient buckler, a skinny nag, and a greyhound for the chase. A stew with more beef than mutton in it, chopped meat for his evening meal, scraps for a Saturday, lentils on Friday, and a young pigeon as a special delicacy for Sunday, went to account for three-quarters of his income. The rest of it he laid out on a broadcloth greatcoat and velvet stockings for feast days, with slippers to match, while the other days of the week he cut a figure in a suit of the finest homespun. Living with him were a housekeeper in her forties, a niece who was not yet twenty, and a lad of the field and market place who saddled his horse for him and wielded the pruning knife.

This gentleman of ours was close on to fifty, of a robust constitution but with little flesh on his bones and a face that was lean and gaunt. He was noted for his early rising, being very fond of the hunt. They will try to tell you that his surname was Quijada or Quesada—there is some difference of opinion among those who have written on the subject—but according to the most likely conjectures we are to understand that it was really Quejana. But all this means very little so far as our story is concerned, providing that in the telling of it we do not depart one iota from the truth.

You may know, then, that the aforesaid gentleman, on those occasions when he was at leisure, which was most of the year around, was in the habit of reading books of chivalry with such pleasure and devotion as to lead him almost wholly to forget the life of a hunter and even the administration of his estate. So great was his curiosity and infatuation in this regard that he even sold many acres of tillable land in order to be able to buy and read the books that he loved, and he would carry home with him as many of them as he could obtain.

Of all those that he thus devoured none pleased him so well as the ones that had been composed by the famous Feliciano de Silva, whose lucid prose style and involved conceits were as precious to him as pearls; especially when he came to read those tales of love and amorous challenges that are to be met with in many places, such a passage as the following, for example: "The reason of the unreason that afflicts my reason, in such a manner weakens my reason that I with reason lament me of your comeliness." And he was similarly affected when his eyes fell upon such lines at these: ". . . the high Heaven of your divinity divinely fortifies you with the stars and renders you deserving of that desert your greatness doth deserve."

The poor fellow used to lie awake nights in an effort to disentangle the meaning and make sense out of passages such as these, although Aristotle himself would not have been able to understand them, even if he had been resurrected for that sole purpose. He was not at ease in his mind over those wounds that Don Belianís gave and received; for no matter how great the surgeons who treated him, the poor fellow must have been left with his face and his entire body covered with marks and scars. Nevertheless, he was grateful to the author for closing the book with the promise of an interminable adventure to come; many a time he was tempted to take up his pen and literally finish the tale as had been promised, and he undoubtedly would have done so, and would have succeeded at it very well, if his thoughts had not been constantly occupied with other things of greater moment.

He often talked it over with the village curate, who was a learned man, a graduate of Sigüenza, and they would hold long discussions as to who had been the better knight, Palmerin of England or Amadis of Gaul; but Master Nicholas, the barber of the same village, was in the habit of saying that no one could come up to the Knight of Phoebus, and that if anyone *could* compare with him it was Don Galaor, brother of Amadis of Gaul, for Galaor was ready for anything—he was none of your finical knights, who went around whimpering as his brother did, and in point of valor he did not lag behind him.

In short, our gentleman became so immersed in his reading that he spent whole nights from sundown to sunup and his days from dawn to dusk in poring over his books, until, finally, from so little sleeping and so much reading, his brain dried up and he went completely out of his mind. He had filled his imagination with everything that he had read, with enchantments, knightly encounters, battles, challenges, wounds, with tales of love and its torments, and all sorts of impossible things, and as a result had come to believe that all these fictitious happenings were true; they were more real to him than anything else in the world. He would remark that the Cid Ruy Díaz had been a very good knight, but there was no comparison between him and the Knight of the Flaming Sword, who with a single backward stroke had cut in half two fierce and monstrous giants. He preferred Bernardo del Carpio, who at Roncesvalles had slain Roland despite the charm the latter bore, availing himself of the stratagem which Hercules employed when he strangled Antaeus, the son of Earth, in his arms.

He had much good to say for Morgante who, though he belonged to the haughty, overbearing race of giants, was of an affable disposition and well brought up. But, above all, he cherished an admiration for Rinaldo of Montalbán, especially as he beheld him sallying forth from his castle to rob all those that crossed his path, or when he thought of him overseas stealing the image of Mohammed which, so the story has it, was all of gold. And he woud have liked very well to have had his fill of kicking that traitor Galalón, a privilege for which he would have given his housekeeper with his niece thrown into the bargain.

At last, when his wits were gone beyond repair, he came to conceive the strangest idea that ever occurred to any madman in this world. It now appeared to him fitting and necessary, in order to win a greater amount of honor for himself and serve his country at the same time, to become a knight-errant and roam the world on horseback, in a suit of armor; he would go in quest of adventures, by way of putting into practice all that he had read in his books; he would right every manner of wrong, placing himself in situations of the greatest peril such as would redound to the eternal glory of his name. As a reward for his valor and the might of his arm, the poor fellow could already see himself crowned Emperor of Trebizond at the very least; and so, carried away by the strange pleasure that he found in such thoughts as these, he at once set about putting his plan into effect.

The first thing he did was to burnish up some old pieces of armor, left him by his great-grandfather, which for ages had lain in a corner, moldering and forgotten. He polished and adjusted them as best he could, and then he noticed that one very important thing was lacking: there was no closed helmet, but only a morion, or visorless headpiece, with turned-up brim of the kind foot soldiers wore. His ingenuity, however, enabled him to remedy this, and he proceded to fashion out of cardboard a kind of half-helmet, which, when attached to the morion, gave the appearance of a whole one. True, when he went to see if it was strong enough to withstand a good slashing blow, he was somewhat disappointed; for when he drew his sword and gave it a couple of thrusts, he succeeded only in undoing a whole week's labor. The ease with which he had hewed it to bits disturbed him no little, and he decided to make it over. This time he placed a few strips of iron on the inside, and then, convinced that it was strong enough, refrained from putting it to any further test; instead, he adopted it then and there as the finest helmet ever made.

After this, he went out to have a look at his nag; and although the animal had more *cuartos,* or cracks, in its hoof than there are quarters in a real, and more blemishes than Gonela's steed which *tantum pellis et ossa fuit,* it nonetheless looked to its master like a far better horse than Alexander's Bucephalus or the Babicca of the Cid. He spent all of four days in trying to think up a name for his mount; for—so he told himself—seeing that it belonged to so famous and worthy a knight, there was no reason why it should not have a name of equal renown. The kind of name he wanted was one that would at once indicate what the nag had been before it came to belong to a knight-errant and what its present status was; for it stood to reason that, when the master's worldly condition changed, his horse also ought to have a famous, high-sounding appellation, one suited to the new order of things and the new profession that it was to follow.

After he in his memory and imagination had made up, struck out, and discarded many names, now adding to and now subtracting from the list, he finally hit upon "Rocinante," a name that impressed him as being sonorous and at the same time indicative of what the steed had been when it was but a hack, whereas now it was nothing other than the first and foremost of all the hacks in the world.

Having found a name for his horse that pleased his fancy, he then desired to do as much for himself, and this required another week, and by the end of that period he had made up his mind that he was henceforth to be known as Don Quixote, which, as has been stated, has led the authors of this veracious history to assume that his real name must undoubtedly have been Quijada, and not Quesada as others would have it. But remembering that the valiant Amadis was not content to call himself that and nothing more, but added the name of his kingdom and fatherland that he might make it famous also, and thus came to take the name of Amadis of Gaul, so our good knight chose to add his place of origin and become "Don Quixote de la Mancha"; for by this means, as he saw it, he was making very plain his lineage and was conferring honor upon his country by taking its name as his own.

And so, having polished up his armor and made the morion over into a closed helmet, and having given himself and his horse a name, he naturally found but one thing lacking still: he must seek out a lady of whom he could become enamored; for a knight-errant without a lady-love was like a tree without leaves or fruit, a body without a soul.

"If," he said to himself, "as a punishment for my sins or by a stroke of fortune I should come upon some giant hereabouts, a thing that very commonly happens to knights-errant, and if I should slay him in a hand-to-hand encounter or perhaps cut him in two, or, finally, if I should vanquish and subdue him, would it not be well to have someone to whom I may send him as a present, in order that he, if he is living, may come in, fall upon his knees in front of my sweet lady, and say in a humble and submissive tone of voice, 'I, lady, am the giant Caraculiambro, lord of the island Malindrania, who has been overcome in single combat by that knight who never can be praised enough, Don Quixote de la Mancha, the same who sent me to present myself before your Grace that your Highness may dispose of me as you see fit'?"

Oh, how our good knight reveled in this speech, and more than ever when he came to think of the name that he shoud give his lady! As the story goes, there was a very good-looking farm girl who lived near by, with whom he had once been smitten, although it is generally believed that she never knew or suspected it. Her name was Aldonza Lorenzo, and it seemed to him that she was the one upon whom he should bestow the title of mistress of his thoughts. For her he wished a name that should not be incongruous with his own and that would convey the suggestion of a princess or a great lady; and, accordingly, he resolved to call her "Dulcinea del Toboso," she being a native of that place. A musical name to his ears, out of the ordinary and significant, like the others he had chosen for himself and his appurtenances.

The first sally that the ingenious Don Quixote made from his native heath

Having, then, made all these preparations, he did not wish to lose any time in putting his plan into effect, for he could not but blame himself for what the world was losing by his delay, so many were the wrongs that were to be righted, the grievances to be redressed, the abuses to be done away with, and the duties to be performed. Accordingly, without informing anyone of his intention and without letting anyone see him, he set out one morning before daybreak on one of those very hot days in July. Donning all his armor, mounting Rocinante, adjusting his ill-contrived helmet, bracing his shield on his arm, and taking up his lance, he sallied forth by the back gate of his stable yard into the open countryside. It was with great contentment and joy that he saw how easily he had made a beginning toward the fulfillment of his desire.

No sooner was he out on the plain, however, than a terrible thought assailed him, one that all but caused him to abandon the enterprise he had undertaken. This occurred when he suddenly remembered that he had never formally been dubbed a knight, and so, in accordance with the law of knighthood, was not permitted to bear arms against one who had a right to that title. And even if he had been, as a novice knight he would have had to wear white armor, without any device on his shield, until he should have earned one by his exploits. These thoughts led him to waver in his purpose, but, madness prevailing over reason, he resolved to have himself knighted by the first person he met, as many others had done if what he had read in those books that he had at home was true. And so far as white armor was concerned, he would scour his own the first chance that offered until it shone whiter than any ermine. With this he became more tranquil and continued on his way, letting his horse take whatever path it chose, for he believed that therein lay the very essence of adventures.

And so we find our newly fledged adventurer jogging along and talking to himself. "Undoubtedly," he is saying, "in the days to come, when the true history of my famous deeds is published, the learned chronicler who records them, when he comes to describe my first sally so early in the morning, will put down something like this: 'No sooner had the rubicund Apollo spread over the face of the broad and spacious earth the gilded filaments of his beauteous locks, and no sooner had the little singing birds of painted plumage greeted with their sweet and mellifluous harmony the coming of the Dawn, who, leaving the soft couch of her jealous spouse, now showed herself to mortals at all the doors and balconies of the horizon that bounds La Mancha—no sooner had this happened than the famous knight, Don Quixote de la Mancha, forsaking his own downy bed and mounting his famous steed, Rocinante, fared forth and began riding over the ancient and famous Campo de Montiel.' "

And this was the truth, for he was indeed riding over that stretch of plain.

"O happy age and happy century," he went on, "in which my famous exploits shall be published, exploits worthy of being engraved in bronze, sculptured in marble, and depicted in paintings for the benefit of posterity. O wise magician, whoever you be, to whom shall fall the task of chronicling this extraordinary history of mine! I beg of you not to forget my good Rocinante, eternal companion of my wayfarings and my wanderings."

Then, as though he really had been in love: "O Princess Dulcinea, lady of this captive heart! Much wrong have you done me in thus sending me forth with your reproaches and sternly commanding me not to appear in your beauteous presence. O lady, deign to be mindful of this your subject who endures so many woes for the love of you."

And so he went on, stringing together absurdities, all of a kind that his books had taught him, imitating insofar as he was able the language of their authors. He rode slowly, and the sun came up so swiftly and with so much heat that it would have been sufficient to melt his brains if he had had any. He had been on the road almost the entire day without anything happening that is worthy of being set down here; and he was on the verge of despair, for he wished to meet someone at once with whom he might try the valor of his good right arm. Certain authors say that his first adventure was that of Puerto Lápice, while others state that it was that of the windmills; but in this particular instance I am in a position to affirm what I have read in the annals of La Mancha; and that is to the effect that he went all that day until nightfall, when he and his hack found themselves tired to death and famished. Gazing all around him to see if he could discover some castle or shepherd's hut where he might take shelter and attend to his pressing needs, he caught sight of an inn not far off the road along which they were traveling, and this to him was like a star guiding him not merely to the gates, but rather, let us say, to the palace of redemption. Quickening his pace, he came up to it just as night was falling.

By chance there stood in the doorway two lasses of the sort known as "of the district"; they were on their way to Seville in the company of some mule drivers who were spending the night in the inn. Now, everything that this adventurer of ours thought, saw, or imagined seemed to him to be directly out of one of the storybooks he had read, and so, when he caught sight of the inn, it at once became a castle with its four turrets and its pinnacles of gleaming silver, not to speak of the drawbridge and moat and all the other things that are commonly supposed to go with a castle. As he rode up to it, he accordingly reined in Rocinante and sat there waiting for a dwarf to appear upon the battlements and blow his trumpet by way of announcing the arrival of a knight. The dwarf, however, was slow in coming, and as Rocinante was anxious to reach the stable, Don Quixote drew up to the door of the hostelry and surveyed the two merry maidens, who to him were a pair of beauteous damsels or gracious ladies taking their ease at the castle gate.

And then a swineherd came along, engaged in rounding up his drove of hogs—for, without any apology, that is what they were. He gave a blast on his horn to bring them together, and this at once became for Don Quixote just what he wished it to be: some dwarf who was heralding his coming; and so it was with a vast deal of satisfaction that he presented himself before the ladies in question, who, upon beholding a man in full armor like this, with lance and buckler, were filled with fright and made as if to flee indoors. Realizing that they were afraid, Don Quixote raised his pasteboard visor and revealed his withered, dust-covered face.

"Do not flee, your Ladyships," he said to them in a courteous manner and gentle voice. "You need not fear that any wrong will be done you, for it is not in accordance with the order of knighthood which I profess to wrong anyone, much less such highborn damsels as your appearance shows you to be."

The girls looked at him, endeavoring to scan his face, which was half-hidden by his ill-made visor. Never having heard women of their profession called damsels before, they were unable to restrain their laughter, at which Don Quixote took offense.

"Modesty," he observed, "well becomes those with the dower of beauty, and, moreover, laughter that has not good cause is a very foolish thing. But I do not say this to be discourteous or to hurt your feelings; my only desire is to serve you."

The ladies did not understand what he was talking about, but felt more than ever like laughing at our knight's unprepossessing figure. This increased his annoyance, and there is no telling what would have happened if at that moment the innkeeper had not come out. He was very fat and very peaceably inclined; but upon sighting this grotesque personage clad in bits of armor that were quite as oddly matched as were his bridle, lance, buckler, and corselet, mine host was not at all indisposed to join the lasses in their merriment. He was suspicious, however, of all this paraphernalia and decided that it would be better to keep a civil tongue in his head.

"If, Sir Knight," he said, "your Grace desires a lodging, aside from a bed—for there is none to be had in this inn—you will find all else that you may want in great abundance."

When Don Quixote saw how humble the governor of the castle was—for he took the innkeeper and his inn to be no less than that —he replied, "For me, Sir Castellan, anything will do, since

Arms are my only ornament,
My only rest the fight, etc."

The landlord thought that the knight had called him a castellan because he took him for one of those worthies of Castile, whereas the truth was, he was an Andalusian from the beach of Sanlúcar, no less a thief than Cacus himself, and as full of tricks as a student or a page boy.

"In that case," he said,

"Your bed will be the solid rock,
Your sleep: to watch all night.

This being so, you may be assured of finding beneath this roof enough to keep you awake for a whole year, to say nothing of a single night."

With this, he went up to hold the stirrup for Don Quixote, who encountered much difficulty in dismounting, not having broken his fast all day long. The knight then directed his host to take good care of the steed, as it was the best piece of horseflesh in all the world. The innkeeper looked it over, and it did not impress him as being half as good as Don Quixote had said it was. Having stabled the animal, he came back to see what his guest would have and found the latter being relieved of his armor by the damsels, who by now had made their peace with the new arrival. They had already removed his breastplate and backpiece but had no idea how they were going to open his gorget or get his improvised helmet off. That piece of armor had been tied on with green ribbons which it would be necessary to cut, since the knots could not be undone, but he would not hear of this, and so spent all the rest of that night with his headpiece in place, which gave him the weirdest, most laughable appearance that could be imagined.

Don Quixote fancied that these wenches who were assisting him must surely be the chatelaine and other ladies of the castle, and so proceeded to address them very gracefully and with much wit:

Never was knight so served
By any noble dame
As was Don Quixote
When from his village he came,
With damsels to wait on his every need
While princesses cared for his hack . . .

"By hack," he explained, "is meant my steed Rocinante, for that is his name, and mine is Don Quixote de la Mancha. I had no intention of revealing my identity until my exploits done in your service should have made me known to you; but the necessity of adapting to present circumstances that old ballad of Lancelot has led to your becoming acquainted with it prematurely. However, the time will come when your Ladyships shall command and I will obey and with the valor of my good right arm show you how eager I am to serve you."

The young women were not used to listening to speeches like this and had not a word to say, but merely asked him if he desired to eat anything.

"I could eat a bite of something, yes," replied Don Quixote. "Indeed, I feel that a little food would go very nicely just now."

He thereupon learned that, since it was Friday, there was nothing to be had in all the inn except a few portions of codfish, which in Castile is called *abadejo,* in Andalusia *bacalao,* in some places *cura-*

dillo, and elsewhere *truchuella* or small trout. Would his Grace, then, have some small trout, seeing that was all there was that they could offer him?

"If there are enough of them," said Don Quixote, "they will take the place of a trout, for it is all one to me whether I am given in change eight reales or one piece of eight. What is more, those small trout may be like veal, which is better than beef, or like kid, which is better than goat. But however that may be, bring them on at once, for the weight and burden of arms is not to be borne without inner sustenance."

Placing the table at the door of the hostelry, in the open air, they brought the guest a portion of badly soaked and worse cooked codfish and a piece of bread as black and moldy as the suit of armor that he wore. It was a mirth-provoking sight to see him eat, for he still had his helmet on with his visor fastened, which made it impossible for him to put anything into his mouth with his hands, and so it was necessary for one of the girls to feed him. As for giving him anything to drink, that would have been out of the question if the innkeeper had not hollowed out a reed, placing one end in Don Quixote's mouth while through the other end he poured the wine. All this the knight bore very patiently rather than have them cut the ribbons of his helmet.

At this point a gelder of pigs approached the inn, announcing his arrival with four or five blasts on his horn, all of which confirmed Don Quixote in the belief that this was indeed a famous castle, for what was this if not music that they were playing for him? The fish was trout, the bread was of the finest, the wenches were ladies, and the innkeeper was the castellan. He was convinced that he had been right in his resolve to sally forth and roam the world at large, but there was one thing that still distressed him greatly, and that was the fact that he had not as yet been dubbed a knight; as he saw it, he could not legitimately engage in any adventure until he had received the order of knighthood.

Of the amusing manner in which Don Quixote had himself dubbed a knight

Wearied of his thoughts, Don Quixote lost no time over the scanty repast which the inn afforded him. When he had finished, he summoned the landlord and, taking him out to the stable, closed the doors and fell on his knees in front of him.

"Never, valiant knight," he said, "shall I arise from here until you have courteously granted me the boon I seek, one which will redound to your praise and to the good of the human race."

Seeing his guest at his feet and hearing him utter such words as these, the innkeeper could only stare at him in bewilderment, not knowing what to say or do. It was in vain that he entreated him to rise, for Don Quixote refused to do so until his request had been granted.

"I expected nothing less of your great magnificence, my lord," the latter then continued, "and so I may tell you that the boon I asked and which you have so generously conceded me is that tomorrow morning you dub me a knight. Until that time, in the chapel of this your castle, I will watch over my armor, and when morning comes, as I have said, that which I so desire shall then be done, in order that I may lawfully go to the four corners of the earth in quest of adventures and to succor the needy, which is the chivalrous duty of all knights-errant such as I who long to engage in deeds of high emprise."

The innkeeper, as we have said, was a sharp fellow. He already had a suspicion that his guest was not quite right in the head, and he was now convinced of it as he listened to such remarks as these. However, just for the sport of it, he determined to humor him; and so he went on to assure Don Quixote that he was fully justified in his request and that such a desire and purpose was only natural on the part of so distinguished a knight as his gallant bearing plainly showed him to be.

He himself, the landlord added, when he was a young man, had followed the same honorable calling. He had gone through various parts of the world seeking adventures, among the places he had visited being the Perchcles of Málaga, the Isles of Riarán, the District of Seville, the Little Market Place of Segovia, the Olivera of Valencia, the Rondilla of Granada, the beach of Sanlúcar, the Horse Fountain of Cordova, the Small Taverns of Toledo, and numerous other localities where his nimble feet and light fingers had found much exercise. He had done many wrongs, cheated many widows, ruined many maidens, and swindled not a few minors until he had finally come to be known in almost all the courts and tribunals that are to be found in the whole of Spain.

At last he had retired to his castle here, where he lived upon his own income and the property of others; and here it was that he received all knights-errant of whatever quality and condition, simply out of the great affection that he bore them and that they might share with him their possessions in payment of his good will. Unfortunately, in this castle there was no chapel where Don Quixote might keep watch over his arms, for the old chapel had been torn down to make way for a new one; but in case of necessity, he felt quite sure that such a vigil could be maintained anywhere, and for the present occasion the courtyard of the castle would do; and then in the morning, please God, the requisite ceremony could be performed and his guest be duly dubbed a knight, as much a knight as anyone ever was.

He then inquired if Don Quixote had any money on his person, and the latter replied that he had not a cent, for in all the storybooks he had never read of knights-errant carrying any. But the innkeeper told him he was mistaken on this point: supposing the authors of those stories had not set down the fact in black and white, that was because they did not deem it necessary to speak of things as indispensable as money and a clean shirt, and one was not to assume for that reason that those knights-errant of whom the books were so full did not have any. He looked upon it as an absolute certainty that they all had well-stuffed purses, that they might be prepared for any emergency; and they also carried shirts and a little box of ointment for healing the wounds that they received.

For when they had been wounded in combat on the plains and in desert places, there was not always someone at hand to treat them, unless they had some skilled enchanter for a friend who then would succor them, bringing to them through the air, upon a cloud, some damsel or dwarf bearing a vial of water of such virtue that one had but to taste a drop of it and at once his wounds were healed and he was as sound as if he had never received any.

But even if this was not the case, knights in times past saw to it that their squires were well provided with money and other necessities, such as lint and ointment for healing purposes; and if they had no squires—which happened very rarely—they themselves carried these objects in a pair of saddle bags very cleverly attached to their horses' croups in such a manner as to be scarcely noticeable, as if they held something of greater importance than that, for among the knights-errant saddlebags as a rule were not favored. Accordingly, he would advise the novice before him, and inasmuch as the latter was soon to be his godson, he might even command him, that henceforth he should not go without money and a supply of those things that have been mentioned, as he would find that they came in useful at a time when he least expected it.

Don Quixote promised to follow his host's advice punctiliously; and so it was arranged that he should watch his armor in a large barnyard at one side of the inn. He gathered up all the pieces, placed them in a horse trough that stood near the well, and bracing his shield on his arm, took up his lance and with stately demeanor began pacing up and down in front of the trough even as night was closing in.

The innkeeper informed his other guests of what was going on, of Don Quixote's vigil and his expectation of being dubbed a knight; and, marveling greatly at so extraordinary a variety of madness, they all went out to see for themselves and stood there watching from a distance. For a while the knight-to-be, with tranquil mien, would merely walk up and down; then, leaning on his lance, he would pause to survey his armor, gazing fixedly at it for a considerable length of time. As has been said, it was night now, but the brightness of the moon, which well might rival that of Him who lent it, was such that everything the novice knight did was plainly visible to all.

At this point one of the mule drivers who were stopping at the inn came out to water his drove, and in order to do this it was necessary to remove the armor from the trough.

As he saw the man approaching, Don Quixote cried out to him, "O bold knight, whoever you may be, who thus would dare to lay hands upon the accouterments of the most valiant man of arms that ever girded on a sword, look well what you do and desist if you do not wish to pay with your life for your insolence!"

The muleteer gave no heed to these words—it would have been better for his own sake had he done so—but, taking it up by the straps, tossed the armor some distance from him. When he beheld this, Don Quixote rolled his eyes heavenward and with his thoughts apparently upon his Dulcinea exclaimed, "Succor, O lady mine, this vassal heart in this my first encounter; let not your favor and protection fail me in the peril in which for the first time I now find myself."

With these and other similar words, he loosed his buckler, grasped his lance in both his hands, and let the mule driver have such a blow on the head that the man fell to the ground stunned; and had it been followed by another one, he would have had no need of a surgeon to treat him. Having done this, Don Quixote gathered up his armor and resumed his pacing up and down with the same calm manner as before. Not long afterward, without knowing what had happened—for the first muleteer was still lying there unconscious—another came out with the same intention of watering his mules, and he too was about to remove the armor from the trough when the knight, without saying a word or asking favor of anyone, once more adjusted his buckler and raised his lance, and if he did not break the second mule driver's head to bits, he made more than three pieces of it by dividing it into quarters. At the sound of the fracas everybody in the inn came running out, among them the innkeeper; whereupon Don Quixote again lifted his buckler and laid his hand on his sword.

"O lady of beauty," he said, "strength and vigor of this fainting heart of mine! Now is the time to turn the eyes of your greatness upon this captive knight of yours who must face so formidable an adventure."

By this time he had worked himself up to such a pitch of anger that if all the mule drivers in the world had attacked him he would not have taken one step backward. The comrades of the wounded men, seeing the plight those two were in, now began showering stones on Don Quixote, who shielded himself as best he could with his buckler, although he did not dare stir from the trough for fear of leaving his armor unprotected. The landlord, meanwhile, kept calling to them to stop, for he had told them that this was a madman who would be sure to go free even though he killed them all. The knight was shouting louder than ever, calling them knaves and traitors. As for the lord of the castle, who allowed knights-errant to be treated in this fashion, he was a lowborn villain, and if he, Don Quixote, had but received the order of knighthood, he would make him pay for his treachery.

"As for you others, vile and filthy rabble, I take no account of you; you may stone me or come forward and attack me all you like; you shall see what the reward of your folly and insolence will be."

He spoke so vigorously and was so undaunted in bearing as to strike terror in those who would assail him; and for this reason, and owing also to the persuasions of the innkeeper, they ceased stoning him. He then permitted them to carry away the wounded, and went back to watching his armor with the same tranquil, unconcerned air that he had previously displayed.

The landlord was none too well pleased with these mad pranks on the part of his guest and determined to confer upon him that accursed order of knighthood before something else happened. Going up to him, he begged Don Quixote's pardon for the insolence which, without his knowledge, had been shown the knight by those of low degree. They, however, had been well punished for their impudence. As he had said, there was no chapel in this castle, but for that which remained to be done there was no need of any. According to what he had read of the ceremonial of the order, there was nothing to this business of being dubbed a knight except a slap on the neck and one across the shoulder, and that could be performed in the middle of a field as well as anywhere else. All that was required was for the knight-to-be to keep watch over his armor for a couple of hours, and Don Quixote had been at it more than four. The latter believed all this and announced that he was ready to obey and get the matter over with as speedily as possible. Once dubbed a knight, if he were attacked one more time, he did not think that he would leave a single person in the castle alive, save such as he might command be spared, at the bidding of his host and out of respect to him.

Thus warned, and fearful that it might occur, the castellan brought out the book in which he had jotted down the hay and barley for which the mule drivers owed him, and, accompanied by a lad bearing the butt of a candle and the two aforesaid damsels, he came up to where Don Quixote stood and commanded him to kneel. Reading from the account book—as if he had been saying a prayer—he raised his hand and, with the knight's own sword, gave him a good thwack upon the neck and another lusty one upon the shoulder, muttering all the while between his teeth. He then directed one of the ladies to gird on Don Quixote's sword, which she did with much gravity and composure; for it was all they could do to keep from laughing at every point of the ceremony, but the thought of the knight's prowess which they had already witnessed was sufficient to restrain their mirth.

"May God give your Grace much good fortune," said the worthy lady as she attached the blade, "and prosper you in battle."

Don Quixote thereupon inquired her name, for he desired to know to whom it was he was indebted for the favor he had just received, that he might share with her some of the honor which his strong right arm was sure to bring him. She replied very humbly that her name was Tolosa and that she was the daughter of a shoemaker, a native of Toledo who lived in the stalls of Sancho Bienaya. To this the knight replied that she would do him a very great favor if from then on she would call herself Doña Tolosa, and she promised to do so. The other girl then helped him on with his spurs, and practically the same conversation was repeated. When asked her name, she stated that it was La Molinera and added that she was the daughter of a respectable miller of Antequera. Don Quixote likewise requested her to assume the "don" and become Doña Molinera and offered to render her further services and favors.

These unheard-of ceremonies having been dispatched in great haste, Don Quixote could scarcely wait to be astride his horse and sally forth on his quest for adventures. Saddling and mounting Rocinante, he embraced his host, thanking him for the favor of having dubbed him a knight and saying such strange things that it would be quite impossible to record them here. The innkeeper, who was only too glad to be rid of him, answered with a speech that was no less flowery, though somewhat shorter, and he did not so much as ask him for the price of a lodging, so glad was he to see him go.

Of the good fortune which the valorous Don Quixote had in the terrifying and never-before-imagined adventure of the windmills, along with other events that deserve to be suitably recorded

At this point they caught sight of thirty or forty windmills which were standing on the plain there, and no sooner had Don Quixote laid eyes upon them than he turned to his squire and said, "Fortune is guiding our affairs better than we could have wished; for you see there before you, friend Sancho Panza, some thirty or more lawless giants with whom I mean to do battle. I shall deprive them of their lives, and with the spoils from this encounter we shall begin to enrich ourselves; for this is righteous warfare, and it is a great service to God to remove so accursed a breed from the face of the earth."

"What giants?" said Sancho Panza.

"Those that you see there," replied his master, "those with the long arms some of which are as much as two leagues in length."

"But look, your Grace, those are not giants but windmills, and what appear to be arms are their wings which, when whirled in the breeze, cause the millstone to go."

"It is plain to be seen," said Don Quixote, "that you have had little experience in this matter of adventures. If you are afraid, go off to one side and say your prayers while I am engaging them in fierce, unequal combat."

Saying this, he gave spurs to his steed Rocinante, without paying any heed to Sancho's warning that these were truly windmills and not giants that he was riding forth to attack. Nor even when he was close upon them did he perceive what they really were, but shouted at the top of his lungs, "Do not seek to flee, cowards and vile creatures that you are, for it is but a single knight with whom you have to deal!"

At that moment a little wind came up and the big wings began turning.

"Though you flourish as many arms as did the giant Briareus," said Don Quixote when he perceived this, "you still shall have to answer to me."

He thereupon commended himself with all his heart to his lady Dulcinea, beseeching her to succor him in this peril; and, being well covered with his shield and with his lance at rest, he bore down upon them at a full gallop and fell upon the first mill that stood in his way, giving a thrust at the wing, which was whirling at such a speed that his lance was broken into bits and both horse and horseman went rolling over the plain, very much battered indeed. Sancho upon his donkey came hurrying to his master's assistance as fast as he could, but when he reached the spot, the knight was unable to move, so great was the shock with which he and Rocinante had hit the ground.

"God help us!" exclaimed Sancho, "did I not tell your Grace to look well, that those were nothing but windmills, a fact which no one could fail to see unless he had other mills of the same sort in his head?"

"Be quiet, friend Sancho," said Don Quixote. "Such are the fortunes of war, which more than any other are subject to constant change. What is more, when I come to think of it, I am sure that this must be the work of that magician Frestón, the one who robbed me of my study and my books, and who has thus changed the giants into windmills in order to deprive me of the glory of overcoming them, so great is the enmity that he bears me; but in the end his evil arts shall not prevail against this trusty sword of mine."

"May God's will be done," was Sancho Panza's response. And with the aid of his squire the knight was once more mounted on Rocinante, who stood there with one shoulder half out of joint. And so, speaking of the adventure that had just befallen them, they continued along the Puerto Lápice highway; for there, Don

Quixote said, they could not fail to find many and varied adventures, this being a much traveled thoroughfare. The only thing was, the knight was exceedingly downcast over the loss of his lance.

"I remember," he said to his squire, "having read of a Spanish knight by the name of Diego Pérez de Vargas, who, having broken his sword in battle, tore from an oak a heavy bough or branch and with it did such feats of valor that day, and pounded so many Moors, that he came to be known as Machuca, and he and his descendants from that day forth have been called Vargas y Machuca. I tell you this because I too intend to provide myself with just such a bough as the one he wielded, and with it I propose to do such exploits that you shall deem yourself fortunate to have been found worthy to come with me and behold and witness things that are almost beyond belief."

"God's will be done," said Sancho. "I believe everything that your Grace says; but straighten yourself up in the saddle a little, for you seem to be slipping down on one side, owing, no doubt, to the shaking-up that you received in your fall."

"Ah, that is the truth," replied Don Quixote, "and if I do not speak of my sufferings, it is for the reason that it is not permitted knights-errant to complain of any wound whatsoever, even though their bowels may be dropping out."

"If that is the way it is," said Sancho, "I have nothing more to say; but, God knows, it would suit me better if your Grace did complain when something hurts him. I can assure you that I mean to do so, over the least little thing that ails me—that is, unless the same rule applies to squires as well."

Don Quixote laughed long and heartily over Sancho's simplicity, telling him that he might complain as much as he liked and where and when he liked, whether he had good cause or not; for he had read nothing to the contrary in the ordinances of chivalry. Sancho then called his master's attention to the fact that it was time to eat. The knight replied that he himself had no need of food at the moment, but his squire might eat whenever he chose. Having been granted this permission, Sancho seated himself as best he could upon his beast, and, taking out from his saddlebags the provisions that he had stored there, he rode along leisurely behind his master, munching his victuals and taking a good, hearty swig now and then at the leather flask in a manner that might well have caused the biggest-bellied tavernkeeper of Málaga to envy him. Between draughts he gave not so much as a thought to any promise that his master might have made him, nor did he look upon it as any hardship, but rather as good sport, to go in quest of adventures however hazardous they might be.

The short of the matter is, they spent the night under some trees, from one of which Don Quixote tore off a withered bough to serve him as a lance, placing it in the lance head from which he had removed the broken one. He did not sleep all night long for thinking of his lady Dulcinea; for this was in accordance with what he had read in his books, of men of arms in the forest or desert places who kept a wakeful vigil, sustained by the memory of their ladies fair. Not so with Sancho, whose stomach was full, and not with chicory water. He fell into a dreamless slumber, and had not his master called him, he would not have been awakened either by the rays of the sun in his face or by the many birds who greeted the coming of the new day with their merry song.

Upon arising, he had another go at the flask, finding it somewhat more flaccid than it had been the night before, a circumstance which grieved his heart, for he could not see that they were on the way to remedying the deficiency within any very short space of time. Don Quixote did not wish any breakfast; for, as has been said, he was in the habit of nourishing himself on savorous memories. They then set out once more along the road to Puerto Lápice, and around three in the afternoon they came in sight of the pass that bears that name.

"There," said Don Quixote as his eyes fell upon it, "we may plunge our arms up to the elbow in what are known as adventures. But I must warn you that even though you see me in the greatest peril in the world, you are not to lay hand upon your sword to defend me, unless it be that those who attack me are rabble and men of low degree, in which case you may very well come to my aid; but if they be gentlemen, it is in no wise permitted by the laws of chivalry that you should assist me until you yourself shall have been dubbed a knight."

"Most certainly, sir," replied Sancho, "your Grace shall be very well obeyed in this; all the more so for the reason that I myself am of a peaceful disposition and not fond of meddling in the quarrels and feuds of others. However, when it comes to protecting my own person, I shall not take account of those laws of which you speak, seeing that all laws, human and divine, permit each one to defend himself whenever he is attacked."

"I am willing to grant you that," assented Don Quixote, "but in this matter of defending me against gentlemen you must restrain your natural impulses."

"I promise you I shall do so," said Sancho. "I will observe this precept as I would the Sabbath day."

As they were conversing in this manner, there appeared in the road in front of them two friars of the Order of St. Benedict, mounted upon dromedaries—for the she-mules they rode were certainly no smaller than that. The friars wore travelers' spectacles and carried sunshades, and behind them came a coach accompanied by four or five men on horseback and a couple of muleteers on foot. In the coach, as was afterwards learned, was a lady of Biscay, on her way to Seville to bid farewell to her husband, who had been appointed to some high post in the Indies. The religious were not of her company although they were going by the same road.

The instant Don Quixote laid eyes upon them he turned to his squire. "Either I am mistaken or this is going to be the most famous adventure that ever was seen; for those black-clad figures that you behold must be, and without any doubt are, certain enchanters who are bearing with them a captive princess in that coach, and I must do all I can to right this wrong."

"It will be worse than the windmills," declared Sancho. "Look you, sir, those are Benedictine friars and the coach must be that of some travelers. Mark well what I say and what you do, lest the devil lead you astray."

"I have already told you, Sancho," replied Don Quixote, "that you know little where the subject of adventures is concerned. What I am saying to you is the truth, as you shall now see."

With this, he rode forward and took up a position in the middle of the road along which the friars were coming, and as soon as they appeared to be within earshot he cried out to them in a loud voice, "O devilish and monstrous beings, set free at once the highborn princesses whom you bear captive in that coach, or else prepare at once to meet your death as the just punishment of your evil deeds."

The friars drew rein and sat there in astonishment, marveling as much at Don Quixote's appearance as at the words he spoke. "Sir Knight," they answered him, "we are neither devilish nor monstrous but religious of the Order of St. Benedict who are merely going our way. We know nothing of those who are in that coach, nor of any captive princesses either."

"Soft words," said Don Quixote, "have no effect on me. I know you for what you are, lying rabble!" And without waiting for any further parley he gave spur to Rocinante and, with lowered lance, bore down upon the first friar with such fury and intrepidity that, had not the fellow tumbled from his mule of his own accord, he would have been hurled to the ground and either killed or badly wounded. The second religious, seeing how his companion had been treated, dug his legs into his she-mule's flanks and scurried away over the countryside faster than the wind.

Seeing the friar upon the ground, Sancho Panza slipped lightly from his mount and, falling upon him, began stripping him of his habit. The two mule drivers accompanying the religious thereupon came running up and asked Sancho why he was doing this. The latter replied that the friar's garments belonged to him as legitimate spoils of the battle that his master Don Quixote had just won. The muleteers, however, were lads with no sense of humor, nor did they know what all this talk of spoils and battles was about; but, perceiving that Don Quixote had ridden off to one side to converse with those inside the coach, they pounced upon Sancho, threw him to the ground, and proceeded to pull out the hair of his beard and kick him to a pulp, after which they went off and left him stretched out there, bereft at once of breath and sense.

Without losing any time, they then assisted the friar to remount. The good brother was trembling all over from fright, and there was not a speck of color in his face, but when he found himself in the saddle once more, he quickly spurred his beast to where his companion, at some little distance, sat watching and waiting to see what the result of the encounter would be. Having no curiosity as to the final outcome of the fray, the two of them now resumed their journey, making more signs of the cross than the devil would be able to carry upon his back.

Meanwhile Don Quixote, as we have said, was speaking to the lady in the coach.

"Your beauty, my lady, may now dispose of your person as best may please you, for the arrogance of your abductors lies upon the ground, overthrown by this good arm of mine; and in order that you may not pine to know the name of your liberator, I may inform you that I am Don Quixote de la Mancha, knight-errant and adventurer and captive of the peerless and beauteous Doña Dulcinea del Toboso. In payment of the favor which you have received from me, I ask nothing other than that you return to El Toboso and on my behalf pay your respects to this lady, telling her that it was I who set you free."

One of the squires accompanying those in the coach, a Biscayan, was listening to Don Quixote's words, and when he saw that the knight did not propose to let the coach proceed upon its way but was bent upon having it turn back to El Toboso, he promptly went up to him, seized his lance, and said to him in bad Castilian and worse Biscayan, "Go, *caballero,* and bad luck go with you; for by the God that created me, if you do not let this coach pass, me kill you or me no Biscayan."

Don Quixote heard him attentively enough and answered him very mildly, "If you were a *caballero,* which you are not, I should already have chastised you, wretched creature, for your foolhardiness and your impudence."

"Me no *caballero?*" cried the Biscayan. "Me swear to God, you lie like a Christian. If you will but lay aside your lance and unsheath your sword, you will soon see that you are carrying water to the cat! Biscayan on land, gentleman at sea, but a gentleman in spite of the devil, and you lie if you say otherwise."

" ' "You shall see as to that presently," said Agrajes,' " Don Quixote quoted. He cast his lance to the earth, drew his sword, and, taking his buckler on his arm, attacked the Biscayan with intent to slay him. The latter, when he saw his adversary approaching, would have liked to dismount from his mule, for she was one of the worthless sort that are let for hire and he had no confidence in her; but there was no time for this, and so he had no choice but to draw his own sword in turn and make the best of it. However, he was near enough to the coach to be able to snatch a cushion from it to serve him as a shield; and then they fell upon each other as though they were mortal enemies. The rest of those present sought to make peace between them but did not succeed, for the Biscayan with his disjointed phrases kept muttering that if they did not let him finish the battle then he himself would have to kill his mistress and anyone else who tried to stop him.

The lady inside the carriage, amazed by it all and trembling at what she saw, directed her coachman to drive on a little way; and there from a distance she watched the deadly combat, in the course of which the Biscayan came down with a great blow on Don Quixote's shoulder, over the top of the latter's shield, and had not the knight been clad in armor, it would have split him to the waist.

Feeling the weight of this blow, Don Quixote cried out, "O lady of my soul, Dulcinea, flower of beauty, succor this your champion who out of gratitude for your many favors finds himself in so perilous a plight!" To utter these words, lay hold of his sword, cover himself with his buckler, and attack the Biscayan was but the work of a moment; for he was now resolved to risk everything upon a single stroke.

As he saw Don Quixote approaching with so dauntless a bearing, the Biscayan was well aware of his adversary's courage and forthwith determined to imitate the example thus set him. He kept himself protected with his cushion, but he was unable to get his she-mule to budge to one side or the other, for the beast, out of sheer exhaustion and being, moreover, unused to such childish play, was incapable of taking a single step. And so, then, as has been stated, Don Quixote was approaching the wary Biscayan, his sword raised on high and with the firm resolve of cleaving his enemy in two; and the Biscayan was awaiting the knight in the same posture, cushion in front of him and with uplifted sword. All the bystanders were trembling with suspense at what would happen as a result of the terrible blows that were threatened, and the lady in the coach and her maids were making a thousand vows and offerings to all the images and shrines in Spain, praying that God would save them all and the lady's squire from this great peril that confronted them.

But the unfortunate part of the matter is that at this very point the author of the history breaks off and leaves the battle pending, excusing himself upon the ground that he has been unable to find anything else in writing concerning the exploits of Don Quixote beyond those already set forth. It is true, on the other hand, that the second author of this work could not bring himself to believe that so unusual a chronicle would have been consigned to oblivion, nor that the learned ones of La Mancha were possessed of so little curiosity as not to be able to discover in their archives or registry offices certain papers that have to do with this famous knight. Being convinced of this, he did not despair of coming upon the end of this pleasing story, and Heaven favoring him, he did find it, as shall be related in the second part.

John Colet: *Sermon to the Convocation at St. Paul's*

One of the most earnest of the English humanists, John Colet was a close friend of Thomas More and Desiderius Erasmus, a Neoplatonist of sorts, a student of the Bible, a promoter of education, and a church reformer. Born around 1467, he was the only survivor among the twenty-two children sired by his father Sir Henry Colet, a merchant and lord mayor of London. In school he studied the traditional subjects, grammar, rhetoric, dialectic, and mathematics, and he later took his A.B. and M.A. degrees at Cambridge. At the university he heard lectures by Grocyn and Linacre, pioneers of humanist learning and the study of Greek, who inspired him to make the humanist pilgrimage to Italy. In the homeland of the Renaissance in 1493 he fell under the spell of Florentine Neoplatonism. He corresponded with the Neoplatonist philosopher Marsiglio Ficino, studied the mystical writings of Dionysius the Areopagite, and read St. Augustine. On his return in 1496 he began at Oxford his famous lectures on St. Paul's epistle to the Romans. He stressed sin as the root condition of man, his need for God's grace, and for faith in Christ the Redeemer of fallen man.

Colet won his doctorate and was made the Dean of St. Paul's Cathedral. He inherited a sizable fortune from his father in the year 1508. With it he endowed St. Paul's School, built to the east of the great church, modeled after the humanist schools of Italy. William Lilly, the headmaster, stressed the importance of classical Latin, Greek, religion, and moral instruction. Colet himself was a fearless preacher, scoring the abuses in church and society, criticizing England's continental wars, and even laying out the duties of a cardinal for the benefit of Wolsey. He died in 1519 when the Reformation was just beginning to stir on the continent.

The Sermon of Doctor Colet Made to the Convocation at St. Paul's has been assigned to the year 1511; it was printed by Thomas Berthelet, royal printer. It is reproduced here in somewhat modernized English from J. H. Lupton, *A Life of John Colet, D.D.,*

Dean of St. Paul's, and Founder of St. Paul's School (London: George Bell and Sons, 1887), 293–304.

You are come together today, fathers and right wise men, to enter counsel; in the which, what we will do, and what matters you will handle, yet we understand not. But we wish that once, remembering your name and profession, you would mind the reformation of the church's matter. For it was nevermore need, and the state of the church did never desire more your endeavors. For the spouse of Christ, the church, which you would should be *without spot or wrinkle,* is made foul and ill-favored, as Isaiah says, *The faithful city is made a harlot.* And as Jeremiah says, *She has done lechery with many lovers, whereby she has conceived many seeds of wickedness, and daily brings forth very foul fruit.*

Wherefore I came hither today, fathers, to warn you that in this your council, with all your mind, you think upon the reformation of the church. But forsooth I came not willingly, for I knew my unworthiness. I saw besides how hard it was to please the precise judgment of so many men. For I judged it utterly unworthy and unmeet, yes, and almost too malapert, that I, a servant, should counsel my lords; that I, a son, should teach you, my fathers. Truly it would have been more meet for some one of the fathers, that is to say, you prelates might have done it with more grave authority and graver wisdom. But the commandment was to be obeyed of the most reverend father and lord the archbishop, president of this council, which laid upon me this burden truly too heavy for me. We read that the prophet Samuel said: *Obedience is better than sacrifice.* Wherefore, fathers and right worthy men, I pray you and beseech you that this day you would sustain my weakness with your goodness and patience; furthermore, to help me at the beginning with your good prayers.

And before all things let us pray unto God the Father Almighty, first remembering our most holy father the pope, and all spiritual pastors, with all Christian people; furthermore the most reverend father and lord the archbishop, president of this council, and all bishops, and all the clergy, and all the people of England; remembering, finally, this your congregation, desiring God to inspire your minds so accordingly to agree, to such profit and fruit of the church that you seem not, after the council finished, to have been gathered together in vain and without cause. Let us all say *Pater noster.*

To exhort you, reverend fathers, to the endeavor of reformation of the church's estate (because that nothing has so disfigured the face of the church as has the fashion of secular and worldly living in clerics and priests) I know not where more conveniently to take beginning of my tale than of the apostle Paul, in whose temple you are gathered together. For he, writing to the Romans, and under their name to you, says: *Be you not conformed to this world, but be you reformed in the newness of your understanding that you may prove what is the good will of God, well pleasing and perfect.* This did the apostle write to all Christian men, but most chiefly unto priests and bishops. Priests and bishops are the light of the world. For unto them said our Savior: *you are the light of the world.* And he said also: *If the light that is in you be darkness, how dark shall the darkness be?* That is to say, if priests and bishops that should be as lights, run in the dark way of the world, how dark then shall the secular people be? Wherefore St. Paul said chiefly to priests and bishops: *Be you not conformable to this world, but be you reformed.*

In which words the apostle does two things. First, he forbids us to be conformable to the world and to be made carnal. Furthermore, he commands that we be reformed in the spirit of God, whereby we are spiritual.

I intend to follow this order; I will speak first of confirmation, then afterwards of reformation.

Be you not, he says, *conformable to this world.*

The apostle calls the *world* the ways and manner of secular living, which chiefly rest in four evils of this world, that is to say, in devilish pride, in carnal concupiscence, in worldly covetousness, in secular business. These are in the world, as St. John the apostle witnesses in his canonical epistle. For he says: *Everything that is in the world* is either the *concupiscence of the flesh,* or the *concupiscence of the eyes,* or *pride of life.* The same are now and reign in the church, and in men of the church, so that we may seem truly to say, everything that is in the church is either concupiscence of flesh, or eyes, or pride of life.

And first to speak of pride of life, how much greediness and appetite of honor and dignity is nowadays in men of the church? How run they, yes, almost out of breath, from one benefice to another, from the less to the more, from the lower to the higher? Who does not see this? Who, seeing this, does not sorrow? Moreover, these that are in the same dignities, the most part of them go with so stately a countenance and with such high looks that they seem not to be put into the humble bishopric of Christ, but rather into the high lordship and power of the world, not knowing nor advertising what

Christ the master of all meekness said to his disciples, whom he called to be bishops and priests: *The princes of people,* says he, *have lordship of them, and those that be in authority have power; but do you not so: but he that is greater among you, let him be minister; he that is highest in dignity, let him be the servant of all men. The son of man came not to be ministered to but to minister.* By which words our Savior plainly teaches that the mastery in the church is nothing else than a ministry, and the high dignity in a man of the church is nothing else than a meek service.

The second secular evil is carnal concupiscence. Has not this vice so grown and waxed in the church as a flood of their lust, so that there is nothing looked for more diligently in this most busy time of the most part of the priests than what delights and pleases the senses? They give themselves to feasts and banquetting; they spend themselves in vain babbling; they give themselves to sports and plays; they apply themselves to hunting and hawking; they drown themselves in the delights of this world. Procurers and finders of lusts they set by. Against which kind of men Jude the apostle cries out in his epistle, saying: *Woe unto those who have gone the way of Cain. They are foul and beastly, feasting in their meats, without fear feeding themselves; floods of the wild sea, foaming out their confusions; unto whom the storm of darkness is reserved for everlasting.*

Covetousness is the third secular evil, which St. John the apostle calls concupiscence of the eyes. St. Paul calls it idolatry. This abominable pestilence has so entered into the mind almost of all priests, and has so blinded the eyes of the mind, that we are blind to all things except to those which seem to bring to us some gains. For what other things seek we nowadays in the church than fat benefices and high promotions? Yes, and in the same promotions, of what other thing do we pass upon than of our tithes and rents? So that we care not how many, how chargeful [costly], how great the benefices we take, if only they are of great value. O covetousness! St. Paul justly called you the root of all evil. From you comes this heaping of benefices upon benefices. From you such great pensions assigned from many benefices resigned. Of you all the suing for tithes, for offering, for mortuaries, for delapidations, by the right and title of the church. For which thing we strive no less than for our own life. O covetousness! From you come these chargeful visitations of bishops. From you comes the corruptness of courts, and these daily new inventions with which the silly people are so sorely vexed. Of you comes the deceit and wantonness of officials. O covetousness! Mother of all iniquity, from you comes this fervent study of the ordinaries to dilate their jurisdictions. From you comes this mad and raging contention in ordinaries; from you the insinuation of testaments; from you comes the undue sequestration of fruits; from you comes the superstitious observing of all those laws that sound to any lucre, setting aside and despising those that concern the amendment of manners. Why should I rehearse the rest? To be short and to conclude with one word: all corruptness, all the decay of the church, all the offences of the world, come from the covetousness of priests, according to that word of St. Paul which here I repeat again and beat into your ears: *covetousness is the root of all evil.*

The fourth secular evil that spots and makes ill-favored the face of the church is the continual secular occupation, wherein priests and bishops nowadays busy themselves, the servants rather of me than of God, the warriors rather of this world than of Christ. For the apostle Paul writes unto Timothy: *No man, being God's soldier, turmoil himself with secular business.* The warring of them is not carnal but spiritual. For our warring is to pray, to read and study Scriptures, to preach the Word of God, to minister the sacraments of health, to do sacrifice for the people, and to offer the host for their sins. For we are mediators and means unto God for men. The which St. Paul witnesses, writing to the Hebrews: *Every bishop* (he says) *taken of men, is ordained for men in those things that be unto God, that he may offer gifts and sacrifices for sins.* Wherefore those apostles that were the first priests and bishops did so much abhor from all manner of meddling of secular things that they would not minister the meat that was necessary to poor people, although that were a great work of virtue, but they said: *It is not meet that we should leave the word of God and serve tables; we will be continually in prayer, and preaching the word of God.* And St. Paul cries unto the Corinthians: If you have any secular business, ordain them to be judges that are most in contempt in the church. Without doubt, of this secularity, and that clerics and priests, leaving all spiritualness, do turmoil themselves with earthly occupations, many evils do follow.

First, the dignity of priesthood is dishonored, the which is greater than either the kings' or emperors'; it is equal with the dignity of angels. But the brightness of this great dignity is sore shadowed when priests are occupied with earthly things, whose conversation ought to be in heaven.

Secondly, priesthood is despised when there is no difference between such priests and lay people, but, according to the prophecy of Hosea: *as the people be, so are the priests.*

Thirdly, the beautiful order and holy dignity in the church is confused, when the highest in the church meddle with vile and earthly things, and in their stead vile and abject persons do exercise high and heavenly things.

Fourthly, the lay people have great occasion of evils, and cause to fall, when those men whose duty is to draw men from the affection of this world, by their continual conversation in this world teach men to love this world, and of the love of the world cast them down headlong into hell.

Moreover, in such priests that are so busied there must needs follow hypocrisy. For when they are so mixed and confused with the lay people, under the garment and habit of a priest, they live plainly after the lay fashion. Also by spiritual weakness and bondage fear, when they are made weak with the waters of this world, they dare neither do nor say but such things as they know to be pleasant and thankful to their princes.

At last, ignorance and blindness: when they are blinded with the darkness of this world they see nothing but earthly things. Wherefore our Savior Christ, not without cause, did warn the prelates of his church: *Take heed,* said he, *lest your hearts be grieved with gluttony and drunkenness and with the cares of this world. With the cares,* says he, *of this world,* wherewith the hearts of priests being sore charged they cannot hold and lift up their minds to high and heavenly things.

Many other evils there are beside those that follow on the secularity of priests, which would be long to rehearse here. But I make an end.

These are the four evils that I have spoken of, O fathers, O priests, by which we are conformable to this world, by which the face of the church is made evil favored, by which the state of it is destroyed truly much more than it was in the beginning by the persecution of tyrants, or afterward by the invasion that followed of heretics. For, in the persecution of tyrants the church being vexed was made stronger and brighter. In the invasion of heretics, the church being shaken was made wiser and more cunning in Holy Writ. But since this secularity was brought in, after that the secular manner of living crept in in the men of the church, the root of all spiritual life—that is to say, charity—was extinct. The which taken away, there can neither wise nor strong church be in God.

In this time also we perceive contradiction of the lay people. But they are not so much contrary unto us, as we are ourselves; nor does their contrariness hurt us so much as the contrariness of our evil life, which is contrary both to God and Christ. For he said: *He that is not with me is against me.*

We are also nowadays grieved of heretics, men mad with marvellous foolishness. But their heresies are not so pestilent and pernicious unto us and the people, as the evil and wicked life of priests; which, if we believe St. Bernard, is a certain kind of heresy, and chief of all and most perilous. For that same holy father, in a certain convocation, preaching unto the priests of his time, in a certain sermon so he said by these words: "There are many catholic and faithful men in speaking and preaching, which same men are heretics in working. For what heretics do by evil teaching, that same thing do they through evil example: they lead the people out of the right way, and bring them in to error of life. And so much are they worse than heretics, as much as their works prevail over their words." This that holy father St. Bernard, with a great and fervent spirit, said against the sect of evil priests in his time. By which words he shows plainly that there are two manners of heresies; the one being perverse teaching and the other naughty life: of which this latter is worse and more perilous. This reigns now in the church in priests not living priestly but secularly to the utter and miserable destruction of the church.

Therefore, you fathers, you priests, and all you of the clergy, at the last look up and awake from this your sleep in this forgetful world; and at the last being well awakened, hear Paul crying unto you: Be you not conformable unto this world.

And this for the first part. Now let us come to the second.

The second part, of Reformation.

But be you reformed in the newness of your understanding.

The second thing that St. Paul commands is that we be reformed into a new understanding; that we smell those things that be of God. Be we reformed unto those things that are contrary to those I spoke of even now: that is to say, to meekness, to soberness, to charity, to spiritual occupation; that, as St. Paul writes to Titus, *denying all wickedness and worldly desires, we live in this world soberly, truly, and virtuously.*

This reformation and restoring of the church's estate must needs begin with you our fathers, and so follow in us, your priests, and in all the clergy. You are our heads, you are an example of living for us. Unto you we look as unto marks of our direction. In you and in your life we desire to read, as in lively books, how and after what fashion we may live. Therefore, if you will ponder and look upon our notes, first take away the blocks out of your eyes. It is an old proverb: *Physician, heal thyself.* You spiritual physicians, first taste you this medicine of purgation of manners, and then after offer us the same to taste.

The way whereby the church may be reformed into better fashion is not by making new laws. For there are laws enough, many and out of number, as Solomon says: *nothing is new under the sun.* For the evils that are now in the church were before in time past; and there is no fault but the fathers have provided very good remedies for it. There are no trespasses, but there are laws against them in the body of the canon law. Therefore, there is no need that new laws and constitutions be made, but that those that are made already be kept. Therefore in this your assembly let those laws that are made be called before you and rehearsed: those laws, I say, that restrain vice and those that further virtue.

First, let those laws be rehearsed that warn you fathers that you not too soon put your hands on every man or admit to holy orders. For there is the well of evils that the broad gate of holy orders opened, every man who offers himself is always admitted without pulling back. From this spring and come out the people in the church who are both unlearned and evil priests. It is not enough for a priest after my judgment to construe a collect, to put forth a question, or to answer a sophism; but much more a good, a pure, and a holy life, approved manners, properly learning of Holy Scriptures, some knowledge of the sacraments; chiefly and above all the fear of God and love of the heavenly life.

Let the laws be rehearsed that command that benefices of the church be given to those that are worthy; and that promotions be made in the church by the right balance of virtue, not by carnal affection, not by the acceptance of persons, whereby it happens nowadays that boys for old men, fools for wise men, evil for good, do reign and rule.

Let the laws be rehearsed that war against the spot of simony. The which corruption, the which infection, the which cruel and odible pestilence so creeps now abroad as the canker evil in the minds of priests that many of them are not afraid nowadays both by prayer and service, rewards and promises, to get them great dignities.

Let the laws be rehearsed that command personal residence of curates in their churches. For of this many evils grow, because all things nowadays are done by vicaries and parish priests, yes, and those foolish also and unsuitable, and oftentimes wicked, that seek no other thing in the people than foul lucre, from which comes occasion for evil heresies and ill christendom in the people.

Let be rehearsed the laws and holy rules given of fathers, of the life and honesty of clerics; that forbid that a cleric be no merchant, that he be no usurer, that he be no hunter, that he be no common player, that he bear no weapon; the laws that forbid clerics to haunt taverns, that forbid them to have suspect familiarity with women; the laws that command soberness, and a measurableness in apparel, and temperance in adorning the body.

Let be rehearsed also to my lords these monks, canons, and religious men, the laws that command them to go the straight way that leads unto heaven, leaving the broad way of the world; that command them not to turmoil themselves in business neither secular nor other; that command that they sue not in princes courts for earthly things. For it is in the council of Chalcedon that monks ought only to give themselves to prayer and fasting and to the chastening of their flesh, and observing of their rules.

Above all things let the laws be rehearsed that pertain to and concern you, my reverend fathers and lord bishops, laws of your just and canonical election, in the chapters of your churches, with the calling of the Holy Ghost. For because that is not done nowadays, and because prelates are chosen oftentimes more by favor of men than by the grace of God, therefore we truly have not a few times bishops who are very little spiritual men, rather worldly than heavenly, savoring more the spirit of this world than the spirit of Christ.

Let the laws be rehearsed of the good bestowing of the patrimony of Christ: the laws that command that the goods of the church be spent, not in costly building, not in sumptuous apparel and pompous, not in feasting and banquetting, not in excess and wantonness, not in enriching of kinsfolk, not in keeping of dogs, but in things profitable and necessary to the church. For when St. Augustine, sometime bishop of England, did ask the pope Gregory how the bishops and prelates of England should spend their goods that were the offerings of faithful people, the said pope answered (and his answer is put in the Decrees, in the 12th chapter and second question), that the goods of bishops ought to be divided into four parts; whereof one part ought to be to the bishop and his household, another to his clerics, the third to repair and uphold his tenements, the fourth to the poor people.

Let the laws be rehearsed, yes, and that often times, that take away the filths and uncleanness of courts, that take away those daily new-found crafts for lucre, that busy them to pull away this foul covetousness, which is the spring and cause of all evils, which is the well of all iniquity.

At the last let be renewed those laws and constitutions of fathers about the celebration of councils, that command provincial councils to be oftener used for the reformation of the church. For there never happens anything more hurtful to the church of Christ than the lack both of council general and provincial.

When these laws and such others are rehearsed that are for us and that concern the correction of manners, nothing is lacking but that the same be put into execution with all authority and power; that once seeing we have a law, we live after the law. For which things, with all due reverence, I call chiefly upon you fathers. For this execution of the laws and observing of the constitutions must needs begin with you, so that you may teach us priests to follow you by lively examples, or else truly it will be said of you: *They lay grievous burdens upon other men's backs and they themselves will not as much as touch it with their little finger.*

Forsooth, if you keep the laws and if you reform first your life to the rules of the canon laws, then shall you give us light, in which we may see what is to be done on our part, that is to say the light of your good example. And we, seeing our fathers so keeping the laws, will gladly follow the steps of our fathers.

The clergy and spiritual part once reformed in the church, then may we with a just order proceed to the reformation of the lay part, which truly will be very easy to do, if we first be reformed. For the body follows the soul, and just as the rulers in the city are, so the dwellers in it are. Therefore if priests that have the charge of souls be good, straight the people will be good. Our goodness shall teach them more clearly to be good than all other teachings and preachings. Our goodness shall compel them into the right way truly more effectually than all your suspendings and cursings.

Therefore, if you will have the lay people live after your wish and will, first live yourselves after the will of God, and so, trust me, you shall get in them whatsoever you will.

You will be obeyed by them, and right it is. For in the epistle to the Hebrews these are the words of St. Paul to the lay people: *Obey, says he, your rulers, and be you under them.* But if you will have this obedience, first perform in yourselves the reason and cause of obedience, which the said Paul teaches, and it follows in the text: that is, *Take you heed also diligently, as though you should give a reckoning for their souls:* and they will obey you.

You will be honored by the people. It is reason. For St. Paul writes to Timothy: *Priests that rule well are worthy of double honors, chiefly those who labor in word and teaching.* Therefore, if you desire to be honored, first look that you rule well, and that you labor in word and teaching, and then shall the people have you in all honor.

You will reap their carnal things and gather tithes and offerings without any striving. Right it is. For St. Paul, writing to the Romans, says: *They are debtors, and ought to minister unto you in carnal things.* First sow your spiritual things, and then you shall reap plentifully their carnal things. For truly that man is very hard and unjust that will *reap where he never did sow* and that will *gather where he never scattered.*

You will have the church's liberty, and not be drawn before secular judges: and that also is right. For it is in the psalms: *Touch you not my anointed.* But if you desire this liberty, first unloose yourselves from worldly bondage, and from the services of men; and lift up yourself into the true liberty, the spiritual liberty of Christ, into grace from sins, and serve God and reign in him. And then, believe me, the people will not touch the anointed of their Lord God.

You would be out of business in rest and peace, and that is convenient. But if you will have peace, come again to the God of peace and love. Come again to Christ, in whom is the very true peace of the Holy Ghost which surpasses all understanding. Come again to yourselves and to your priestly living. And, to make an end, as St. Paul says: *Be you reformed in the newness of your understanding that you savor those things that are of God; and the peace of God shall be with you.*

These are the things, reverend father and right famous men, that I thought to be said for the reformation of the church's estate. I trust you will take them of your gentleness to the best. And if peradventure it be thought that I have passed my bounds in this sermon, or have said anything out of temper, forgive me; and you shall forgive a man speaking from very zeal, a man sorrowing over the decay of the church. And consider the thing itself, not regarding my foolishness. Consider the miserable form and state of the church, and endeavor yourselves with all your minds to reform it. Suffer not, fathers, this your great gathering to depart in vain. Suffer not this your congregation to slip for naught. Truly you are gathered oftentimes together, but by your favor to speak the truth, yet I see not what fruit comes of your assembling, namely to the church.

Go now in the spirit that you have called on, so that by its help you may in this your council find out, discern, and ordain those things that may be profitable to the church, praise to you, and honor to God. *Unto whom be all honor and glory forevermore. Amen.*

Thomas More: from *Utopia*

The most famous of the English humanists was Thomas More, renowned as a distinguished man of letters, as lord chancellor of the realm and as a man of conviction who gave up his life for the sake of his conscience. Born in London in 1478 he was destined for a legal career, but about the age of twenty he suffered an acute spiritual crisis and contemplated earnestly withdrawing from the world to a monastery, and actually did for some years live voluntarily according to the discipline of the Carthusians. He was made undersheriff of London in 1502. He became treasurer of the exchequer in 1521 and speaker of the House of Commons in 1523. When the lord chancellor Cardinal Wolsey lost favor in 1529 because of his failure to secure an annulment of Henry VIII's marriage to Catherine of Aragon, Thomas More reluctantly succeeded him in his high office. The king freed himself of Queen Catherine by staging a divorce trial in England and married Anne Boleyn. More could not accept the king's denial of papal supremacy and resigned as chancellor on May 16, 1532. When by the Act of Supremacy two years later Henry VIII was declared to be the "supreme head" of the English church, More refused to swear the oath acknowledging the king's ecclesiastical supremacy. More was convicted of treason in a show trial and was beheaded in the Tower of London on July 7, 1535, steadfast to the end.

At Oxford Thomas More had encountered Renaissance humanist ideas and his interest in the classics and church fathers was stimulated further by his close associations with Colet and Erasmus. The best known of all his writings was *The Best State of a Commonwealth and the New Island of Utopia; A Truly Golden Handbook, No Less Beneficial than Entertaining, by the Distinguished and Eloquent Author Thomas More Citizen and Sheriff of the Famous City of London,* which he wrote in 1516. In Book One he recorded the discourse of the "extraordinary character" Raphael Hythlodaeus criticizing the political and social abuses of his times such as the hardships resulting from the enclosure system, the harsh punishments of the criminal code, warfare among Christian states, and other evils. Book Two describes the make-believe island of Utopia, a land ruled by reason and righteousness, where property is held in common, where the state provides for every person who does the amount of work required of him, where arms are used only for defense or to take possession of unused lands, and religion is enlightened and constructive.

The selection which follows is taken from Book Two of the Yale Edition of More's Selected Works, *St. Thomas More: Utopia*, ed. Edward Surtz, S.J. (New Haven: Yale University Press, 1964), 59–81. Reprinted by permission of the Yale University Press.

The Best State of a Commonwealth, the Discourse of Raphael Hythlodaeus as Reported by Thomas More, Citizen and Sheriff of London. BOOK II

The island of the Utopians extends in the center (where it is broadest) for two hundred miles and is not much narrower for the greater part of the island, but toward both ends it begins gradually to taper. These ends form a circle five hundred miles in circumference and so make the island look like a new moon, the horns of which are divided by straits about eleven miles across. The straits then unfold into a wide expanse. As the winds are kept off by the land which everywhere surrounds it, the bay is like a huge lake, smooth rather than rough, and thus converts almost the whole center of the country into a harbor which lets ships cross in every direction to the great convenience of the inhabitants.

The mouth of this bay is rendered perilous here by shallows and there by reefs. Almost in the center of the gap stands one great crag which, being visible, is not dangerous. A tower built on it is occupied by a garrison. The other rocks are hidden and therefore treacherous. The channels are known only to the natives, and so it does not easily happen that any foreigner enters the bay except with a Utopian pilot. In fact, the entrance is hardly safe even for themselves, unless they guide themselves by landmarks on the shore. If these were removed to other positions, they could easily lure an enemy's fleet, however numerous, to destruction.

On the outer side of the island, harbors are many. Everywhere, however, the landing is so well defended by nature or by engineering that a few defenders can prevent strong forces from coming ashore.

As the report goes and as the appearance of the ground shows, the island once was not surrounded by sea. But Utopus, who as conqueror gave the island its name (up to then it had been called Abraxa) and who brought the rude and rustic people to such a perfection of culture and humanity as makes them now superior to almost all other mortals, gained a victory at his very first landing. He then ordered the excavation of fifteen miles on the side where the land was connected with the continent and caused the sea to flow around the land. He set to the task not only the natives but, to prevent them from thinking the labor a disgrace, his own soldiers also. With the work divided among so many hands, the enterprise was finished with incredible speed and struck the neighboring peoples, who at first had derided the project as vain, with wonder and terror at its success.

The island contains fifty-four city-states, all spacious and magnificent, identical in language, traditions, customs, and laws. They are similar also in layout and everywhere, as far as the nature of the ground permits, similar even in appearance. None of them is separated by less than twenty-four miles from the nearest, but none is so isolated that a person cannot go from it to another in a day's journey on foot. From each city three old and experienced citizens meet to discuss the affairs of common interest to the island once a year at Amaurotum, for this city, being in the very center of the country, is situated most conveniently for the representatives of all sections. It is considered the chief as well as the capital city.

The lands are so well assigned to the cities that each has at least twelve miles of country on every side, and on some sides even much more, to wit, the side on which the cities are farther apart. No city has any desire to extend its territory, for they consider themselves the tenants rather than the masters of what they hold.

Everywhere in the rural districts they have, at suitable distances from one another, farmhouses well equipped with agricultural implements. They are inhabited by citizens who come in succession to live there. No rural household numbers less than forty men and women, besides two serfs attached to the soil. Over them are set a master and a mistress, serious in mind and ripe in years. Over every group of thirty households rules a phylarch.

Twenty from each household return every year to the city, namely, those having completed two years in the country. As substitutes in their place, the same number are sent from the city. They are to be trained by those who have been there a year and who therefore are more expert in farming; they themselves will teach others in the following years. There is thus no danger of anything going wrong with the annual food supply through want of skill, as might happen if all at one time were newcomers and novices at farming. Though this system of changing farmers is the rule, to prevent any individual's being forced against his will to continue too long in a life of rather hard work, yet many men who take a natural pleasure in agricultural pursuits obtain leave to stay several years.

The occupation of the farmers is to cultivate the soil, to feed the animals, and to get wood and convey it to the city either by land or by water, whichever way is more convenient. They breed a vast quantity of poultry by a wonderful contrivance. The hens do not brood over the eggs, but the farmers, by keeping a great number of them at a uniform heat, bring them to life and hatch them. As soon as they come out of the shell, the chicks follow and acknowledge humans as their mothers!

They rear very few horses, and these only high-spirited ones, which they use for no other purpose than for exercising their young men in horsemanship. All the labor of cultivation and transportation is performed by oxen, which they admit are inferior to horses in a sudden spurt but which are far superior to them in staying power and endurance and not liable to as many diseases. Moreover, it requires less trouble and expense to feed them. When they are past work, they finally are of use for food.

They sow grain only for bread. Their drink is wine or cider or perry, or it is even water. The latter is sometimes plain and often that in which they have boiled honey or licorice, whereof they have a great abundance.

Though they are more than sure how much food the city with its adjacent territory consumes, they produce far more grain and cattle than they require for their own use: they distribute the surplus among their neighbors. Whenever they need things not found in the country, they send for all the materials from the city and, having to give nothing in exchange, obtain it from the municipal officials without the bother of bargaining. For very many go there every single month to observe the holyday.

When the time of harvest is at hand, the agricultural phylarchs inform the municipal officials what number of citizens they require to be sent. The crowd of harvesters, coming promptly at the appointed time, dispatch the whole task of harvesting almost in a single day of fine weather.

The Cities, Especially Amaurotum

The person who knows one of the cities will know them all, since they are exactly alike insofar as the terrain permits. I shall therefore picture one or other (nor does it matter which), but which should I describe rather than Amaurotum? First, none is worthier, the rest deferring to it as the meeting place of the national senate; and, secondly, none is better known to me, as being one in which I had lived for five whole years.

To proceed. Amaurotum is situated on the gentle slope of a hill and is almost four-square in outline. Its breadth is about two miles starting just below the crest of the hill and running down to the river Anydrus; its length along the river is somewhat more than its breadth.

The Anydrus rises eighty miles above Amaurotum from a spring not very large; but, being increased in size by several tributaries, two of which are of fair size, it is half a mile broad in front of the city. After soon becoming still broader and after running farther for sixty miles, it falls into the ocean. Through the whole distance between the city and the sea, and even above the city for some miles, the tide alternately flows in for six whole hours and then ebbs with an equally speedy current. When the sea comes in, it fills the whole bed of the Anydrus with its water for a distance of thirty miles, driving the river back. At such times it turns the water salt for some distance farther, but above that point the river grows gradually fresh and passes the city uncontaminated. When the ebb comes, the fresh and pure water extends down almost to the mouth of the river.

The city is joined to the opposite bank of the river not by a bridge built on wooden pillars or piles but by one magnificently arched with stonework. It is situated in the quarter which is farthest from the sea so that ships may pass along the whole of that side of the city without hindrance.

They have also another river, not very large, but very gentle and pleasant, which rises out of the same hill whereon the city is built and runs down through its middle into the river Anydrus. The head and source of this river just outside the city has been connected with it by outworks, lest in case of hostile attack the water might be cut off and diverted or polluted. From this point the water is distributed by conduits made of baked clay into various parts of the lower town. Where the ground makes that course impossible, the rain water collected in capacious cisterns is just as useful.

The city is surrounded by a high and broad wall with towers and ravelins at frequent intervals. A moat, dry but deep and wide and made impassable by thorn hedges, surrounds the fortifications on three sides; on the fourth the river itself takes the place of the moat.

The streets are well laid out both for traffic and for protection against the winds. The buildings, which are far from mean, are set together in a long row, continuous through the block and faced by a corresponding one. The house fronts of the respective blocks are divided by an avenue twenty feet broad. On the rear of the houses, through the whole length of the block, lies a broad garden enclosed on all sides by the backs of the blocks. Every home has not only a door into the street but a back door into the garden. What is more, folding doors, easily opened by hand and then closing of themselves, give admission to anyone. As a result, nothing is private property anywhere. Every ten years they actually exchange their very homes by lot.

The Utopians are very fond of their gardens. In them they have vines, fruits, herbs, flowers, so well kept and flourishing that I never saw anything more fruitful and more tasteful anywhere. Their zest in keeping them is increased not merely by the pleasure afforded them but by the keen competition between blocks as to which will have the best kept garden. Certainly you cannot readily find anything in the whole city more productive of profit and pleasure to the citizens. There is nothing which their founder seems to have cared so much for as these gardens.

In fact, they report that the whole plan of the city had been sketched at the very beginning by Utopus himself. He left to posterity, however, to add the adornment and other improvements for which he saw one lifetime would hardly suffice. Their annals, embracing the history of 1760 years, are preserved carefully and conscientiously in writing. Here they find stated that at first the houses were low, mere cabins and huts, haphazardly made with any wood to hand, with mud-plastered walls. They had thatched the steeply sloping roofs with straw.

But now all the homes are of handsome appearance with three stories. The exposed faces of the walls are made of stone or cement or brick, rubble being used as filling for the empty space between the walls. The roofs are flat and covered with a kind of cement which is cheap but so well mixed that it is impervious to fire and superior to lead in defying the damage caused by storms. They keep the winds out of their windows by glass (which is in very common use in Utopia) or sometimes by thin linen smeared with translucent oil or amber. The advantage is twofold: the device results in letting more light in and keeping more wind out.

The Officials

Every thirty families choose annually an official whom in their ancient language they call a syphogrant but in their newer a phylarch. Over ten syphogrants with their families is set a person once called a tranibor but now a protophylarch. The whole body of syphogrants, in number two hundred, having sworn to choose the man whom they judge most useful, by secret balloting appoint a governor, specifically one of the four candidates named to them by the people, for one is selected out of each of the four quarters of the city to be commended to the senate.

The governor holds office for life, unless ousted on suspicion of aiming at a tyranny. The tranibors are elected annually but are not changed without good reason. The other officials all hold their posts for one year.

The tranibors enter into consultation with the governor every other day and sometimes, if need arises, oftener. They take counsel about the commonwealth. If there are any disputes between private persons—there are very few—they settle them without loss of time. They always admit to the senate chamber two syphogrants, and different ones every day. It is provided that nothing concerning the commonwealth be ratified if it has not been discussed in the senate three days before the passing of the decree. To take counsel on matters of common interest outside the senate or the popular assembly is considered a capital offense. The object of these measures, they say, is to prevent it from being easy, by a conspiracy between the governor and the tranibors and by tyrannous oppression of the people, to change the order of the commonwealth. Therefore whatever is considered important is laid before the assembly of the syphogrants who, after informing their groups of families, take counsel together and report their decision to the senate. Sometimes the matter is laid before the council of the whole island.

In addition, the senate has the custom of debating nothing on the same day on which it is first proposed but of putting it off till the next meeting. This is their rule lest anyone, after hastily blurting out the first thought that popped into his head, should afterwards give more thought to defending his opinion than to supporting what is for the good of the commonwealth, and should prefer to jeopardize the public welfare rather than to risk his reputation through a wrongheaded and misplaced shame, fearing he might be thought to have shown too little foresight at the first—though he should have been enough foresighted at the first to speak with prudence rather than with haste!

Occupations

Agriculture is the one pursuit which is common to all, both men and women, without exception. They are all instructed in it from childhood, partly by principles taught in school, partly by field trips to the farms closer to the city as if for recreation. Here they do not merely look on, but, as opportunity arises for bodily exercise, they do the actual work.

Besides agriculture (which is, as I said, common to all), each is taught one particular craft as his own. This is generally either wool-working or linen-making or masonry or metal-working or carpentry. There is no other pursuit which occupies any number worth mentioning. As for clothes, these are of one and the same pattern throughout the island and down the centuries, though there is a distinction between the sexes and between the single and married. The garments are comely to the eye, convenient for bodily movement, and fit for wear in heat and cold. Each family, I say, does its own tailoring.

Of the other crafts, one is learned by each person, and not the men only, but the women too. The latter as the weaker sex have the lighter occupations and generally work wool and flax. To the men are committed the remaining more laborious crafts. For the most part, each is brought up in his father's craft, for which most have a natural inclination. But if anyone is attracted to another occupation, he is transferred by adoption to a family pursuing that craft for which he has a liking. Care is taken not only by his father but by the authorities, too, that he will be assigned to a grave and honorable householder. Moreover, if anyone after being thoroughly taught one craft desires another also, the same permission is given. Having acquired both, he practices his choice unless the city has more need of the one than of the other.

The chief and almost the only function of the syphogrants is to manage and provide that no one sit idle, but that each apply himself industriously to his trade, and yet that he be not wearied like a beast of burden with constant toil from early morning till late at night. Such wretchedness is worse than the lot of slaves, and yet it is almost everywhere the life of workingmen—except for the Utopians. The latter divide the day and night into twenty-four equal hours and assign only six to work. There are three before noon, after which they go to dinner. After dinner, when they have rested for two hours in the afternoon, they again give three to work and finish up with supper. Counting one o'clock as beginning at midday, they go to bed about eight o'clock, and sleep claims eight hours.

The intervals between the hours of work, sleep, and food are left to every man's discretion, not to waste in revelry or idleness, but to devote the time free from work to some other occupation according to taste. These periods are commonly devoted to intellectual pursuits. For it is their custom that public lectures are daily delivered in the hours before daybreak. Attendance is compulsory only for those who have been specially chosen to devote themselves to learning. A great number of all classes, however, both males and females, flock to hear the lectures, some to one and some to another, according to their natural inclination. But if anyone should prefer to devote this time to his trade, as is the case with many minds which do not reach the level for any of the higher intellectual disciplines, he is not hindered; in fact, he is even praised as useful to the commonwealth.

After supper they spend one hour in recreation, in summer in the gardens, in winter in the common halls in which they have their meals. There they either play music or entertain themselves with conversation. Dice and that kind of foolish and ruinous game they are not acquainted with. They do play two games not unlike chess. The first is a battle of numbers in which one number plunders another. The second is a game in which the vices fight a pitched battle with the virtues. In the latter is exhibited very cleverly, to begin with, both the strife of the vices with one another and their concerted opposition to the virtues; then, what vices are opposed to what virtues, by what forces they assail them openly, by what stratagems they attack them indirectly, by what safeguards the virtues check the power of the vices, by what arts they frustrate their designs; and, finally, by what means the one side gains the victory.

But here, lest you be mistaken, there is one point you must examine more closely. Since they devote but six hours to work, you might possibly think the consequence to be some scarcity of necessities. But so far is this from being the case that the aforesaid time is not only enough but more than enough for a supply of all that is requisite for either the necessity or the convenience of living. This phenomenon you too will understand if you consider how large a part of the population in other countries exists without working. First, there are almost all the women, who constitute half the whole; or, where the women are busy, there as a rule the men are snoring in their stead. Besides, how great and how lazy is the crowd of priests and so-called religious! Add to them all the rich, especially the masters of estates, who are commonly termed gentlemen and noblemen. Reckon with them their retainers—I mean, that whole rabble of good-for-nothing swashbucklers. Finally, join in the lusty and sturdy beggars who make some disease an excuse for idleness. You will certainly find far less numerous than you had supposed those whose labor produces all the articles that mortals require for daily use.

Now estimate how few of those who do work are occupied in essential trades. For, in a society where we make money the standard of everything, it is necessary to practice many crafts which are quite vain and superfluous, ministering only to luxury and licentiousness. Suppose the host of those who now toil were distributed over only as few crafts as the few needs and conveniences demanded by nature. In the great abundance of commodities which must then arise, the prices set on them would be too low for the craftsmen to earn their livelihood by their work. But suppose all those fellows who are now busied with unprofitable crafts, as well as all the lazy and idle throng, any one of whom now consumes as much of the fruits of other men's labors as any two of the workingmen, were all set to work and indeed to useful work. You can easily see how small an allowance of time would be enough and to spare for the production of all that is required by necessity or comfort (or even pleasure, provided it be genuine and natural).

The very experience of Utopia makes the latter clear. In the whole city and its neighborhood, exemption from work is granted to hardly five hundred of the total of men and women whose age and strength make them fit for work. Among them the syphogrants, though legally exempted from work, yet take no advantage of this privilege so that by their example they may the more readily attract the others to work. The same exemption is enjoyed by those whom the people, persuaded by the recommendation of the priests, have given perpetual freedom from labor through the secret vote of the syphogrants so that they may learn thoroughly the various branches of knowledge. But if any of these scholars falsifies the hopes entertained of him, he is reduced to the rank of workingman. On the other hand, not seldom does it happen that a craftsman so industriously employs his spare hours on learning and makes such progress by his diligence that he is relieved of his manual labor and advanced into the class of men of learning. It is out of this company of scholars that they choose ambassadors, priests, tranibors, and finally the governor himself, whom they call in their ancient tongue Barzanes but in their more modern language Ademus.

Nearly all the remaining populace being neither idle nor busied with useless occupations, it is easy to calculate how much good work can be produced in a very few hours. Besides the points mentioned, there is this further convenience that in most of the necessary crafts they do not require as much work as other nations. In the first place the erection or repair of buildings requires the constant labor of so many men elsewhere because what a father has built, his extravagant heir allows gradually to fall into ruin. As a result, what might have been kept up at small cost, his successor is obliged to erect anew at great expense. Further, often even when a house has cost one man a large sum, another is so fastidious that he thinks little of it. When it is neglected and therefore soon becomes dilapidated, he builds a second elsewhere at no less cost. But in the land of the Utopians, where everything has its proper place and the general welfare is carefully regulated, a new home on a new site is a rare event, for not only do they promptly repair any damage, but they even take care to prevent damage. What is the result? With the minimum of labor, buildings last very long, and masons and carpenters sometimes have scarcely anything to do, except that they are set to hew out timber at home and to square and prepare stone meantime so that, if any work be required, a building may the sooner be erected.

In the matter of clothing, too, see how little toil and labor is needed. First, while at work, they are dressed unpretentiously in leather or hide, which lasts for seven years. When they go out in public, they put on a cape to hide their comparatively rough working clothes. This garment is of one color throughout the island and that the natural color. Consequently not only is much less woolen cloth needed than elsewhere, but what they have is much less expensive. On the other hand, since linen cloth is made with less labor, it is more used. In linen cloth only whiteness, in woolen cloth only cleanliness, is considered. No value is set on fineness of thread. So it comes about that, whereas elsewhere one man is not satisfied with four or five woolen coats of different colors and as many silk shirts, and the more fastidious not even with ten, in Utopia a man is content with a single cape, lasting generally for two years. There is no reason, of course, why he should desire more, for if he had them he would not be better fortified against the cold nor appear better dressed in the least.

Wherefore, seeing that they are all busied with useful trades and are satisfied with fewer products from them, it even happens that when there is an abundance of all commodities, they sometimes take out a countless number of people to repair whatever public roads are in bad order. Often, too, when there is nothing even of this kind of work to be done, they announce publicly that there will be fewer hours of work. For the authorities do not keep the citizens against their will at superfluous labor since the constitution of their commonwealth looks in the first place to this sole object: that for all the citizens, as far as the public needs permit, as much time as possible should be withdrawn from the service of the body and devoted to the freedom and culture of the mind. It is in the latter that they deem the happiness of life to consist.

Social Relations

But now, it seems, I must explain the behavior of the citizens toward one another, the nature of their social relations, and the method of distribution of goods. Since the city consists of households, households as a rule are made up of those related by blood. Girls, upon reaching womanhood and upon being settled in marriage, go to their husbands' domiciles. On the other hand, male children and then grandchildren remain in the family and are subject to the oldest parent, unless he has become a dotard with old age. In the latter case the next oldest is put in his place.

But that the city neither be depopulated nor grow beyond measure, provision is made that no household shall have fewer than ten or more than sixteen adults; there are six thousand such households in each city, apart from its surrounding territory. Of children under age, of course, no number can be fixed. This limit is easily observed by transferring those who exceed the number in larger families into those that are under the prescribed number. Whenever all the families of a city reach their full quota, the adults in excess of that number help to make up the deficient population of other cities.

And if the population throughout the island should happen to swell above the fixed quotas, they enroll citizens out of every city and, on the mainland nearest them, wherever the natives have much unoccupied and uncultivated land, they found a colony under their own laws. They join with themselves the natives if they are willing to dwell with them. When such a union takes place, the two parties gradually and easily merge and together absorb the same way of life and the same customs, much to the great advantage of both peoples. By their procedures they make the land sufficient for both, which previously seemed poor and barren to the natives. The inhabitants who refuse to live according to their laws, they drive from the territory which they carve out for themselves. If they resist, they wage war against them. They consider it a most just cause for war when a people which does not use its soil but keeps it idle and waste nevertheless forbids the use and possession of it to others who by the rule of nature ought to be maintained by it.

If ever any misfortune so diminishes the number in any of their cities that it cannot be made up out of other parts of the island without bringing other cities below their proper strength (this has happened, they say, only twice in all the ages on account of the raging of a fierce pestilence), they are filled up by citizens returning from colonial territory. They would rather that the colonies should perish than that any of the cities of the island should be enfeebled.

But to return to the dealings of the citizens. The oldest, as I have said, rules the household. Wives wait on their husbands, children on their parents, and generally the younger on their elders.

Every city is divided into four equal districts. In the middle of each quarter is a market of all kinds of commodities. To designated market buildings the products of each family are conveyed. Each kind of goods is arranged separately in storehouses. From the latter any head of a household seeks what he and his require and, without money or any kind of compensation, carries off what he seeks. Why should anything be refused? First, there is a plentiful supply of all things and, secondly, there is no underlying fear that anyone will demand more than he needs. Why should there be any suspicion that someone may demand an excessive amount when he is certain of never being in want? No doubt about it, avarice and greed are aroused in every kind of living creature by the fear of want, but only in man are they motivated by pride alone—pride which counts it a personal glory to excel others by superfluous display of possessions. The latter vice can have no place at all in the Utopian scheme of things.

Next to the market place that I have mentioned are the food markets. Here are brought not only different kinds of vegetables, fruit, and bread but also fish and whatever is edible of bird and four-footed beast. Outside the city are designated places where all gore and offal may be washed away in running water. From these places they transport the carcasses of the animals slaughtered and cleaned by the hands of slaves. They do not allow their citizens to accustom themselves to the butchering of animals, by the practice of which they think that mercy, the finest feeling of our human nature, is gradually killed off. In addition, they do not permit to be brought inside the city anything filthy or unclean for fear that the air, tainted by putrefaction, should engender disease.

To continue, each street has spacious halls, located at equal distance from one another, each being known by a special name of its own. In these halls live the syphogrants. To each hall are assigned thirty families, fifteen on either side, to take their meals in common. The managers of each hall meet at a fixed time in the market and get food according to the number of persons in their individual charge.

Special care is first taken of the sick who are looked after in public hospitals. They have four at the city limits, a little outside the walls. These are so roomy as to be comparable to as many small towns. The purpose is twofold: first, that the sick, however numerous, should not be packed too close together in consequent discomfort and, second, that those who have a contagious disease likely to pass from one to another may be isolated as much as possible from the rest. These hospitals are very well furnished and equipped with everything conducive to health. Besides, such tender and careful treatment and such constant attendance of expert physicians are provided that, though no one is sent to them against his will, there is hardly anybody in the whole city who, when suffering from illness, does not prefer to be nursed there rather than at home.

After the supervisor for the sick has received food as prescribed by the physicians, then the finest of everything is distributed equally among the halls according to the number in each, except that special regard is paid to the governor, the high priest, and the tranibors, as well as to ambassadors and all foreigners (if there are any, but they are few and far between). Yet the latter, too, when they are in Utopia, have definite homes got ready for them.

To these halls, at the hours fixed for dinner and supper, the entire syphograncy assembles, summoned by the blast of a brazen trumpet, excepting persons who are taking their meals either in the hospitals or at home. No one is forbidden, after the halls have been served, to fetch food from the market to his home: they realize that no one would do it without good reason. For, though nobody is forbidden to dine at home, yet no one does it willingly since the practice is considered not decent and since it is foolish to take the trouble of preparing an inferior dinner when an excellent and sumptuous one is ready at hand in the hall nearby.

In this hall all menial offices which to some degree involve heavy labor or soil the hands are performed by slaves. But the duty of cooking and preparing the food and, in fine, of arranging the whole meal is carried out by the women alone, taking turns for each family. Persons sit down at three or more tables according to the number of the company. The men sit with their backs to the wall, the women on the outside, so that if they have any sudden pain or sickness, such as often happens to women with child, they may rise without disturbing the arrangements and go to the nurses.

The nurses sit separately with the infants in a dining room assigned for the purpose, never without a fire and a supply of clean water nor without cradles. Thus they can both lay the infants down and, when they wish, undo their wrappings and let them play freely by the fire. Each woman nurses her own offspring, unless prevented by either death or disease. When that happens, the wives of the syphogrants quickly provide a nurse and find no difficulty in doing so. The reason is that women who can do the service offer themselves with the greatest readiness since everybody praises this kind of pity and since the child who is thus fostered looks on his nurse as his natural mother. In the nurses' quarters are all children up to five years of age. All other minors, among whom they include all of both sexes below the age of marriage, either wait at table on the diners or, if they are not old and strong enough, stand by—and that in absolute silence. Both groups eat what is handed them from the table and have no other separate time for dining.

The syphogrant and his wife sit in the middle of the first table, which is the highest place and which allows them to have the whole company in view, for it stands crosswise at the farthest end of the dining room. Alongside them are two of the eldest, for they always sit four by four at all tables. But if there is a temple in the syphograncy, the priest and his wife so sit with the syphogrant as to preside. On both sides of them sit younger people, and next to them old people again, and so through the house those of the same age sit together and yet mingle with those of a different age. The reason for this practice, they say, is that the grave and reverend behavior of the old may restrain the younger people from mischievous freedom in word and gesture, since nothing can be done or said at table which escapes the notice of the old present on every side.

The trays of food are not served in order from the first place and so on, but all the old men, who are seated in conspicuous places, are served first with the best food, and then equal portions are given to the rest. The old men at their discretion give a share of their delicacies to their neighbors when there is not enough to go around to everybody in the house. Thus, due respect is paid to seniority, and yet all have an equal advantage.

They begin every dinner and supper with some reading which is conducive to morality but which is brief so as not to be tiresome. Taking their cue from the reading, the elders introduce approved subjects of conversation, neither somber nor dull. But they do not monopolize the whole dinner with long speeches: they are ready to hear the young men too, and indeed deliberately draw them out that they may test each one's ability and character, which are revealed in the relaxed atmosphere of a feast.

Their dinners are somewhat short, their suppers more prolonged, because the former are followed by labor, the latter by sleep and a night's rest. They think the night's rest to be more efficacious to wholesome digestion. No supper passes without music, nor does the dessert course lack delicacies. They burn spices and scatter perfumes and omit nothing that may cheer the company. For they are somewhat too much inclined to this attitude of mind: that no kind of pleasure is forbidden, provided no harm comes of it.

This is the common life they live in the city. In the country, however, since they are rather far removed from their neighbors, all take their meals in their own homes. No family lacks any kind of edible inasmuch as all the food eaten by the city dwellers comes from those who live in the country.

Roger Ascham: from *The Schoolmaster*

Roger Ascham was the author of *The Schoolmaster* (1570), one of the most famous treatises on education written by an Englishman during the Renaissance. Ascham was born in 1515 or 1516, the second son of John Ascham, overseer of estates for a prominent Yorkshire baron. He was while very young placed in the household of Sir Humphrey Wingfield, a Suffolk jurist, who held very advanced views about the proper education of children. In 1530 he entered St. John's College at Cambridge University, which rivalled Oxford for Greek and Latin studies and was a center for the discussion of continental evangelical theology. He took his A. B. degree in 1534, his M.A. degree in 1537, and stayed on as a reader in Greek and public orator of the university. In 1548 he left the university to become the tutor of fifteen-year-old Princess Elizabeth. He had on occasion taught the boy King Edward VI, but now he was the regular tutor of the future queen for a little less than two years. He found her intelligent and industrious and read Greek with her in the mornings, beginning with readings from the New Testament and patristic writers, and Latin in the afternoons. He tried to bring her up in the best tradition of Christian humanism, developing both her mind and her character by the most useful instruction from the classics and the essential teachings of the Christian faith.

Upon dismissal from the royal household he returned to Cambridge. He met the reformer Martin Bucer, who put him into contact with the great Strassburg educator Johannes Sturm, with whom he corresponded for eighteen years. In September, 1550, he accompanied Sir Richard Morrison, the English ambassador to the court of Emperor Charles V, to Augsburg and spent three years on the continent. In September, 1553, he returned briefly to Cambridge and then became Latin Secretary to Queen Mary and, after her death in 1558, to Queen Elizabeth, in whom he saw the full flowering of his early educational efforts. Ascham died of a devastating fever on December 30, 1568, leaving behind the manuscript of his great educational masterpiece, which his widow had published two years later.

In *The Schoolmaster* Ascham held up Elizabeth as a model according to which all well-born youth should be fashioned. The idea for the treatise grew out of a conversation which he had with another courtier in the Queen's chamber at Windsor Castle about whether a gentle approach or severe discipline is educationally the sounder method. When the courtier, Sir Richard Sackville asked Ascham to find an excellent tutor for his grandson, he came upon the idea of writing *The Schoolmaster,* describing what should be sought for in both teacher and pupil. The first half is concerned with fundamental principles of education and the second with "teaching the ready way to the Latin tongue." Ascham's theories of pedagogy were influenced by the Italian Renaissance views of Vittorino da Feltre, Battista Guarino, and the like. Like them he was concerned about the intellectual and moral development of pupils who would rule the state or advise rulers and who would hold high office in the church. The study of the liberal arts would not only help to cultivate the artistic and social graces, but would contribute to wisdom and character, and should be combined with a knowledge of public affairs. He added to the moral philosophy derived from the classics the Christian virtues and religious faith. The passages selected for inclusion here present his argument in favor of love and gentleness in teaching. Ascham believed in education, for, he wrote "Learning teacheth more in one year than experience in twenty, and learning teacheth safely, when experience maketh more miserable than wise."

The following selections are taken from *The Schoolmaster (1570) by Roger Ascham,* ed. Lawrence V. Ryan (Ithaca, New York: The Folger Shakespeare Library, 1967), 20–27, 31–45. Reprinted by permission of the Folger Shakespeare Library.

I will now declare at large why, in mine opinion, love is fitter than fear, gentleness better than beating, to bring up a child rightly in learning.

With the common use of teaching and beating in common schools of England I will not greatly contend; which if I did, it were but a small grammatical controversy neither belonging to heresy nor treason nor greatly touching God nor the prince, although, in very deed, in the end the good or ill bringing-up of children doth as much serve to the good or ill service of God, our prince, and our whole country as any one thing doth beside.

I do gladly agree with all good schoolmasters in these points: to have children brought to good perfectness in learning, to all honesty in manners; to have all faults rightly amended; to have every vice severely corrected; but for the order and way that leadeth rightly to these points we somewhat differ. For commonly many schoolmasters, some, as I have seen, more, as I have heard tell, be of so crooked a nature as, when they meet with a hard-witted scholar, they rather break him than bow him, rather mar him than mend him. For when the schoolmaster is angry with some other matter, then will he soonest fall to beat his scholar, and though he himself should be punished for his folly, yet must he beat some scholar for his pleasure, though there be no cause for him to do so nor yet fault in the scholar to deserve so. These, ye will say, be fond schoolmasters, and few they be that be found to be such. They be fond indeed, but surely overmany such be found everywhere. But this will I say, that even the wisest of your great beaters do as oft punish nature as they do correct faults. Yea, many times the better nature is sorer punished, for if one by quickness of wit take his lesson readily, another, by hardness of wit, taketh it not so speedily, the first is always commended, the other is commonly punished, when a wise schoolmaster should rather discreetly consider the right disposition of both their natures and not so much weigh what either of them is able to do now as what either of them is likely to do hereafter. For this I know, not only by reading of books in my study but also by experience of life abroad in the world, that those which be commonly the wisest, the best learned, and best men also, when they be old, were never commonly the quickest of wit when they were young. The causes why, amongst other, which be many, that move me thus to think, be these few which I will reckon. Quick wits commonly be apt to take, unapt to keep; soon hot and desirous of this and that, as cold and soon weary of the same again; more quick to enter speedily than able to pierce far, even like oversharp tools, whose edges be very soon turned. Such wits delight themselves in easy and pleasant studies and never pass far forward in high and hard sciences. And therefore the quickest wits commonly may prove the best poets but not the wisest orators—ready of tongue to speak boldly, not deep of judgment either for good counsel or wise writing. Also, for manners and life quick wits commonly be in desire newfangled, in purpose unconstant; light to promised anything, ready to forget everything, both benefit and injury, and thereby neither fast to friend nor fearful to foe; inquisitive of every trifle, not secret in greatest affairs; bold with any person, busy in every matter; soothing such as be present, nipping any that is absent; of nature, also, always flattering their betters, envying their equals, despising their inferiors; and by quickness of wit very quick and ready to like none so well as themselves.

Moreover, commonly men very quick of wit be also very light of conditions and thereby very ready of disposition to be carried overquickly by any light company to any riot and unthriftiness when they be young, and therefore seldom either honest of life or rich in living when they be old. For quick in wit and light in manners be either seldom troubled or very soon weary in carrying a very heavy purse. Quick wits also be, in most part of all their doings, overquick, hasty, rash, heady, and brainsick. These two last words, *heady* and *brainsick,* be fit and proper words, rising naturally of the matter and termed aptly by the condition of overmuch quickness of wit. In youth also they be ready scoffers, privy mockers, and ever over light and merry. In age, soon testy, very waspish, and always overmiserable. And yet few of them come to any great age by reason of their misordered life when they were young, but a great deal fewer of them come to show any great countenance or bear any great authority abroad in the world, but either live obscurely, men know not how, or die obscurely, men mark not when. They be like trees that show forth fair blossoms and broad leaves in springtime, but bring out small and not long lasting fruit in harvest time, and that only such as fall and rot before they be ripe and so never, or seldom, come to any good at all. For this ye shall find most true by experience, that amongst a number of quick wits in youth, few be found, in the end, either very fortunate for themselves or very profitable to serve the commonwealth, but decay and vanish, men know not which way, except a very few to whom peradventure blood and happy parentage may perchance purchase a long standing upon the stage. The which felicity, because it cometh by others' procuring, not by their own deserving, and stand by other men's feet and not by their own, what outward brag soever is borne by them is indeed, of itself and in wise men's eyes, of no great estimation.

Some wits, moderate enough by nature, be many times marred by overmuch study and use of some sciences, namely, music, arithmetic, and geometry. These sciences, as they sharpen men's wits overmuch, so they change men's manners oversore, if they be not moderately mingled and wisely applied to some good use of life. Mark all mathematical heads which be only and wholly bent to those sciences, how solitary they be themselves, how unfit to live with others, and how unapt to serve in the world. This is not only known now by common experience, but uttered long before by wise men's judgment and sentence. Galen saith, "Much music marreth men's manners," and Plato hath a notable place of the same thing in his books *De republica,* well marked also and excellently translated by Tully himself. Of this matter I wrote once more at large twenty years ago in my book of shooting. Now I thought but to touch it, to prove that overmuch quickness of wit, either given by nature or sharpened by study, doth not commonly bring forth either greatest learning, best manners, or happiest life in the end.

Contrariwise, a wit in youth that is not overdull, heavy, knotty, and lumpish, but hard, rough, and though somewhat staffish—as Tully wisheth, *otium quietum, non languidum,* and *negotium cum labore, non cum periculo*—such a wit, I say, if it be at first well handled by the mother and rightly smoothed and wrought as it should, not overthwartly and against the wood, by the schoolmaster, both for learning and whole course of living proveth always the best. In wood and stone, not the softest, but hardest, be always aptest for portraiture, both fairest for pleasure and most durable for profit. Hard wits be hard to receive but sure to keep, painful without weariness, heedful without wavering, constant without newfangledness; bearing heavy things, though not lightly, yet willingly; entering hard things, though not easily, yet deeply; and so come to that perfectness of learning in the end that quick wits seem in hope, but do not in deed, or else very seldom, ever attain unto. Also, for manners and life hard wits commonly are hardly carried either to desire every new thing or else to marvel at every strange thing, and therefore they be careful and diligent in their own matters, not curious and busy in other men's affairs; and so they become wise themselves and also are counted honest by others. They be grave, steadfast, silent of tongue, secret of heart; not hasty in making, but constant in keeping, any promise; not rash in uttering, but ware in considering, every matter, and thereby not quick in speaking, but deep of judgment, whether they write or give counsel, in all weighty affairs. And these be the men that become in the end both most happy for themselves and always best esteemed abroad in the world.

I have been longer in describing the nature, the good or ill success, of the quick and hard wit than perchance some will think this place and matter doth require. But my purpose was hereby plainly to utter what injury is offered to all learning and to the commonwealth also, first, by the fond father in choosing but, chiefly, by the lewd schoolmaster in beating and driving away the best natures from learning. A child that is still, silent, constant, and somewhat hard of wit is either never chosen by the father to be made a scholar, or else, when he cometh to the school, he is smally regarded, little looked unto. He lacketh teaching, he lacketh couraging, he lacketh all things; only he never lacketh beating, nor any word that may move him to hate learning, nor any deed that may drive him from learning to any other kind of living.

And when this sad-natured and hard-witted child is beat from his book and becometh after either student of the common law, or page in the court, or servingman, or bound prentice to a merchant or to some handicraft, he proveth in the end wiser, happier, and many times honester, too, than many of these quick wits do by their learning.

Learning is both hindered and injured too by the ill choice of them that send young scholars to the universities, of whom needs must come all our divines, lawyers, and physicians.

These young scholars be chosen commonly as young apples be chosen by children in a fair garden about St. James's tide. A child will choose a sweeting because it is presently fair and pleasant, and refuse a rennet because it is then green, hard, and sour, when the one if it be eaten doth breed both worms and ill humors, the other if it stand his time, be ordered and kept as it should, is wholesome of itself and helpeth to the good digestion of other meats. Sweetings will receive worms, rot and die on the tree, and never or seldom come to the gathering for good and lasting store.

For very grief of heart I will not apply the similitude, but hereby is plainly seen how learning is robbed of her best wits, first, by the great beating and, after, by the ill choosing of scholars to go to the universities. Whereof cometh partly that lewd and spiteful proverb, sounding to the great hurt of learning and shame of learned men, that "the greatest clerks be not the wisest men."

And though I, in all this discourse, seem plainly to prefer hard and rough wits before quick and light wits both for learning and manners, yet am I not ignorant that some quickness of wit is a singular gift of God, and so most rare amongst men, and namely such a wit as is quick without lightness, sharp without brittleness, desirous of good things without newfangledness, diligent in painful things without wearisomeness, and constant in good will to do all things well, as I know was in Sir John Cheke, and is in some that yet live, in whom all these fair qualities of wit are fully met together.

But it is notable and true that Socrates saith in Plato to his friend Crito: that that number of men is fewest which far exceed, either in good or ill, in wisdom or folly, but the mean betwixt both be the greatest number; which he proveth true in diverse other things, as in greyhounds, amongst which few are found exceeding great or exceeding little, exceeding swift or exceeding slow. And therefore, I speaking of quick and hard wits, I meant the common number of quick and hard wits, amongst the which for the most part the hard wit proveth many times the better learned, wiser, and honester man, and therefore do I the more lament that such wits commonly be either kept from learning by fond fathers or beat from learning by lewd schoolmasters.

And speaking thus much of the wits of children for learning, the opportunity of the place and goodness of the matter might require to have here declared the most special notes of a good wit for learning in a child, after the manner and custom of a good horseman who is skillful to know and able to tell others how, by certain sure signs, a man may choose a colt that is like to prove another day excellent for the saddle. And it is pity that commonly more care is had, yea, and that amongst very wise men, to find out rather a cunning man for their horse than a cunning man for their children. They say nay in word, but they do so in deed. For to the one they will gladly give a stipend of two hundred crowns by year and loathe to offer the other two hundred shillings. God that sitteth in heaven laugheth their choice to scorn and rewardeth their liberality as it should, for he suffereth them to have tame and well-ordered horse but wild and unfortunate children; and therefore in the end they find more pleasure in their horse than comfort in their children.

* * *

He that loveth to be praised for well-doing at his father's or master's hand. A child of this nature will earnestly love learning, gladly labor for learning, willingly learn of other, boldly ask any doubt. And thus, by Socrates' judgment, a good father and a wise schoolmaster should choose a child to make a scholar of that hath by nature the foresaid perfect qualities and comely furniture, both of mind and body; hath memory quick to receive, sure to keep, and ready to deliver; hath love to learning; hath lust to labor; hath desire to learn of others; hath boldness to ask any question; hath mind wholly bent to win praise by well-doing.

The two first points be special benefits of nature which nevertheless be well preserved and much increased by good order. But as for the five last, love, labor, gladness to learn of others, boldness to ask doubts, and will to win praise be won and maintained by the only wisdom and discretion of the schoolmaster. Which five points, whether a schoolmaster shall work sooner in a child by fearful beating or courteous handling, you that be wise judge.

Yet some men, wise indeed but in this matter, more by severity of nature than any wisdom at all, do laugh at us when we thus wish and reason that young children should rather be allured to learning by gentleness and love than compelled to learning by beating and fear. They say our "reasons serve only to breed forth talk and pass away time, but we never saw schoolmaster do so, nor never read of wise man that thought so."

Yes, forsooth, as wise as they be, either in other men's opinion or in their own conceit, I will bring the contrary judgment of him who, they themselves shall confess, was as wise as they are, or else they may be justly thought to have small wit at all; and that is Socrates, whose judgment in Plato is plainly this in these words: "No learning ought to be learned with bondage, for bodily labors wrought by compulsion hurt not the body, but any learning learned by compulsion tarrieth not long in the mind." And why? For whatsoever the mind doth learn unwillingly with fear, the same it doth quickly forget without care. And lest proud wits, that love not to be contraried but have lust to wrangle or trifle away truth, will say that Socrates meaneth not this of children's teaching, but of some other higher learning, hear what Socrates in the same place doth more plainly say: "And therefore, my dear friend, bring not up your children in learning by compulsion and fear, but by playing and pleasure." And you that do read Plato as ye should do well perceive that these be no questions asked by Socrates as doubts, but they be sentences, first affirmed by Socrates as mere truths, and after given forth by Socrates as right rules, most necessary to be marked and fit to be followed of all them that would have children taught as they should. And in this counsel, judgment, and authority of Socrates I will repose myself until I meet with a man of the contrary mind whom I may justly take to be wiser than I think Socrates was. Fond schoolmasters neither can understand nor will follow this good counsel of Socrates, but wise riders, in their office, can and will do both; which is the only cause that commonly the young gentlemen of England go so unwillingly to school and run so fast to the stable. For in very deed fond schoolmasters, by fear, do beat into them the hatred of learning, and wise riders, by gentle allurements, do breed up in them the love of riding. They find fear and bondage in schools; they feel liberty and freedom in stables; which causeth them utterly to abhor the one and most gladly to haunt the other. And I do not write this that, in exhorting to the one, I would dissuade young gentlemen from the other. Yea, I am sorry with all my heart that they be given no more to riding than they be, for of all outward qualities, to ride fair is most comely for himself, most necessary for his country, and the greater he is in blood, the greater is his praise, the more he doth exceed all other therein. It was one of the three excellent praises amongst the noble gentlemen the old Persians: always to say truth, to ride fair, and shoot well; and so it was engraven upon Darius' tomb, as Strabo beareth witness:

> Darius the king lieth buried here,
> Who in riding and shooting had never peer.

But to our purpose. Young men, by any means losing the love of learning, when by time they come to their own rule, they carry commonly from the school with them a perpetual hatred of their master and a continual contempt of learning. If ten gentlemen be asked why they forget so soon in court that which they were learning so long in school, eight of them, or let me be blamed, will lay the fault on their ill-handling by their schoolmasters.

Cuspinian doth report that that noble Emperor Maximilian would lament very oft his misfortune herein.

Yet some will say that children of nature love pastime and mislike learning because, in their kind, the one is easy and pleasant, the other hard and wearisome; which is an opinion not so true as some men ween. For the matter lieth not so much in the disposition of them that be young as in the order and manner of bringing-up by them that be old, nor yet in the difference of learning and pastime. For beat a child if he dance not well and cherish him though he learn not well, ye shall have him unwilling to go to dance and glad to go to his book. Knock him always when he draweth his shaft ill and favor him again though he fault at his book, ye shall have him very loath to be in the field and very willing to be in the school. Yea, I say more, and not of myself but by the judgment of those from whom few wise men will gladly dissent, that if ever the nature of man be given at any time more than other to receive goodness, it is in innocency of young years before that experience of evil have taken root in him. For the pure clean wit of a sweet young babe is, like the newest wax, most able to receive the best and fairest printing and, like a new bright silver dish never occupied, to receive and keep clean any good thing that is put into it.

And thus will in children, wisely wrought withal, may easily be won to be very willing to learn. And wit in children by nature, namely memory, the only key and keeper of all learning, is readiest to receive and surest to keep any manner of thing that is learned in youth; this, lewd and learned, by common experience, know to be most true. For we remember nothing so well when we be old as those things which we learned when we were young, and this is not strange but common in all nature's works. Every man sees (as I said before) new wax is best for printing, new clay fittest for working, new shorn wool aptest for soon and surest dyeing, new fresh flesh for good and durable salting. And this similitude is not rude, nor borrowed of the larder house, but out of his schoolhouse of whom the wisest in England need not be ashamed to learn. Young grafts grow not only soonest but also fairest, and bring always forth the best and sweetest fruit; young whelps learn easily to carry; young popinjays learn quickly to speak—and so, to be short, if in all other things, though they lack reason, sense, and life, the similitude of youth is fittest to all goodness surely nature in mankind is most beneficial and effectual in this behalf.

Therefore, if to the goodness of nature be joined the wisdom of the teacher in leading young wits into a right and plain way of learning, surely children, kept up in God's fear and governed by his grace, may most easily be brought well to serve God and country both by virtue and wisdom.

But if will and wit, by farther age, be once allured from innocency, delighted in vain sights, filed with foul talk, crooked with willfulness, hardened with stubbornness, and let loose to disobedience, surely it is hard with gentleness, but unpossible with severe cruelty, to call them back to good frame again. For where the one perchance may bend it, the other shall surely break it, and so instead of some hope leave an assured desperation and shameless contempt of all goodness, the farthest point in all mischief, as Xenophon doth most truly and most wittily mark.

Therefore, to love or to hate, to like or contemn, to ply this way or that way to good or to bad, ye shall have as ye use a child in his youth.

And one example, whether love or fear doth work more in a child for virtue and learning, I will gladly report; which may be heard with some pleasure and followed with more profit. Before I went into Germany, I came to Broadgate in Leicestershire to take my leave of that noble Lady Jane Grey, to whom I was exceeding much beholding. Her parents, the duke and the duchess, with all the household, gentlemen and gentlewomen, were hunting in the park. I found her in her chamber reading *Phaedon Platonis* in Greek, and that with as much delight as some gentleman would read a merry tale in Boccaccio. After salutation and duty done, with some other talk, I asked her why she would lose such pastime in the park. Smiling she answered me, "Iwis, all their sport in the park is but a shadow to that pleasure that I find in Plato. Alas, good folk, they never felt what true pleasure meant." "And how came you, madame," quoth I, "to this deep knowledge of pleasure, and what did chiefly allure you unto it, seeing not many women, but very few men, have attained thereunto?" "I will tell you," quoth she, "and tell you a truth which perchance ye will marvel at. One of the greatest benefits that ever God gave me is that he sent me so sharp and severe parents and so gentle a schoolmaster. For when I am in presence either of father or mother, whether I speak, keep silence, sit, stand, or go, eat, drink, be merry or sad, be sewing, playing, dancing, or doing anything else, I must do it, as it were, in such weight, measure, and number, even so perfectly as God made the world, or else I am so sharply taunted, so cruelly threatened, yea, presently sometimes, with pinches, nips, and bobs, and other ways which I will not name for the honor I bear them, so without measure misordered, that I think myself in hell till time come that I must go to Master Aylmer, who teacheth me so gently, so pleasantly, with such fair allurements to learning, that I think all the time nothing whilst I am with him. And when I am called from him, I fall on weeping because whatsoever I do else but learning is full of grief, trouble, fear, and whole misliking unto me. And thus my book hath been so much my pleasure, and bringeth daily to me more pleasure and more, that in respect of it all other pleasures in very deed be but trifles and troubles unto me." I remember this talk gladly, both because it is so worthy of memory and because also it was the last talk that ever I had, and the last time that ever I saw, that noble and worthy lady.

I could be overlong, both in showing just causes and in reciting true examples, why learning should be taught rather by love than fear. He that would see a perfect discourse of it, let him read that learned treatise which my friend Joannes Sturmius wrote *De institutione principis* to the Duke of Cleves.

The godly counsels of Solomon and Jesus, the son of Sirach, for sharp keeping-in and bridling of youth are meant rather for fatherly correction than masterly beating, rather for manners than for learning, for other places than for schools. For God forbid but all evil touches, wantonness, lying, picking, sloth, will, stubbornness, and disobedience should be with sharp chastisement daily cut away.

This discipline was well known and diligently used among the Grecians and old Romans, as doth appear in Aristophanes, Isocrates, and Plato, and also in the comedies of Plautus, where we see that children were under the rule of three persons: *praceptore, paedagogo, parente*. The schoolmaster taught him learning with all gentleness; the governor corrected his manners with much sharpness; the father held the stern of his whole obedience. And so he that used to teach did not commonly use to beat but remitted that over to another man's charge. But what shall we say when now in our days the schoolmaster is used both for *praeceptor* in learning and *paedagogus* in manners? Surely, I would he should not confound their offices but discreetly use the duty of both so that neither ill touches should be left unpunished nor gentleness in teaching any wise omitted. And he shall well do both if wisely he do appoint diversity of time and separate place for either purpose, using always such discreet moderation as the schoolhouse should be counted a sanctuary against fear, and very well learning a common pardon for ill-doing, if the fault of itself be not overheinous.

And thus the children, kept up in God's fear and preserved by his grace, finding pain in ill-doing and pleasure in well studying, should easily be brought to honesty of life and perfectness of learning, the only mark that good and wise fathers do wish and labor that their children should most busily and carefully shoot at.

There is another discommodity, besides cruelty in schoolmasters in beating away the love of learning from children, which hindereth learning and virtue and good bringing-up of youth, and namely young gentlemen, very much in England. This fault is clean contrary to the first. I wished before to have love of learning bred up in children; I wish as much now to have young men brought up in good order of living and in some more severe discipline than commonly they be. We have lack in England of such good order as the old noble Persians so carefully used, whose children to the age of twenty-one year were brought up in learning and exercises of labor, and that in such place where they should neither see that was uncomely nor hear that was unhonest. Yea, a young gentleman was never free to go where he would and do what he list himself, but under the keep and by the counsel of some grave governor, until he was either married or called to bear some office in the commonwealth.

And see the great obedience that was used in old time to fathers and governors. No son, were he never so old of years, never so great of birth, though he were a king's son, might not marry but by his father's, and mother's also, consent. Cyrus the Great, after he had conquered Babylon and subdued rich King Croesus with whole Asia Minor, coming triumphantly home, his uncle Cyaxares offered him his daughter to wife. Cyrus thanked his uncle and praised the maid, but for marriage he answered him with these wise and sweet words, as they be uttered by Xenophon: "Uncle Cyaxares, I commend the stock, I like the maid, and I allow well the dowry, but (saith he) by the counsel and consent of my father and mother I will determine farther of these matters."

Strong Samson also, in Scripture, saw a maid that liked him, but he spake not to her, but went home to his father and his mother and desired both father and mother to make the marriage for him. Doth this modesty, doth this obedience that was in great King Cyrus and stout Samson remain in our young men at this day? No, surely, for we live not longer after them by time than we live far different from them by good order. Our time is so far from that old discipline and obedience as now not only young gentlemen, but even very girls, dare without all fear, though not without open shame, where they list, and how they list, marry themselves in spite of father, mother, God, good order, and all. The cause of this evil is that youth is least looked unto when they stand most need of good keep and regard. It availeth not to see them well taught in young years and after, when they come to lust and youthful days, to give them license to live as they lust themselves. For if we suffer the eye of a young gentleman once to be entangled with vain sights, and the ear to be corrupted with fond or filthy talk, the mind shall quickly fall sick and soon vomit and cast up all the wholesome doctrine that he received in childhood, though he were never so well brought up before. And being once englutted with vanity, he will straightway loathe all learning and all good counsel to the same. And the parents, for all their great cost and charge, reap only in the end the fruit of grief and care.

This evil is not common to poor men, as God will have it, but proper to rich and great men's children, as they deserve it. Indeed from seven to seventeen young gentlemen commonly be carefully enough brought up, but from seventeen to seven-and-twenty (the most dangerous time of all a man's life and most slippery to stay well in) they have commonly the rein of all license in their own hand, and specially such as do live in the court. And that which is most to be marveled at, commonly the wisest and also best men be found the fondest fathers in this behalf. And if some good father would seek some remedy herein, yet the mother (if the house hold of our lady) had rather, yea, and will, too, have her son cunning and bold in making him to live trimly when he is young, than by learning and travail to be able to serve his prince and country both wisely in peace and stoutly in war when he is old.

The fault is in yourselves, ye noblemen's sons, and therefore ye deserve the greater blame that commonly the meaner men's children come to be the wisest counselors and greatest doers in the weighty affairs of this realm. And why? For God will have it so of his providence because ye will have it no otherwise by your negligence.

And God is a good God, and wisest in all his doings, that will place virtue and displace vice in those kingdoms where he doth govern. For he knoweth that nobility without virtue and wisdom is blood indeed but blood, truly, without bones and sinews, and so of itself, without the other, very weak to bear the burden of weighty affairs.

The greatest ship indeed commonly carrieth the greatest burden, but yet always with the greatest jeopardy, not only for the persons and goods committed unto it, but even for the ship itself, except it be governed with the greater wisdom.

But nobility governed by learning and wisdom is indeed most like a fair ship, having tide and wind at will, under the rule of a skillful master, when contrariwise a ship carried, yea, with the highest tide and greatest wind, lacking a skillful master, most commonly doth either sink itself upon sands or break itself upon rocks. And even so, how many have been either drowned in vain pleasure or overwhelmed by stout willfulness, the histories of England be able to afford overmany examples unto us. Therefore, ye great and noble men's children, if ye will have rightfully that praise and enjoy surely that place which your fathers have, and elders had and left unto you, ye must keep it as they gat it, and that is by the only way of virtue, wisdom, and worthiness.

For wisdom and virtue there be many fair examples in this court for young gentlemen to follow. But they be like fair marks in the field, out of a man's reach, too far off to shoot at well. The best and worthiest men, indeed, be sometimes seen but seldom talked withal; a young gentleman may sometime kneel to their person, smally use their company for their better instruction.

But young gentlemen are fain commonly to do in the court as young archers do in the field; that is, take such marks as be nigh them, although they be never so foul to shoot at. I mean, they be driven to keep company with the worst, and what force ill company hath to corrupt good wits the wisest men know best.

And not ill company only, but the ill opinion also of the most part, doth much harm, and namely of those which should be wise in the true deciphering of the good disposition of nature, of comeliness in courtly manners, and all right doings of men.

But error and fantasy do commonly occupy the place of truth and judgment. For if a young gentleman be demure and still of nature, they say he is simple and lacketh wit; if he be bashful and will soon blush, they call him a babyish and ill-brought-up thing, when Xenophon doth precisely note in Cyrus that his bashfulness in youth was the very true sign of his virtue and stoutness after; if he be innocent and ignorant of ill, they say he is rude and hath no grace, so ungraciously do some graceless men misuse the fair and godly word *grace*.

But if ye would know what grace they mean, go, and look, and learn amongst them, and ye shall see that it is, first, to blush at nothing. And blushing in youth, saith Aristotle, is nothing else but fear to do ill, which fear being once lustily frayed away from youth, then followeth to dare do any mischief, to contemn stoutly any goodness, to be busy in every matter, to be skillful in everything, to acknowledge no ignorance at all. To do thus in court is counted of some the chief and greatest grace of all and termed by the name of a virtue, called courage and boldness, when Crassus in Cicero teacheth the clean contrary, and that most wittily, saying thus: *Audere, cum bonis etiam rebus conjunctum, per se ipsum est magnopere fugiendum*. Which is to say, "To be bold, yea, in a good matter, is for itself greatly to be eschewed."

Moreover, where the swing goeth, there to follow, fawn, flatter, laugh, and lie lustily at other men's liking. To face, stand foremost, shove back, and, to the meaner man or unknown in the court, to seem somewhat solemn, coy, big, and dangerous of look, talk, and answer; to think well of himself, to be lusty in contemning of others, to have some trim grace in a privy mock. And in greater presence to bear a brave look; to be warlike, though he never looked enemy in the face in war; yet some warlike sign must be used, either a slovenly busking or an overstaring frounced head, as though out of every hair's top should suddenly start out a good big oath when need requireth. Yet praised be God, England hath at this time many worthy captains and good soldiers which be indeed so honest of behavior, so comely of conditions, so mild of manners, as they may be examples of good order to a good sort of others which never came in war. But to return where I left. In place, also, to be able to raise talk and make discourse of every rush; to have a very good will to hear himself speak; to be seen in palmistry, whereby to convey to chaste ears some fond or filthy talk.

And if some Smithfield ruffian take up some strange going, some new mowing with the mouth, some wrenching with the shoulder, some brave proverb, some fresh new oath that is not stale but will run round in the mouth, some new disguised garment or desperate hat, fond in fashion or garish in color, whatsoever it cost, how small soever his living be, by what shift soever it be gotten, gotten must it be and used with the first, or else the grace of it is stale and gone. Some part of this graceless grace was described by me in a little rude verse long ago:

> To laugh, to lie, to flatter, to face,
> Four ways in court to win men grace.
> If thou be thrall to none of these,
> Away, good peak-goose, hence, John Cheese!
> Mark well my word, and mark their deed,
> And think this verse part of thy creed.

Would to God this talk were not true and that some men's doings were not thus. I write not to hurt any, but to profit some; to accuse none, but monish such who, allured by ill counsel and following ill example, contrary to their good bringing-up and against their own good nature, yield overmuch to these follies and faults. I know many servingmen of good order and well staid, and again I hear say there be some servingmen do but ill service to their young masters. Yea, read Terence and Plautus advisedly over and yet shall find in those two wise writers, almost in every comedy, no unthrifty young man that is not brought thereunto by the subtle enticement of some lewd servant. And even now in our days Getae and Davi, Gnathos and many bold, bawdy Phormios, too, be pressing in to prattle on every stage, to meddle in every matter, when honest Parmenos shall not be heard, but bear small swing with their masters. Their company, their talk, their overgreat experience in mischief doth easily corrupt the best natures and best-brought-up wits.

But I marvel the less that these misorders be amongst some in the court, for commonly in the country also everywhere innocency is gone, bashfulness is banished, much presumption in youth, small authority in age, reverence is neglected, duties be confounded, and, to be short, disobedience doth overflow the banks of good order, almost in every place, almost in every degree of man.

Mean men have eyes to see, and cause to lament, and occasion to complain of these miseries, but other have authority to remedy them, and will do so, too, when God shall think time fit. For all these misorders be God's just plagues, by his sufferance brought justly upon us for our sins, which be infinite in number and horrible in deed, but namely, for the great abominable sin of unkindness. But what unkindness? Even such unkindness as was in the Jews in contemning God's voice, in shrinking from his word, in wishing back again for Egypt, in committing adultery and whoredom, not with the women, but with the doctrine, of Babylon, did bring all the plagues, destructions, and captivities that fell so oft and horribly upon Israel.

We have cause also in England to beware of unkindness, who have had in so few years the candle of God's word so oft lightened, so oft put out, and yet will venture by our unthankfulness in doctrine and sinful life to lose again light, candle, candlestick, and all.

God keep us in his fear; God graft in us the true knowledge of his word, with a forward will to follow it, and so to bring forth the sweet fruits of it, and then shall he preserve us by his grace from all manner of terrible days.

Desiderius Erasmus: from the *Colloquies*

The near perfect embodiment of nearly all the finest aspects of Christian humanism, Desiderius Erasmus belonged to all the nations of the North. He was born in 1469 in the Netherlands, studied in France, taught and visited in England several times, travelled and published in Italy, taught in Louvain, spent some fourteen years on the upper Rhine, in Basel and Freiburg, and spoke fondly of "our Germany." He was the prince of the humanists, the arbiter of good letters, honored by offers from the leading universities, and cultivated by the high and mighty such as King Henry VIII and King Francis I, Emperor Charles V, who put him on a pension, and Popes Leo X and Adrian VI. He carried on an enormous correspondence with people in all parts of Europe. No one equalled his knowledge of classical and patristic writings, which he edited in many volumes. He was a prolific author and wrote in a variety of literary forms.

His program of religious enlightenment called for sharp criticism of superstitious practices, replacing scholastic philosophy with Biblical moral philosophy, and promoting the simple philosophy of Christ. By way of criticism of abuses Erasmus wrote his *Praise of Folly,* which mocked idle ceremonies and superstition. In the *Colloquies,* which he began as an exercise book for boys studying Latin, he ridiculed superstitious religious practices, the veneration of relics, repetitious prayers, monkish ignorance, social fopperies, the false pride and belligerance of rulers. Two of the most famous of the *Colloquies,* a work which has been published in more than three hundred editions, *The Shipwreck* and *Charon,* are presented here.

The Shipwreck, one of the most popular of the *Colloquies* is an exquisite satire on medieval doctrine, scorning pretended piety and superstition. *Charon* expressed Erasmus' hatred of war and bloodshed in a way reminiscent of his treatise entitled *The Complaint of Peace.* The "three rulers of the world" are Emperor Charles V, Francis I of France, and Henry VIII of England. During the years preceding the publication of this colloquy in 1529, they had kept the world embroiled in nearly constant warfare. Erasmus attacks the folly and cupidity of rulers, compliant ecclesiastics who flatter rulers instead of opposing unjust wars, and mercenaries who lose their lives fighting for gold. Charon is ferrying the souls of the dead across the river Styx to the underworld.

Two of Erasmus' writings more than any others bring out the main emphases of his "philosophy of Christ," the *Enchiridion,* or *Handbook of a Christian Knight,* which he wrote in 1501, and the *Paraclesis* or *Entreaty,* which he published in 1516 as an introduction to his great edition of the New Testament.

The two selections are from *The Colloquies of Erasmus,* trans. Craig R. Thompson (Chicago: University of Chicago Press, 1965), 139–46, 390–94. Reprinted by permission of the University of Chicago Press. The *Paraclesis* is presented here in a new translation from the Latin by Dr. Lewis W. Spitz, Sr., based upon the text in *Desiderius Erasmus Roterodamus Ausgewählte Werke,* ed. Hajo Holborn (Munich: C. H. Beck'sche Verlagsbuchhandlung, 1964), 139–49.

The Shipwreck

satire of medieval doctrine

ANTONY, ADOLPH

ANTONY: Terrible tales you tell! That's what going to sea is like? God forbid any such notion should ever enter *my* head!

ADOLPH: Oh, no, what I've related up to this point is mere sport compared with what you'll hear now.

ANTONY: I've heard more than enough of disasters. When you're recalling them I shudder as if I myself were sharing the danger.

ADOLPH: To me, on the contrary, troubles over and done with are enjoyable.—On that same night something happened which in large part robbed the skipper of his hope of safety.

ANTONY: What, I beseech you?

ADOLPH: The night was partially clear, and on the topmast, in the "crow's-nest" (as I think they call it), stood one of the crew, looking out for land. Suddenly a fiery ball appeared beside him—a very bad sign to sailors when it's a single flame, lucky when it's double. Antiquity believed these were Castor and Pollux.

ANTONY: What's their connection with sailors? One was a horseman, the other a boxer.

ADOLPH: This is the poets' version. The skipper, who was by the helm, spoke up: "Mate"—that's what sailors call one another—"see your company alongside there?" "I see it," the man replied, "and I hope it's good luck!" Soon the blazing ball slid down the ropes and rolled straight up to the skipper.

ANTONY: Wasn't he scared out of his wits?

ADOLPH: Sailors get used to marvels. After stopping there a moment, it rolled the whole way round the ship, then dropped through the middle hatches and disappeared. Toward noon the storm began to rage more and more.—Ever seen the Alps?

ANTONY: Yes, I've seen them.

ADOLPH: Those mountains are warts compared with the waves of the sea. Whenever we were borne on the crest, we could have touched the moon with a finger; whenever dipped, we seemed to plunge through the gaping earth to hell.

ANTONY: What fools they are who trust themselves to the sea!

ADOLPH: Since the crew's struggle with the storm was hopeless, the skipper, pale as a ghost, at last came up to us.

ANTONY: His pallor portends some great disaster.

ADOLPH: "Friends," he says, "I'm no longer master of my ship; the winds have won. The only thing left to do is to put our hope in God and each one prepare himself for the end."

ANTONY: Truly a Scythian speech.

ADOLPH: "But first of all," he says, "the ship must be unloaded; deadly necessity compels it. Better to save life at the cost of goods than for both to perish together." The plain fact convinced them. A lot of luggage filled with costly wares was tossed overboard.

ANTONY: This was sacrificing for sure!

ADOLPH: On board was a certain Italian who had served as legate to the King of Scotland. He had a chest full of silver plate, rings, cloth, and silk robes.

ANTONY: He didn't want to come to terms with the sea?

ADOLPH: No, instead he wanted to go down with his beloved treasures or else be saved along with them. So he protested.

ANTONY: What did the skipper do?

ADOLPH: "We're quite willing to let you perish alone with your goods," said he, "but it's not fair for all of us to be endangered because of your chest. Rather, we'll throw you and the chest together into the sea."

ANTONY: True sailor's talk!

ADOLPH: So the Italian, too, threw his goods overboard, cursing away by heaven and hell because he had entrusted his life to so barbarous an element.

ANTONY: I recognize the Italian accent.

ADOLPH: Soon afterward the winds, unappeased by our offerings, broke the ropes and tore the sails to pieces.

ANTONY: Catastrophe!

ADOLPH: At that moment the skipper comes to us again.

ANTONY: To make a speech?

ADOLPH: "Friends"—he begins by way of greeting—"the hour warns each of us to commend himself to God and prepare for death." Questioned by some familiar with seamanship as to how many hours he thought he could keep the ship afloat, he replied that he couldn't promise anything, but not more than three hours.

ANTONY: This speech was even sterner than the first one.

ADOLPH: After saying this, he orders all the shrouds to be slashed and the mast sawn off down to its socket and thrown into the sea, together with the spars.

ANTONY: Why this?

ADOLPH: With the sail ruined or torn, the mast was a useless burden. Our whole hope was in the tiller.

ANTONY: What about the passengers meanwhile?

ADOLPH: There you'd have seen what a wretched plight we were in: the sailors singing *Salve Regina,* praying to the Virgin Mother, calling her Star of the Sea, Queen of Heaven, Mistress of the World, Port of Salvation, flattering her with many other titles the Sacred Scriptures nowhere assign to her.

ANTONY: What has she to do with the sea? She never went voyaging, I believe.

ADOLPH: Formerly Venus was protectress of sailors, because she was believed to have been born of the sea. Since she gave up guarding them, the Virgin Mother has succeeded this mother who was not a virgin.

ANTONY: You're joking.

ADOLPH: Prostrating themselves on the deck, some worshiped the sea, pouring whatever oil they had on the waves, flattering it no differently from the way we do a wrathful sovereign.

ANTONY: What did they say?

ADOLPH: "O most merciful sea, O most kind sea, O most splendid sea, O most lovely sea, have pity on us! Save us!" Many songs of this kind they sang to the sea—which was deaf.

ANTONY: Absurd superstition! What did the rest do?

ADOLPH: Some did nothing but get sick. Many made vows. There was an Englishman who promised heaps of gold to the Virgin of Walsingham if he reached shore alive. Some promised many things to the wood of the Cross at such and such a place; others, again, to that in some other place. The same with respect to the Virgin Mary, who reigns in many places; and they think the vow worthless unless you specify the place.

ANTONY: Ridiculous! As if saints don't dwell in heaven.

ADOLPH: Some pledged themselves to become Carthusians. There was one who promised to journey to St. James at Compostella barefoot, bareheaded, clad only in a coat of mail, begging his bread besides.

ANTONY: Did nobody remember Christopher?

ADOLPH: I couldn't help laughing as I listened to one chap, who in a loud voice (for fear he wouldn't be heard) promised a wax taper as big as himself to the Christopher in the tallest church in Paris—a mountain rather than a statue. While he was proclaiming this at the top of his lungs, insisting on it again and again, an acquaintance who chanced to be standing by nudged him with his elbow and cautioned: "Be careful what you promise. Even if you sold all your goods at auction, you couldn't pay for it." Then the other, lowering his voice—so Christopher wouldn't overhear him, of course!—said, "Shut up, you fool. Do you suppose I'm serious? If I once touch land, I won't give him a tallow candle."

ANTONY: Blockhead! Batavian, I suppose.

ADOLPH: No, a Zeelander.

ANTONY: I'm surprised nobody thought of the apostle Paul, who was once shipwrecked himself, and when the ship broke leaped overboard and reached land. No stranger to misfortune, he knew how to help those in distress.

ADOLPH: Paul wasn't mentioned.

ANTONY: Did they pray all the while?

ADOLPH: Strenuously. One chanted *Salve Regina,* another *Credo in Deum.* Some had certain queer beads, like charms, to ward off danger.

ANTONY: How devout men are made by suffering! In prosperity the thought of God or saint never enters their heads. What were you doing all this time? Making vows to any of the saints?

ADOLPH: Not at all.

ANTONY: Why?

ADOLPH: Because I don't make deals with saints. For what else is that but a bargain according to the form "I'll give this if you do that" or "I'll do this if you'll do that"; "I'll give a taper if I can swim"; "I'll go to Rome if you save me."

ANTONY: But you called on some saint for help?

ADOLPH: Not even that.

ANTONY: But why?

ADOLPH: Because heaven's a large place. If I entrust my safety to some saint—St. Peter, for example, who perhaps will be first to hear, since he stands at the gate—I may be dead before he meets God and pleads my cause.

ANTONY: What did you do, then?

ADOLPH: Went straight to the Father himself, reciting the Pater Noster. No saint hears sooner than he or more willingly grants what is asked.

ANTONY: But didn't your conscience accuse you when you did this? Weren't you afraid to entreat the Father, whom you had offended by so many sins?

ADOLPH: To speak frankly, my conscience did deter me somewhat. But I soon recovered my spirits, thinking to myself, "No father is so angry with his son that, if he sees him in danger in a stream or lake, he won't grasp him by the hair and pull him out." Of all the passengers, none behaved more calmly than a certain woman who was suckling a baby.

ANTONY: What did she do?

ADOLPH: She was the only one who didn't scream, weep, or make promises; she simply prayed in silence, clasping her little boy.—While the ship was continually battered by the sea, the skipper undergirded it with ropes both fore and aft, for fear it might break to pieces.

ANTONY: Miserable protection!

ADOLPH: Meantime an old priest, a man of sixty named Adam, jumped up. Stripped to his underclothes, and with his shoes and leggings removed, he urged us all to prepare likewise for swimming. And standing so in the middle of the ship, he preached to us a sermon from Gerson on the five truths concerning the benefit of confession. He urged everyone to be ready both for life and for death. A Dominican was there, too. Those who wished confessed to these two.

ANTONY: What did you do?

ADOLPH: Seeing everything in an uproar, I confessed silently to God, condemning my unrighteousness before him and imploring his mercy.

ANTONY: Where would you have gone had you died in that condition?

ADOLPH: That I left to God the Judge, for I was unwilling to be judge of my own cause; nevertheless a strong hope possessed my mind the whole time.—While all this is going on, the captain returns to us in tears. "Get ready," says he, "because the ship will be useless to us in a quarter of an hour." It was already shattered in some places and drawing water. Soon afterward a sailor reports seeing a church tower in the distance and beseeches us to appeal to whichever saint took that church under his protection. Everyone falls to his knees and prays to the unknown saint.

ANTONY: If you had invoked him by name, he might have heard.

ADOLPH: We didn't know his name. As much as he could, meanwhile, the skipper steered the ship in that direction. By now it was breaking up, taking in water everywhere, and clearly about to fall to pieces had it not been undergirded with ropes.

ANTONY: A bad state of affairs!

ADOLPH: We were carried far enough in for the inhabitants of the place to see our plight. Groups of them rushed to the shore, and taking off hats and coats and sticking them on poles urged us toward themselves and by lifting their arms to heaven indicated their pity for our lot.

ANTONY: I'm waiting to hear what happened.

ADOLPH: The whole ship was filled with water now, so that thereafter we would be no safer in ship than in sea.

ANTONY: At that moment you had to fall back on your last hope.

ADOLPH: On suffering, rather. The crew released the lifeboat and lowered it into the sea. Everyone tried to hurl himself into it, the sailors protesting in the uproar that the lifeboat would not hold such a crowd, but that everybody should grab what he could and swim. The situation did not allow leisurely plans. One person snatches an oar, another a boathook, another a tub, another a bucket, another a plank; and, each relying on his own resources, they commit themselves to the waves.

ANTONY: What happened during this time to that poor woman, the only one who did not weep and wail?

ADOLPH: She was the first of them all to reach shore.

ANTONY: How could she do that?

ADOLPH: We had put her on a warped plank and tied her in such a way that she couldn't easily fall off. We gave her a small board to use as a paddle, wished her luck, and shoved her off into the waves, pushing with a pole to get her clear of the ship, where the danger lay. Holding her baby with her left hand, she paddled with the right.

ANTONY: Brave woman!

ADOLPH: Since nothing else remained, one man seized a wooden statue of the Virgin Mother, now rotten and mouse-eaten, and, putting his arms around it, began to swim.

ANTONY: Did the lifeboat come through safely?

ADOLPH: The first to go down. And thirty people had thrown themselves into it.

ANTONY: What mishap caused that?

ADOLPH: Before it could get away it was overturned by the lurching of the big ship.

ANTONY: A cruel business! What then?

ADOLPH: While looking out for others, I nearly perished myself.

ANTONY: How so?

ADOLPH: Because there was nothing left for me to swim on.

ANTONY: Cork would have been useful there.

ADOLPH: In that emergency I would rather have had plain cork tree than golden candlestick. Casting about, I finally thought of the stump of the mast. Since I couldn't pry it loose by myself, I enlisted the help of another man. Supporting ourselves on this, we put to sea, I holding the right end and he the left. While we were tossing about in this way, that priest who preached on board threw himself in our midst—on our shoulders. Big fellow, too. "Who's the third?" we yell. "He'll be the death of us all." He, on the other hand, says calmly, "Cheer up, there's plenty of room. God will help us."

ANTONY: Why was he so late in starting to swim?

ADOLPH: Oh, he was to be in the lifeboat along with the Dominican (for everybody conceded this much honor to him), but although they had confessed to each other on the ship, nevertheless some condition—I don't know what—had been forgotten. There on the edge of the ship they confess anew, and each lays his hand on the other. While they're doing this, the lifeboat goes down. Adam told me this.

ANTONY: What became of the Dominican?

ADOLPH: According to Adam, after entreating the aid of the saints he threw off his clothes and began to swim.

ANTONY: Which saints did he invoke?

ADOLPH: Dominic, Thomas, Vincent, and I don't know which Peter, but first and foremost he placed his trust in Catherine of Siena.

ANTONY: Christ didn't come to mind?

ADOLPH: This is what the priest told me.

ANTONY: He'd have swum better if he hadn't thrown off his sacred cowl. With that put aside, how could Catherine of Siena recognize him?—But go on with what happened to you.

ADOLPH: While we were still tossing beside the ship, which was rolling from side to side at the will of the waves, the broken rudder smashed the thigh of the man who was holding on to the left end of the stump. So he was torn away. The priest, saying a prayer *Requiem aeternam* for him, took his place, urging me to keep hold of my end with confidence and kick my feet vigorously. We were swallowing a lot of salt water all this while. Thus Neptune saw to it that we had not only a salty bath but even a salty drink, though the priest showed us a remedy for that.

ANTONY: What, please?

ADOLPH: Every time a wave came rushing upon us, he turned the back of his head to it and kept his mouth closed.

ANTONY: That's a doughty old fellow you describe.

ADOLPH: When we'd made some progress after swimming a while, the priest, who was very tall, said, "Cheer up, I'm touching bottom!" I didn't dare hope for such great luck. "We're too far from shore to hope for bottom." "Oh, no," he replied, "I feel land with my feet." "Maybe it's something from the chests that the sea has rolled this way." "No," he said, "I feel land plainly by the scraping of my toes." After we had swum a while longer in this direction and he again touched bottom, "Do what you think best," he said, "I'm giving up the whole mast to you and trusting myself to the bottom"; and thereupon, after waiting for the waves to subside, he went on foot as fast as he could. When the waves overtook him again, he resisted by clasping his knees with his hands and putting his head under water, as divers and ducks do; when the waves receded, up he popped and moved on. When I saw he was successful at this, I imitated him. Standing on the coast were men—hardy fellows and used to the water—who by means of extremely long poles, held out from one to the other, braced themselves against the force of the waves; so that the one farthest out held his pole to the swimmer. When this was grasped, all heaved toward shore and the swimmer was hauled safely to dry land. A number were rescued by this device.

ANTONY: How many?

ADOLPH: Seven, but two of these died when brought to a fire.

ANTONY: How many were you in the ship?

ADOLPH: Fifty-eight.

ANTONY: O cruel sea! At least it might have been satisfied with a tenth, which is enough for priests. From so large a number how few returned!

ADOLPH: We were treated with wonderful kindness by the people there, who looked after our needs with astonishing eagerness: lodging, fire, food, clothing, money for travel.

ANTONY: What people were they?

ADOLPH: Hollanders.

ANTONY: No people could be more kindly, though they do have savage neighbors. I guess you won't visit Neptune very soon again after this.

ADOLPH: No, not unless God takes my reason from me.

ANTONY: And I for my part would rather hear such tales than experience the events at first hand.

Charon

CHARON, THE SPIRIT ALASTOR

CHARON: Why the hustle and bustle, Alastor?

ALASTOR: Well met, Charon! I was speeding to you.

CHARON: What's new?

ALAS.: I bring news that will delight you and Proserpina.

CHARON: Out with it, then. Unload it.

ALAS.: The Furies have done their work zealously as well as successfully. Not a corner of the earth have they left unravaged by hellish disasters, dissensions, wars, robberies, plagues: so much so that now, with their snakes let loose, they're completely bald. Drained of poisons, they roam about looking for whatever vipers and asps they can find, since they're as smooth-headed as an egg—not a hair on their crowns nor a drop of good poison in their breasts. So have your boat and oars ready, for there'll soon be such a crowd of shades coming that I fear you can't ferry them all.

CHARON: No news to me.

ALAS.: Where did you learn it?

CHARON: Ossa brought it more than two days ago.

ALAS.: Can't get ahead of that goddess! But why are you loitering here without your boat, then?

CHARON: Business trip: I came here to get a good, strong trireme ready. My galley's so rotten with age and so patched up that it won't do for this job if what Ossa told me is true. Though what need was there of Ossa? The plain fact of the matter demands it: I've had a shipwreck.

ALAS.: You *are* dripping wet, undoubtedly. I thought you were coming back from a bath.

CHARON: Oh, no, I've been swimming out of the Stygian swamp.

ALAS.: Where have you left the shades?

CHARON: Swimming with the frogs.

ALAS.: But what did Ossa report?

CHARON: That the three rulers of the world, in deadly hatred, clash to their mutual destruction. No part of Christendom is safe from the ravages of war, for those three have dragged all the rest into alliance.

They're all in such a mood that none of them is willing to yield to another. Neither Dane nor Pole nor Scot nor Turk, in fact, is at peace; catastrophes are building up; the plague rages everywhere, in Spain, Britain, Italy, France. In addition, there's a new epidemic, born of difference of opinion. It has so corrupted everybody's mind that sincere friendship exists nowhere, but brother distrusts brother and husband and wife disagree. I've hopes of a splendid slaughter in the near future, too, if the war of tongues and pens comes to actual blows.

ALAS.: Ossa reported everything quite correctly, for as the constant attendant and assistant of the Furies (who have never shown themselves more deserving of their name) I've seen more than this with my own eyes.

CHARON: But there's danger that some devil may turn up and preach peace all of a sudden—and mortal minds are fickle. I hear there's a certain Polygraphus [Erasmus] up there who's incessantly attacking war with his pen and urging men to peace.

ALAS.: He's sung to deaf ears this long while. He once wrote a "Complaint of Peace O'erthrown"; now he's written the epitaph of peace dead and buried. On the other hand, there are some as helpful to our cause as the Furies themselves.

CHARON: Who are those?

ALAS.: Certain creatures in black and white cloaks and ash-gray tunics, adorned with plumage of various kinds. They never leave the courts of princes. They instil into their ears a love of war; they incite rulers and populace alike; they proclaim in their evangelical sermons that war is just, holy, and right. And—to make you marvel more at the audacity of the fellows—they proclaim the very same thing on both sides. To the French they preach that God is on the French side: he who has God to protect him cannot be conquered! To the English and Spanish they declare this war is not the Emperor's but God's: only let them show themselves valiant men and victory is certain! But if anyone *does* get killed, he doesn't perish utterly but flies straight up to heaven, armed just as he was.

CHARON: And people believe these fellows?

ALAS.: What can a pretense of religion not achieve? Youth, inexperience, thirst for glory, anger, and natural human inclination swallow this whole. People are easily imposed upon. And it's not hard to upset a cart that's ready to collapse of its own accord.

CHARON: I'll be glad to reward these creatures!

ALAS.: Give them a fine dinner. They like nothing better.

CHARON: A dinner of mallows, lupines, and leeks. That's the only fare we have, as you know.

ALAS.: Oh, no, it must be partridges, capons, and pheasants if you wish to be an acceptable host.

CHARON: But what makes them such warmongers? Or what advantage are they afraid of losing?

ALAS.: They make more profit from the dying than from the living.

There are wills, Masses for kinsmen, bulls, and many other sources of revenue not to be despised. In short, they prefer to buzz in camp rather than in their own hives. War spawns many bishops who in peacetime weren't worth a penny.

Charon: They're smart.

Alas.: But why do you need a trireme?

Charon: I don't—if I want to be shipwrecked in the middle of the swamp again.

Alas.: Because of the crowd?

Charon: Of course.

Alas.: But you haul shades, not bodies. Now how light are shades?

Charon: They may be water skippers, but enough water skippers could sink a boat. Then too, you know, the boat is unsubstantial.

Alas.: But sometimes, I remember, when there was a crowd so large the boat couldn't hold them all, I saw three thousand shades hanging from your rudder and you didn't feel any weight.

Charon: Granted there are such souls, which departed little by little from bodies worn away by consumption or hectic fever. But those plucked on the sudden from heavy bodies bring a good deal of corporeal substance along with them. Apoplexy, quinsy, plague, but especially war, send this kind.

Alas.: Frenchmen or Spaniards don't weigh much, I suppose.

Charon: Much less than others, though even their souls are not exactly featherweight. But from well-fed Britons and Germans such shades come at times that lately I've hardly dared to ferry even ten, and unless I'd thrown them overboard I'd have gone down along with boat, rowers, and passage money.

Alas.: A terrible risk!

Charon: Meanwhile what do you think will happen when heavy lords, Thrasos, and swashbucklers come along?

Alas.: None of those who die in a just war come to you, I believe. For these, they say, fly straight to heaven.

Charon: Where they may fly to, I don't know. I *do* know one thing: that whenever a war's on, so many come to me wounded and cut up that I'd be surprised if any had been left on earth. They come loaded not only with debauchery and gluttony but even with bulls, benefices, and many other things.

Alas.: But they don't bring these along with them. The souls come to you naked.

Charon: True, but newcomers bring along dreams of such things.

Alas.: So dreams are heavy?

Charon: They weigh down my boat. Weigh down, did I say? They've already sunk it! Finally, do you imagine so many obols weigh nothing?

Alas.: Well, I suppose they *are* heavy if they're copper ones.

Charon: So I've decided to look out for a vessel strong enough for the load.

ALAS.: Lucky you!

CHARON: How so?

ALAS.: Because you'll soon grow rich.

CHARON: From a lot of shades?

ALAS.: Of course.

CHARON: If only they'd bring their riches with them! As it is, those in the boat who lament the kingdoms, prelacies, abbacies, and countless talents of gold they left up there bring me nothing but an obol. And so everything I've scraped together in three thousand years has to be laid out for one trireme.

ALAS.: If you want to make money you have to spend money.

CHARON: Yet mortals, as I hear, do business better: with Mercury's help they grow rich within three years.

ALAS.: But sometimes those same mortals go broke. Your profit is less but it's more certain.

CHARON: How certain I can't tell. If some god should turn up now and settle the affairs of princes, I'd be utterly ruined.

ALAS.: Don't give the matter a thought; just leave it to me. You've no reason to fear a peace within ten whole years. Only the Roman Pontiff is zealous in urging peace, but his efforts are wasted. Cities, too, weary of their troubles, complain bitterly. People—I don't know who they are —mutter that it's outrageous for human affairs to be turned topsy-turvy on account of the personal grudges or ambitions of two or three men. But the Furies, believe me, will defeat counsel, no matter how good it is.—Yet what need was there for you to ask this favor of those above? Haven't we workmen of our own? We have Vulcan, surely.

CHARON: Fine—if I wanted a bronze ship.

ALAS.: Labor's cheap.

CHARON: Yes, but we're short of timber.

ALAS.: What, aren't there any forests here?

CHARON: Even the groves in the Elysian fields have been used up.

ALAS.: What for?

CHARON: For burning shades of heretics. So that we've been forced of late to mine coal from the bowels of the earth.

ALAS.: What, can't those shades be punished at less expense?

CHARON: This was the decision of Rhadamanthus.

ALAS.: When you've bought your trireme, where will you get rowers?

CHARON: My job is to hold the tiller; the shades must row if they want passage.

ALAS.: But some haven't learned how to handle an oar.

CHARON: No distinction of persons with me: monarchs row and cardinals row, each in their turn, no less than common folk, whether they've learned or not.

ALAS.: Good luck in getting a trireme at a bargain! I won't hold you up any longer. I'll take the good news to Orcus. But say, Charon—

CHARON: What?

ALAS.: Hurry back, so the crowd won't quickly overwhelm you.

CHARON: Oh, you'll meet over two hundred thousand on the bank already, besides those swimming in the swamp. But I'll hurry as much as I can. Tell 'em I'll be there right away.

The Paraclesis of Erasmus

THE ENTREATY OF ERASMUS OF ROTTERDAM TO THE GRACIOUS READER

The noted Lactantius Firmianus [a famous fourth-century Christian author], whose eloquence, esteemed reader, Jerome greatly admired, and who was to become the defender of the Christian faith against the heathen, desired above all that eloquence approximating that of Tully [Cicero] might be given to him, since he regarded it as bold, I think, to wish for equally great eloquence. But if anything is gained by such wishes, I surely, while sounding the trumpet as a charge to battle and exhorting all mortals to the most sacred and salutary study of Christian philosophy, strongly desire that an eloquence might be given to me far different from Cicero's: an eloquence certainly much more effective, even if less embroidered than was his. Or rather, I would surely desire it, if such power of speech were ever given to anyone, which the fables of the ancient poets have recorded with regard to Mercury, who, as with a magic wand and divine cither, imposed sleep at will and took it away again, impelling whom he wished to the underworld and calling them back again from the underworld; or the power of speech which they have reported regarding Amphion and Orpheus, one of whom is pictured as moving rigid stones, the other as pulling up oaks and mountain ashtrees with the cither; or the power of speech which the Gauls attributed to their Ogmius, who led about all mortals anywhere he wished with little chains fastened from his tongue to their ears; or which antiquity, rich in fables, attributed to Marsya [a satyr who played the lute]; or surely, lest we tarry too long on fables, which Alcibiades attributed to Socrates and an old comedy to Pericles. Not such eloquence which merely titillates the ears with pleasure soon to perish, but an eloquence which leaves lasting strings in the minds of the hearers, which overpowers, which transforms, which sends the hearer away a much different person from the one it had received. The famous musician

Timothy, singing Dorian modes, is said habitually to have enflamed Alexander the Great to zeal for war. Nor in times past were people lacking who regarded nothing to be more effective than the entreaties that the Greeks call the epode type of lyric poem. But if there ever was an incantation of this kind, if there ever was a power of harmony which possessed true inspiration, if any Delphic oracle ever truly stirred the heart—that power I crave for my support at this time so that I might convince everyone of the most salutary thing of all. But it is rather to be desired that Christ Himself, whose cause it is, should move the strings of our cither so that this song might deeply affect and move the spirits of all, which no syllogisms or exclamations of rhetoricians are needed to effect. What we desire is that nothing should stand out more surely than truth itself, whose power of speech is the more effective, the simpler it is.

First of all, it is indeed not agreeable to reopen at the present time the complaint (one which is not entirely new, but, alas! only too just, perhaps never more so than in these times) that when mortal men are attending to their respective studies with such fervent spirits, this philosophy of Christ alone is ridiculed even by some Christians, is neglected by many, and is cultivated by a few, but coldly, not to say insincerely. But in all other disciplines that human diligence has produced, nothing is so concealed and backwards that the sagacity of genius has not explored it, nothing so difficult that restless industry has not mastered it. How is it then that we who profess Christ do not embrace this philosophy with equal energy along with His very name? Platonists, Pythagoreans, Academics, Stoics, Cynics, Peripatetics, Epicureans—all have a profound knowledge of the dogmas of their sect, keep them in mind, and contend for them heatedly, and would sooner die than abandon the defence of their author. But why do we not much rather manifest such a spirit for Christ, our Author and Prince? Who would not consider it most detestable for the professor of Aristotelian philosophy not to know what that man held with respect to the causes of lightnings, the prime substance, the infinite? But these, if known, neither make one happy, nor if unknown, unhappy. And we, initiated in so many ways, brought to Christ by so many sacraments, do not consider it detestable and disgraceful not to know His dogmas, though they give to all the surest happiness! What purpose does it serve to emphasize the point with a raised voice, since wanting to compare Christ with Zeno or Aristotle and His doctrine with their tiny precepts, to put it mildly, is in itself a kind of impious folly? Let them extol the leaders of their sect as much as they can or please, He alone is a teacher come from heaven, He alone could teach certainties. Since He is Eternal Wisdom, He alone, the sole Author of man's salvation, taught salutary things, He alone guaranteed absolutely whatever He taught at any time, He alone can produce whatever He promised. Whatever is brought from the Chaldeans or the Egyptians we crave to learn more eagerly for the very reason that it has come from a foreign region, and a part of the value consists in its having come from afar. We are often tortured with such anxiety by the dreams of a small man, not to say an imposter, not only fruitlessly, but at a great loss of time, not to add anything more serious, though this is already by itself most grievous, with nothing added. How is it that such an eager desire does not equally titillate the spirits of Christians, who are persuaded that this doctrine has in fact come not from Egypt or Syria but from heaven itself? Why do we not all think thus by ourselves: It must be a new and admirable kind of philosophy, that in order to proclaim it to mortals, He who was God has been made man, who was immortal has been made mortal, who was in the Father's heart lowered Himself to earth. Whatever it is that this admirable Author came to teach after so many sects of eminent philosophers, after so many famous prophets, must be great indeed and in no sense trivial. Why then do we not here learn them, one and all, with pious curiosity, inquire diligently, investigate? Particularly since this kind of wisdom, so extraordinary that it has once and for all rendered foolish all the wisdom of this world, one may draw from those few books, as from the most limpid fountains, with far less effort than Aristotle's doctrine is drawn from so many thorny volumes, from so many large commentaries of his interpreters, mutually conflicting, not to say with how much more fruit. For here you need not come equipped with so many difficult disciplines. What you need for your journey is simple and ready for anyone. Only see to it that you bring along a pious and ready mind and above all have a simple and pure faith. Only be teachable and you will have accomplished much in this philosophy. It itself supplies in abundance the Spirit as teacher, who imparts Himself to no one more gladly than to simple souls. The disciplines of the others, besides promising a false happiness, obviously discourage the talents of many by the very difficulty of their precepts. The philosophy of Christ accommodates itself equally to all, condescends to the little ones, adjusts itself to their measure, nourishes them with milk, bears, cherishes, sustains, does everything, till we grow up in Christ. On the other hand, it is present in the most lowly in such a manner that it is also admirable for the highest. Indeed, the further you have progressed in its riches, the further you will have moved away from the splendors of the other. For the little ones it is very little, for the great ones it is very great. It turns away no age, no sex, no state, no condition. Here the sun is not so common and open to all as the teaching of Christ. It does not in any way keep anyone away, unless someone, prejudiced against himself, keeps himself distant from it.

I strongly disagree with those who do not want the divine Scriptures translated into the language of the common people to be read by the uneducated, as if Christ had taught things so involved that they can scarcely be understood except by a few theologians, as if the defence of the Christian religion were based on ignorance of it. It may be better to conceal the mysteries of Kings, but Christ would have His mysteries published as widely as possible. I wish that all, even the lowliest of women, would read the Gospel, would read Paul's epistles. O that these were translated into all languages of all people so that they could be read and understood not only by the Scotsmen and the Irish, but also by the Turks and the Saracens! The first step surely is to get to know it in some way. Though many may deride, some may be won. Oh that the farmer would sing something of this at the plow, the weaver would hum something of this at his shuttle, the traveler would lighten the tedium of his journey with tales of this kind! Let all conversations of all Christians be of these things. For we are pretty much as our daily conversations are. Let each attain what he can, each express what he is able. Let not the one behind envy the one who is ahead; let the one ahead urge on the one who follows, so that he does not despair. Why do we restrict the common confession of all to a few? It is not proper, for baptism, in which the first profession of the Christian philosophy is made, is equally the common possession of all Christians, while the other sacraments, although finally this reward of immortality pertains equally to all, are only dogmas that are to be relegated to those very few alone whom the public today calls theologians or monks. Yet I wish that these very ones, although they are a very small part of the Christian people, I wish, I say, that these very ones would be in a larger measure what they are named. For I am afraid that one can find among the theologians those who are far from their title, that is, who talk of earthly, not of divine things, and that also among the monks who profess the poverty of Christ and the contempt of the world, you may find too much of the world. To me he is a true theologian who teaches not by tightly twisted syllogisms, but by affection, by his very mien and eyes, by his very life, that riches are to be spurned, that a Christian is not to trust in the securities of this world, but must depend totally on heaven, that injury must not be retaliated, that good must be invoked upon those who invoke evil, that one must merit well of those that merit evil, that all good men must be loved and cherished equally as members of the same body, that evil men must be tolerated, if they cannot be corrected. Those who are deprived of their goods, who are expelled from their possessions, who mourn, they are blessed and should not be deplored. Even death should be desired by the pious as nothing else than the passage to immortality. If anyone, breathed upon by the Spirit of Christ, preaches these things in this manner, inculcates, exhorts, incites, animates hereto, he is truly a theologian, even if he were a ditch-digger or weaver. If anyone manifests these teachings in his regular behavior, he is a great teacher. Perhaps another doctor or even a non-Christian may discuss more subtly how the angels perceive, but to persuade us here to live an angelic life, pure from all crusts of filth, that is indeed the office of a Christian theologian.

If, however, someone objects that these are vulgar and dull trifles, I shall answer him only that Christ taught mainly these dull trifles, that the apostles inculcated them, that these, however vulgar, produced for us so many faithful Christian people and such multitudes of illustrious martyrs. This very unlearned philosophy, as it seems to them, has attracted the highest princes of the earth, so many kingdoms, so many people to its laws, something no power of tyrants, no erudition of philosophers could do. I do not indeed object to it that among accomplished scholars, if it seems good, they should discuss that other wisdom [scholastic philosophy]. But let the humble mass of Christians console themselves with this plea that if the apostles knew these subtleties and others perceived them, they certainly did not teach them. If, I say, the princes would apply these plebeian ideas to the duties of their office, if the priests inculcated them in their sermons, if the schoolmasters instilled them in the youth, rather than the learning drawn from the fountains of Aristotle and Averroës, Christendom would not be disturbed on all sides by almost perpetual wars, everyone would not seethe with such insane eagerness to amass wealth by right means or wrong, they would not everywhere brawl with so many lawsuits over the sacred and profane alike, and we should, finally, not differ from those who do not profess Christ's philosophy merely in name and in ceremonies. For the task either of establishing or of multiplying the Christian religion is indeed chiefly based on these three orders of mankind: on the princes and on the officials who serve in their stead, on the bishops and their vicars, the priests, and on those who instruct that early age which strives after all knowledge. If it should happen that they would cooperate wholeheartedly for Christ, disregarding their personal interests, we should in not so many years surely see a true and, as Paul says, an authentic race of Christians emerge everywhere that would bring back Christ's philosophy not only by means of ceremonies and propositions, but also in the very heart and the total life. By these arms the enemies of the Christian name might be drawn to Christ much sooner than by threats and weapons. Though we should marshall all military forces, nothing is more powerful than truth itself. A Platonist is not someone who would not read Plato's books, and is he then a theologian, not to say a Christian, who would not read the writings of Christ? "He that loves Me," He says, "keeps my words," a distinctive mark He himself prescribed. If, therefore, we are truly Christian from the heart, if we truly believe that He was sent from heaven to teach us what the wisdom of the philosophers could not, if we truly expect of Him what no princes, however rich, can give, why is anything more important to us than His writings? Why indeed does anything appear erudite that disagrees with His decrees? Why do we allow ourselves the same, I almost said greater, liberty regarding these venerable writings than profane interpreters take regarding Caesar's laws or the books of the physicians, just as though we were engaged in an amusement, to comment on, twist, roll about whatever comes into our mouth? We apply celestial teachings to our life like a Lydian rule, and while we try in every way to avoid appearing as if we do not know much and bring together here from everywhere whatever profane writings there are, we do not exactly corrupt what is important in the Christian philosophy but we do undeniably limit to a few people the reality that Christ wants to have all possess. This kind of philosophy, founded more truly upon affections than on syllogisms, is more truly life than disputation, more an afflation of the Spirit than erudition, more a transformation than a rational theory. Only a few become learned, but everyone can be Christian, everyone can be pious. I shall boldly add: everyone can be a theologian.

Now what is most in accordance with nature enters the minds of all easily. But what else is Christ's philosophy, which He himself calls a rebirth, than the renewal of the nature that had been well created? Accordingly, although no one has presented these more completely, no one more effectively than Christ, it is, nevertheless, possible to find many things in the books of the heathen that agree with His doctrine. No school of philosophy has ever been so crude as to teach that money makes a person happy, none so impudent as to base the ultimate good on such vulgar honors and pleasures. The Stoics perceived that no one is wise save a good man. They saw that nothing is truly good or honorable save true virtue, nothing is dreadful or evil save turpitude alone. According to Plato, Socrates taught in many ways that injury must not be requited with injury, likewise that since the soul is immortal, those are not to be grieved for who depart from this life to a happier one with confidence of having lived morally. Besides that, the soul must by all means be led away from the affections of the body and be led to things that exist in truth, even though they are not seen. Aristotle wrote in his *Politics* that nothing can be delightful for us, even though it is not to be lightly esteemed, except virtue alone. Epicurus likewise confesses that nothing can be sweet to a man in life unless a spirit is present that is conscious of no evil and from which, as from a fountain, true pleasure bubbles out. What of the fact that not a few have presented a large part of His doctrine, principally Socrates, Diogenes, and Epictetus? But inasmuch as Christ taught and presented the same thing so much more fully, is it not like an evil omen that these things are ignored, neglected, or even ridiculed by Christians? If there are things which are closely related to Christianity in these writers of antiquity, let us follow these things. But if these things alone can truly make a Christian, why do we consider them almost more obsolete and abrogated than the books of Moses? The first thing, however, is to know what He has taught, the next is to do it. I think that a man should consider himself to be a Christian not if he disputes with a thorny and strained perplexity of words regarding instances, relations, quiddities, and formalities, but rather if he holds and expresses what Christ taught and manifested. Not that I condemn the industry of those who in a praiseworthy manner exercise the powers of their geniuses with such subtleties, for I do not want anyone to be offended, but according to my judgment, and rightly, unless I am deceived, I hold that the pure and real philosophy of Christ cannot be drawn from elsewhere more happily than from the evangelical books and from the apostolic letters, in which, if anyone philosophizes piously, praying more than arguing and seeking to be transformed rather than armed, he surely shall find that there is nothing that leads to man's happiness, to any function of this life, which is not transmitted, discussed, and brought to a conclusion in them. If we want to learn, why does another author please us more than Christ himself? Or if we require a pattern for life, why do we prefer another example to Christ the very archetype? Or if we desire some medicine against the troublesome desires of the spirit, why do we believe that a remedy is nearer elsewhere? Or if we wish to arouse an inert and languid spirit by reading, where, I pray, will you find sparks equally live and effective? Or if it seems good to lure the spirit away from the toils of this life, why do other delights please us more? Why do we regularly want to learn the wisdom of Christ from the writings of men rather than from Christ himself? Since He promised that He would be with us always, even unto the end of the world, He is present particularly in these writings in which He even now lives, breathes, speaks with us, I should say even more effectively than when He walked among men. The Jews saw less and heard less than you see and hear in the evangelical writings, if only you bring to them your eyes and ears with which He can be discerned and heard.

Finally, what is the point of all this? We keep the letters of a dear friend, kiss them fondly, carry them about, read them again and again, and yet there are so many thousands of Christians who, though they are otherwise learned, have never in their whole life read the Gospels or the books of the apostles. Mohammedans keep their dogmas, Jews also today learn Moses from the very cradle. Why do we not distinguish ourselves in like manner for Christ? Those who profess the monastic way of Benedict keep, learn, and imbibe a rule written by an almost uneducated man and for uneducated men. Those who belong to the Augustinian order understand the rule of their founder. The Franciscans reverence and embrace the humble traditions of their Francis and, taking them along to whichever land they go, do not regard themselves secure, unless the little book is in the pocket of their robe. Why do they attribute more to a rule written by a man than all Christians to their own rule that Christ gave to all and which all have professed together in baptism? Finally, even though you were to add unnumbered more, none could be more sacred. If it would only come about that, just as Paul wrote that the law of Moses was not glorious in comparison with the glory of the Gospel which took its place, so also the Gospels and the writings of the apostles would be kept so sacred by all Christians that the other writings would not appear to be sacred in comparison with them. Whatever others wish to attribute to Albert the Great, to Alexander [of Hales], to Thomas [Aquinas], to Giles [of Rome], to Richard [of St. Victor], or to [William of] Occam, they may freely do so as far as I am concerned, for I do not want to diminish anyone's glory or contend with human studies already of long standing. However erudite these may be, however subtle, however, if they wish, seraphic, the Sacred Scriptures must nevertheless be acknowledged as most dependable. Paul wants the spirits of prophets to be judged, if they are of God. Augustine, reading the books of all men with discretion, demands no more than justice also for his own. Only in these writings do I revere that which I do not grasp. Not a school of theologians, but the Father in heaven himself with the witness of the divine voice approved this author and did so twice: first at the Jordan in His baptism, then at the transfiguration on Mount Tabor. "This," He says, "is my beloved Son, in whom I am well pleased; hear Him." O solid and, as they say, truly irrefragable authority! What does "Hear Him" mean? Here without doubt is the unique teacher; you shall be disciples of Him alone. May each according to his preference magnify his favorite author as much as he wishes, this is said without exception of Christ alone. First the dove descended on Him as approver of the Father's witness. Next Peter bears His spirit, for the Supreme Shepherd committed His sheep once, twice, and a third time entrusted the feeding of His sheep, to be fed, however, without a doubt with the food of Christian teaching. He was reborn, as it were, in Paul, whom He himself called a chosen instrument and an illustrious preacher of His name. What John had drawn from the sacred fountain of His breast, he expressed in his writings. What, I ask, is like it in [Duns] Scotus (I do not want this to appear to be said as a reproach), what like it in Thomas? Nevertheless, I admire the former's genius, I also venerate the latter's holiness. But why do not all of us philosophize on the basis of these great authors? Why do we not carry these about in our bosom and have them always at hand? Why do we not hunt, scrutinize, search in them assiduously? Why is a larger part of life devoted to Averroës than to the Gospels? Why is almost a whole lifetime wasted on decrees of men and mutually conflicting opinions? These may truly now be, if you please, the writings of the loftiest theologians, but surely the basic training of a future great theologian will be in the Sacred Scriptures.

As many of us as have in baptism pledged ourselves on Christ's words, if we have really pledged from the heart, let us be imbued with the teachings of Christ within the very embraces of our parents and the caresses of our nurses. For that which the new vessel of the soul first absorbs retains the firmest hold and sticks most tenaciously. Let the first stammerings praise Christ, let the earliest infancy be shaped by His Gospels, for I wish Him to be so proclaimed above all that He may be loved also by youngsters. For what the austerity of some preceptors achieves, namely that the boys hate literature before they know it, so are those who make Christ's philosophy sad and unattractive, though nothing is sweeter than it. Let them dwell then on those studies until by these silent increments they may each mature into a strong man in Christ. The writings of others are of such a nature that they all too often cause many to repent of the labor expended on them. And it often happens that those who fought throughout their whole life for the defence of their doctrines to the death, in death itself withdraw from the faction of their author. But happy is he whom death claims while he is meditating on these writings about Christ. Let us therefore all long for them with our whole heart, embrace them, walk in them continually, kiss them fondly, at last die in them, be transformed in them, since studies indeed change with habitual behavior. He that cannot attain it (but who cannot do it, if he only wants to?) shall at least reverence these writings as the robe of His divine heart. If anyone shows us a print impressed by Christ's feet, how we Christians prostrate ourselves, how we reverence them! But why do we not rather venerate His living and breathing image in these writings? If anyone were to exhibit Christ's tunic, how we would fly to that corner of the earth in order to kiss it. Yet if you were to bring forth all His garments, there would be nothing to represent Christ more expressively and truly than the gospel writings. Out of love for Christ we embellish a wooden or stone statue with gems and gold. Why not make these writings more distinguished with gold and gems and with whatever may be more precious, writings that bring Christ to us so much more fully than any small image? What else does a statuette finally express than the figure of the body, if indeed it expresses anything at all of Him, but these sacred writings present to you the living image of His most sacred mind and Christ Himself, speaking, healing, dying, rising, and, finally, render Him totally present in such a way that you would see Him less if you saw Him before your very eyes.

THE END OF THE PARACLESIS

Reading List

Artz, Frederick B. *Renaissance Humanism 1300–1550*. Kent, Ohio: Kent State University Press, 1966.

Bainton, Roland H. *Erasmus of Christendom*. New York: Charles Scribner's Sons, 1969.

Bodin, Jean. *Method for the Easy Comprehension of History*. New York: Columbia University Press, 1945.

Borchardt, Frank L., *German Antiquity in Renaissance Myth*. Baltimore and London: The Johns Hopkins Press, 1971.

Bush, Douglas. *The Renaissance and English Humanism*. Toronto: University of Toronto Press, 1939.

Caspari, Fritz. *Humanism and the Social Order in Tudor England*. Chicago: University of Chicago Press, 1954.

Conway, William Martin, ed. *The Writings of Albrecht Dürer*. New York: Philosophical Library, 1958.

De Molen, Richard L., ed. *Erasmus of Rotterdam. A Quincentennial Symposium*. New York: Twayne Publishers, Inc., 1971.

Denieul-Cormier, Anne. *A Time of Glory: The Renaissance in France, 1488–1559*. New York: Doubleday and Company, Inc., 1968.

Einstein, Lewis. *The Italian Renaissance in England*. New York: Columbia University Press, 1902.

Ergang, Robert. *The Renaissance*. New York: Van Nostrand Reinhold Company, 1967.

Ferguson, Wallace K. *Europe in Transition, 1300–1520*. Cambridge, Mass.: Houghton Mifflin Company, 1963.

Ferguson, Wallace K. *The Renaissance in Historical Thought*. Cambridge, Mass.: Houghton Mifflin Company, 1948.

Frame, Donald M. *Montaigne. A Biography*. New York: Harcourt, Brace, Jovanovich Inc., 1965.

Gilmore, Myron P. *The World of Humanism, 1453–1517*. New York: Harper & Row, Publishers, 1952.

Green, James J. and Dolan, John P., eds. *The Essential Thomas More*. New York: New American Library, 1967.

Gundersheimer, Werner L., ed. *French Humanism 1470–1600*. New York: Harper & Row, Publishers, 1969.

Haggis, D. R., et al., eds. *The French Renaissance and its Heritage*. London: Methuen & Co. Ltd., 1968.

Hale, John R. *England and the Italian Renaissance*. London: Faber and Faber, 1954.

Hexter, Jack H. *More's Utopia. The Biography of an Idea*. New York: Harper & Row, Publishers, 1965.

Hillerbrand, Hans. *Erasmus and His Age. Selected Letters of Desiderius Erasmus.* New York: Harper & Row, Publishers, 1970.

Holborn, Hajo, ed. *On the Eve of the Reformation: "Letters of Obscure Men."* New York: Harper & Row, Publishers, 1964.

Holborn, Hajo. *Ulrich von Hutten and the German Reformation.* New York: Harper & Row, Publishers, 1966.

Huizinga, Johan. *Erasmus and the Age of the Reformation.* New York: Harper & Row, Publishers, 1957.

Hunt, Ernest W. *Dean Colet and His Theology.* London: S.P.C.K., 1956.

Koenigsberger, H. G., and Mosse, G. L. *Europe in the Sixteenth Century.* New York: Holt, Rinehart and Winston, Inc., 1968.

Kelley, Donald R. *Foundations of Modern Historical Scholarship: Language, Law, & History in the French Renaissance.* New York: Columbia University Press, 1970.

Levl, A. H. T., ed. *Humanism in France at the end of the Middle Ages and in the Early Renaissance.* New York: Barnes and Noble, Inc., 1970.

Lewis, Archibald, ed. *Aspects of the Renaissance. A Symposium.* Austin: University of Texas Press, 1967.

Lupton, J. H. *A Life of John Colet, D.D.* Hamden, Conn.: The Shoe String Press, Inc., 1961.

Montaigne, Michel de. *The Complete Works of Montaigne. Essays, Travel Journal, Letters.* Translated by Donald M. Frame. Stanford, Calif.: Stanford University Press, 1957.

Nauert, Charles G. *Agrippa and the Crisis of Renaissance Thought.* Urbana: University of Illinois Press, 1965.

Nieto, José C. *Juan de Valdés and the Origins of the Spanish and Italian Reformation.* Geneva: Droz, 1970.

Nugent, Elizabeth M. *The Thought and Culture of the English Renaissance: An Anthology of Early Tudor Prose, 1481–1555.* Cambridge: University Press, 1956.

Olin, John C., ed. *Christian Humanism and the Reformation. Desiderius Erasmus. Selected Writings.* New York: Harper & Row, Publishers, 1965.

Olin, John C., ed. *Luther, Erasmus and the Reformation.* New York: Fordham University Press, 1969.

Panofsky, Erwin. *The Life and Art of Albrecht Dürer.* Princeton, N.J.: Princeton University Press, 1955.

Potter, G. R. *The New Cambridge Modern History,* I: *The Renaissance 1493–1520.* Cambridge: University Press, 1957.

Ryan, Lawrence V. *Roger Ascham.* Stanford, Calif.: Stanford University Press, 1963.

Schwoebel, Robert, ed., *Renaissance Men and Ideas.* New York: St. Martin's Press, 1971.

Simone, Franco. *The French Renaissance. Medieval Tradition and Italian Influence in Shaping the Renaissance in France.* London: Macmillan and Co., 1969.

Smith, Preserved. *Erasmus. A Study of His Life, Ideals and Place in History*. New York: Harper & Row, Publishers, 1923.

Spitz, Lewis W. *Conrad Celtis the German Arch-Humanist*. Cambridge, Mass.: Harvard University Press, 1957.

Spitz, Lewis W. *The Religious Renaissance of the German Humanists*. Cambridge, Mass.: Harvard University Press, 1963.

Spitz, Lewis W. *The Renaissance and Reformation Movements*. Chicago: Rand McNally & Co., 1971.

Starkie, Walter F. *Grand Inquisitor, Being an Account of Cardinal Ximénes de Cisneros and His Times*. London: Hodder and Stoughton, 1940.

Strauss, Gerald. *Sixteenth-Century Germany: Its Topography and Topographers*. Madison, Wis.: University of Wisconsin Press, 1959.

Strauss, Gerald. *Historian in an Age of Crisis: The Life and Work of Johannes Aventinus, 1477–1534*. Cambridge, Mass.: Harvard University Press, 1963.

Tillyard, E. M. W. *The Elizabethan World Picture*. London: Chatto and Windus, 1943.

Tobriner, Sister Marian Leona, ed. *Vives' Introduction to Wisdom*. New York: Columbia Teachers' College Press, 1968.

Weiss, Roberto. *Humanism in England During the Fifteenth Century*, 2d ed. Oxford: B. Blackwell, 1957.